A Passion
for Friends

A Passion for Friends

Toward a Philosophy of Female Affection

JANICE G. RAYMOND

BEACON PRESS

BOSTON

Grateful acknowledgment is made to the following for permission to reprint: to Alix Dobkin, for the excerpt from "The Woman in Your Life Is You," from the album "Lavender Jane Loves Women," Ladyslipper Music, P.O. Box 3130, Durham, NC; lines from "A Letter" by Shao Fei-fei, "To the Tune of 'Flowers Along the Path Through the Field'" by Wu Tsao, "To the Tune 'The River is Red'" and "Two Poems to the Tune 'Narcissus by the River'" by Ch'iu Chin, from *Women Poets of China* translated and edited by Kenneth Rexroth and Ling Chung, ©1972 by Kenneth Rexroth and Ling Chung, used by permission of Bradford Morrow for the Kenneth Rexroth Trust and New Directions Publishing Corporation; for the excerpt from "Women's Rights" by Jiu Jin from *Feminism and Socialism in China* by Elisabeth Croll, by permission of Routledge and Kegan Paul, copyright ©1972; to *The Journal of the China Branch of the Royal Asiatic Society,* XXXIII, for the excerpt from "Song of the Southern Sea"; from "The Space" from *Views from the Intersection* by Catherine Barry, by permission of the author; and from "In Search of a Warm Feminist" by Joan Schwartz, by permission of the author.

Beacon Press
25 Beacon Street
Boston, Massachusetts 02108

Beacon Press books are published under the auspices of the Unitarian Universalist Association of Congregations in North America.

92 91 90 89 88   8 7 6 5 4 3

Library of Congress Cataloging in Publication Data

Raymond, Janice G.
  A passion for friends.

  Bibliography: p.
  Includes index.
  1. Women—Psychology. 2. Friendship.
3. Interpersonal relations. I. Title.
HQ1206.R39 1986   305.4'2   85-47942
ISBN 0-8070-6724-5

For Pat Hynes
who makes these words flesh

The journey would have been pleasant in most circumstances, and interesting in any, but because you were there it was wholly delightful...

"Our actions all have immortality;
Such gladness gives no hostage
unto death."

Thank you, thank you, thank you, for being so completely satisfactory, you most sweet woman.

And we will go again. There are heaps of lovely places to see and things to do. Never doubt that I want to see and do them, and that I ask no better travelling companion than you.

Winifred Holtby to Vera Brittain,
Testament of Friendship

Contents

Acknowledgments

Acknowledgments are always a difficult task. On the one hand, they give the author a chance to thank individuals whose support and work have been crucial to the book's development; on the other hand, acknowledgments do not thank enough or adequately those who are acknowledged or describe their precise role in the gestation of the work.

Having said this, however, I would like to acknowledge many who have been helpful, in various ways, over the course of these last six years of writing. For suggestions, readings, tracking down references and other material, and often for sharing their own work, I thank Marcia Lieberman, Ann Dellenbaugh, Ann Woodhull, Fern Johnson, Denice Yanni, Nancy Richard, Kathy Newman, Elaine Koenig, and Leila Ahmed. Thanks to Sandra Elkin, my agent. Many thanks to Joanne Wyckoff, my editor, for shaping up this book in different ways, and to Barbara Flanagan for a careful and creative copyediting. Julie Melrose dauntlessly read the proofs of this book aloud with me. Charlie Virga, an old friend, helped me put this work in an international context.

My parents have always supported and encouraged my work, even when they have disagreed with some of it. I have been fortunate in the friendship of many women, both new and old friends, whose lives confirm that the ideas in this book have a personal and political reality: Aunt Mae, Wilma Miley, Linda Scaparotti, Marlene Fine, Kathy Alexander, Gena Corea, Emily Culpepper, Kate Lehmann, Linda Barufaldi, Karin Krut, Susan Yarbrough, and Eileen Barrett. For those friends of many years ago in the Sisters of Mercy who were true "companions of the soul," I am grateful.

The courage, work, and friendship of Andrea Dworkin, Robin Morgan, and Kathy Barry have been a source of inspiration and strength to me. They remind me that radical feminism lives and thrives and that female friendship is indeed personal and political. My additional thanks to Kathy Barry for her reading and suggestions on the manuscript. Nelle Morton's spirit and work continue to affect my own.

Mary Daly's vision, work, and friendship have been enspiriting and encouraging for many years. Her Self and her work have always taught me that thinking is where I keep the company of my Self; where I find my original friend, so to speak.

Renate Duelli Klein's friendship has been truly Gyn/affective. Her careful and intelligent reading of this entire work was invaluable. Her attentiveness to the daily and detailed ways of friendship have gladdened not only my life but the lives of hundreds of women worldwide who have passed through her doors.

A Passion
for Friends

Introduction

I like the word affection, because it signifies something habitual.

> Mary Wollstonecraft

I have a passion for friends.

> Socrates in Plato,
> *Lysis*

Philosophising is a process of making sense out of experience.

> Suzanne Langer,
> *Philosophical Sketches*

but I say
that whatever one loves, is.

> Sappho,
> from *Sappho,* a new translation

This is a book about women together. Women together are not women alone.

Hetero-reality, the world view that woman exists always in relation to man, has consistently perceived women together as women alone. Many versions of this hetero-reality assault women in our everyday lives. Lily Tomlin, with her usual wit, "makes light"[1] of one version: "I've actually seen a man walk up to four women sitting in a bar and say: 'Hey, what are you doing here sitting all alone?'"[2] The perception is that women without men are women without company or companionship.

Or, consider the example of two women who go out to eat in a restaurant. A half-hour passes and they have not been waited on. They watch people — men and women together — who came in after them get served. When they tell the attendant that they've been waiting a long time, she or he says, "Oh, I didn't see you!" The perception is that women together are invisible — therefore, not perceived.

A third version of hetero-reality appeared in the *New York Times Sunday Magazine* several years ago in an article entitled "In Praise of Old Nantucket." It was written by a woman, and much of it was devoted to the history of the island, particularly its whaling history. The author told how Nantucket men went away on fishing voyages, often for several years at a time. She also recounted the rich intellectual and social pursuits in which the island women became involved. Out of this island whaling era came some exceptional women: Lucretia Mott, the famous nineteenth-century feminist; Maria Mitchell, the remarkable astronomer; and other women who went back and forth between the island and the mainland to engage in religious, abolitionist, and feminist activities. Associations of island women were formed and grew in numbers. However, the author offered this summation of the wealth of women's activity: "But women left *alone* could not have been altogether happy" (Italics mine).[3] Her perception was that women's activities produce less than happy women. And even when women are engaged in the richest of pursuits, they are impoverished if men are not involved. This sentence would never be written about men's groups that historically were engaged in political, intellectual, and social activities in which no women were involved.

I offer a final version of hetero-reality that appeared in a 1984 review of Simone de Beauvoir's book *Adieux: A Farewell to Sartre,* which is about the last years of Jean-Paul Sartre's life:

[Simone de Beauvoir] was the permanent personal factor in [Sartre's] life...without her Sartre would have been a different person. But as has often been said, Sartre would always have been Sartre all the same. His life followed its own trail and its own logic. Simone de Beauvoir without Sartre is difficult to imagine...Whatever her skills as a writer or her own role as courageous supporter of many causes, she can only be assessed in relation to the Sartrian universe.[4]

The perception here is that women together with their work follow no "trail" or "logic" of their own. No matter how brilliant or creative a woman's work is, it can "only be assessed in relation to" brilliant men. Or, quite simply from the point of view of hetero-relational vision, women's work, like woman herself, is perceived as derivative.

But there is another point of view and another vision—that of *female friendship*. Virginia Woolf tells us how she searched for a tradition of female friendship in literature— "those unsaid or half-said words, which form themselves, no more palpably than the shadows of moths on the ceiling, when women are alone, unlit by the capricious and coloured light of the other sex."[5] In the midst of this search, Woolf found meager evidence that "Chloe liked Olivia," that is, that women are drawn to women. However, the scarcity of evidence is deceiving.

Women have been friends for millennia. Women have been each other's best friends, relatives, stable companions, emotional and economic supporters, and faithful lovers. But this tradition of female friendship, like much else in women's lives, has been distorted, dismantled, destroyed—in summary, to use Mary Daly's term, *dismembered*.[6] The dismembering of female friendship is initially the dismembering of the woman-identified Self.[7] This lack of Self-love is grafted onto the female self under patriarchy. If the graft takes, women who do not love their Selves cannot love others like their Selves.

In spite of the primordial dismembering of female friendship and the enormous pressures put on women to exist for men, all kinds of women have been and are friends. There are women who have been and are *for women*. Women must learn to identify such women. Women must learn to identify their friends. This is a process not realized by anything as simple as the wearing of an identification card.

Within the last decade, we have learned something of the friendships of famous women such as Helen Keller and Annie Sullivan, Margaret Mead and Ruth Benedict, and Eleanor Roosevelt and Lorena Hickok. Much of this knowledge has been mixed with the ambivalence or outright shock of the biographers who discovered the intensity of the female friendships of these women. For example, author Doris

Faber was appalled at the emotional closeness and love revelations that were contained in Eleanor Roosevelt's letters to Lorena Hickock.[8] Faber's Lesbophobia inevitably conditions what we can learn about Roosevelt and Hickok from her treatment of this friendship. However, far fewer women are aware of the traditions of female friendship recorded in the lives and writings of nuns, the religious good books or "precious volumes" that encouraged marriage resistance among women in the rural Kwangtung area of China, and the kind of sisterhood that prevailed among the Beguines of Europe.

A central premise of my book is that buried deep in the past, present, and future of female existence is an original and primary attraction of women for women. This attraction is neither natural nor ontological. It is manifested by many different women in many different ways. Women who have manifested and do manifest this affection for women initially care about their Selves and thus cherish the friendship of others like their Selves.

Female friendship helps create the woman of woman's own inventiveness. Simone de Beauvoir said "if [woman] did not exist, men would have invented her. *But she exists also apart from their inventiveness.*"[9] The last sentence of this citation is far less quoted than the first. Only the woman who is Self-created can be an original woman, not fabricated by man, and a friend to other women. Toni Morrison takes up a similar theme of female inventiveness to describe the originality of Black women: "she had nothing to fall back on; not maleness, not whiteness, not ladyhood, not anything. And out of the profound desolation of her reality she may well have invented herself."[10]

This book is a tribute to the *original woman* — the woman who searches for and claims her relational origins with her vital Self and with other vital women. She is not the creation of men since she does not proceed from their conceit. She is not "the other" of de Beauvoir's *Second Sex* who is man-made. She is not the relative being who has been sired to think of herself always in intercourse with men. And she does not deny her friendship and attraction for other women. She is her *Self*. She is an original woman, who belongs to her Self, who is neither copied, reproduced, nor translated from man's image of her. She is, in the now obsolete meaning of original, a *rare* woman.

It is one of the primary premises of this book that friendship begins with the affinity a woman has with her vital Self. A woman's Self is her original and most enduring friend. In simple yet eloquent words, Alix Dobkin expresses this theme in her song "The Woman in Your Life Is You":

Who is sure to give you courage
And who will surely make you strong
Who will bear all the joy that is coming to you, if not
The woman in your life,
She's someone to pursue
She's patient, and she's waiting,
And she'll take you home now,
The woman in your life
She can wait so easily
She knows everything you do,
Because the woman in your life is you.[11]

Female friendship begins with the companionship of the Self. Aristotle maintained that "the friend is another self." Until the Self is another friend, however, women can easily lose their Selves in the company of others.

I do not wish to romanticize the subject of female friendship. In a woman-hating society, female friendship has been tabooed to the extent that there are women who hate their original Selves and other women or who, at best, are indifferent to women. The obstacles to female friendship have taken solid root in their lives, and it is they who believe and act out the fiction that women never have been and never can be friends. This book does not pretend that all women can befriend other women.

I do believe, however, that all women have the potential to form vital friendships with women. Unfortunately, for many women this potential has been stunted before it grows to any recognizable extent. For others, it has been strangled at some definable or less definable point. In general, the obstacles to female friendship have been one of the silent spheres of feminist writing. Few feminists have wished or known how to explain the lack of women's affection for other women.

There is a maze of obstacles to women becoming and remaining friends. We have all heard the phrase "many women are worse than men" or "women are their own worst enemies." Probably we have also felt the force and reality of such statements in our own associations with some women. It is easier to understand the reasons why women act out anti-woman behavior than to face the reality of this behavior when it is turned against us in our own lives.

The obstacles to female friendship also arise in the lives of committed feminists who supposedly share the spirit and vision of woman-identification. Women have told me, in the course of my writing this work, that they have lost friends over feminism, that is, over personal and political differences that have been inseparably connected with their philosophies of feminist existence. Other women have expressed a sadness of unmet expectations and an inability to connect with the deepest dimensions of the women they would wish for friends. They had expected that a shared feminist vision and reality would create deeper and more caring relationships than those they had experienced in prefeminist friendships. And while they had formed alliances with women over shared political ideals, these same women had not been able to realize deep friendships with their political compeers. Some women even remarked that college friends or friends in other contexts such as the convent or even the army were more caring, respectful, and responsive on a profound existential level than many women they had befriended who shared similar radical feminist ideals.

I knew what these women were trying to describe because I had experienced this same loss in my own radical feminist lifetime: unfulfilled expectations, betrayal, lack of real caring, and the wall of insurmountable differences between friends. In a very real sense, this book has been written, in Elizabeth Gould Davis's words, "to put away [this] grief." What is more important, it is an attempt to re-member a vision of female friendship, in spite of that grief, because the reality of the ideal of friendship lives on in my Self and in other women.

Gyn/Affection and Hetero-relations

Certain words recur throughout my work, the most frequent of which are *Gyn/affection, hetero-relations,* and *hetero-reality.* Generally, Gyn/affection can be defined as woman-to-woman attraction, influence, and movement. *Hetero-relations* expresses the wide range of affective, social, political, and economic relations that are ordained between men and women by men. *Hetero-reality* describes the situation created by hetero-relations.

In many ways, Gyn/affection is a synonym for female friendship. The word *Gyn/affection,* however, has a context of its own which helps to elucidate how I use the term *female friendship* throughout this book. Dictionary definitions of *affection* and *affect* shed further light on the meaning of Gyn/affection.

The more commonly understood meaning of affection is a feeling, emotion, fondness, attachment, and love for another. In this sense, Gyn/affection connotes the passion that women feel for women, that is, the experience of profound attraction for the original vital Self and the movement toward other vital women. There is another meaning to affection, however, which conveys more than the personal movement of one woman toward another. Affection in this sense means the state of influencing, acting upon, moving, and impressing, and of being influenced, acted upon, moved, and impressed by other women. Virginia Woolf expressed this wider meaning of Gyn/affection when she said, "Only women stir my imagination." She might have added, "Only women stir me to action and power."

Women who affect women stimulate response and action; bring about a change in living; stir and arouse emotions, ideas, and activities that defy dichotomies between the personal and political aspects of affection. Thus Gyn/affection means personal and political movement of women toward each other. As "the personal is political," so too "the political is personal."

The society of ancient Greek philosophers and friends taught that politics was the business of friends. Friendship in the Greek male homo-relational tradition was the basis of the state. Aristotle, for example, taught that friendship held states together. However, the citizens of this *polis* were all male. Women had no civic status, and therefore friendship was an affair between men, as was also politics. Neither slaves nor women, who were considered in many ways to be slaves, could be friends or holders of political office.

In any strong sense of the word *friendship,* however, male citizens of the *polis* were not friends. If we regard this friendship of men as homo-affection, as men attracted to men, we see that such affection was at best superficially homosexual and at worst murderously affective. Male citizen-friends killed each other for power and objectified each other, especially young boys, for sexual gratification. The latter tradition has been long sustained in the gay male community's insistent defense of boy love.

Other male political theorists have separated friendship and politics. Michael Walzer espouses this viewpoint: "Friendship, like love, describes a more personal relation, and it is probably a mistake to seek the special delights of that relation in the public arena."[12] While it is true that certain kinds of political activity are and have to be possible between persons who are not friends, both politics and friendship are restored to a deeper meaning when they are brought together—that is, when political activity proceeds from a shared affection, vision, and spirit and when friendship has a more expansive political effect.

Female friendship is much more than the private face of feminist politics. Although politics and friendship cannot always go together, we need to create a feminist politics based on friendship. And we need an ideal of friendship that invests women with personal and socioeconomic power. A genuine friendship goes beyond the world of the Self's relations with other Selves to the society in which the female Self is allowed to grow. Thus, the basic meaning of Gyn/affection is that women affect, move, stir, and arouse each other to full power. One task of feminism has been to show that "the personal is political." Female friendship gives integrity to that claim.

Friendship has become such a vacuous word, so devoid of substance, that one can now speak of home cleaning products as a woman's best friend. This is a prime example of not only depersonalizing but of depoliticizing a word—of taking its personal and political power away. This book aims to restore power and depth to the word and reality of friendship. The word *Gyn/affection* was created with this end in mind. The best feminist politics proceeds from a shared friendship.

This book is also concerned with returning friendship to a primary place as a basis of feminist purpose, passion, and politics. Gyn/affection is not only a loving relationship between two or more women; it is also a freely chosen bond which, when chosen, involves certain reciprocal assurances based on honor, loyalty, and affection. In this sense, one could say that friendship is a social trust. It is an understanding that is continually renewed, revitalized, and entered into not only by two or more individual women but by two or more political beings who claim social and political status for their Selves and others like their Selves.

Hetero-reality has conferred social and political status only on hetero-relations (woman-to-man relationships). In doing so, it has fostered a social context in which friendship, especially female friendship, is regarded as a personal association between individuals who reveal themselves to each other in the intimacy of their private friendly encounters. Of course, some forms of hetero-relations are also considered to be personal and intimate, such as marriage and heterosex, but neither of these is viewed as only a personal association between individuals. Both are given public status and are sustained by the laws, ceremonies, rituals, pacts, and informal consistency of hetero-reality.

I am not suggesting that women work for laws, ceremonies, or rituals to sustain Gyn/affection. Rather, I am advocating that women come to recognize in our friendships with each other the implications beyond the personal nature of this bond so that we ourselves do not underrate its social and political power, a power that, at its deepest level, is an immense force for disintegrating the structures of hetero-reality. The empowering of female friendship can create the conditions for a new feminist politics in which the personal is most passionately political.

The woman who is man-made is primed for hetero-relations. The literature, history, philosophy, and science of patriarchy have reinforced the supposedly mythic and primordial relationship of woman for man. As expressed in Genesis, and henceforth in patriarchal perpetuity, the hetero-relational imperative is one-sided. "Your yearning shall be for your husband, yet he will lord it over you" (Gen. 3:16–17).

It is important to understand that the norms of hetero-reality have intended woman for man and not man for woman. Women are ordained for men in quite different ways than men exist for women. The biblical dictum makes this difference quite clear. It says simply that, within hetero-reality, woman is *ontologically* for man; that is, she is formed by him and cannot do without him. Her man-made destiny and desire are consumed by his voracious appetite. Her essence and existence depend on her being always in relation to him. As Nancy Arnold has phrased it, woman becomes the "essential non-essential."[13]

Man, however, is *accidentally* for woman; that is, man's desire and his destiny, while they include women, are not encompassed by relations with women. Instead, his destiny is that of world-building in the company of his fellow men. His imperative is to create the world and its culture, science, and technology "with the sweat of your brow." And man does this primarily in concert with other men.

Man's destiny is therefore ultimately *homo-relational*. The normative and real power of male homo-relations is disguised by the fact that such man-to-man rapport is institutionalized in every aspect of an apparently hetero-relational culture. It is women who bear the burden of living out the hetero-relational imperative. In truth, this is a male homo-relational society built on male-male relations, transactions, and bonding at all levels. Hetero-relations serve to provide men with sustenance and support from women that they do not get from men. Hetero-reality is the foil for homo-reality.

Clearly, what we observe here is no outright promotion of male homosexuality, although in certain arenas homo-relations and homo-sexuality coexist quite nicely. Most of the time, as Andrea Dworkin has noted, "male homosexuality in male-supremacist societies has always been contained and controlled by men as a class, though the strategies of containment have differed, to protect men from rape by other men, to order male sexuality so that it is, with reference to males, predictable and safe."[14] While heterosexual and hetero-relational standards are being visibly promoted and institutionalized in the family, schools, church, and state, what is really supporting the foundation of patriarchy is, in the words of Mary Daly, "male power bonding, while the erotic component in male mating [is] concealed and denied. The fact that the erotic component [is] present ... but concealed [makes] the apparently nonerotic power bonding message more effective."[15] Gyn/affection, in both its personal and political senses, poses a threat to this oppressive male bonding. It undermines the potential for and the potency of homo-relations.

Hetero-reality institutionalizes hetero-relations. It was expected in the past and still in the present that every woman should be married and, more recently, that every woman's most meaningful and most satisfying relationships are with men. The traditional model for hetero-relations is marriage, but many revolutions in history, sexual and political, have claimed to overthrow the hegemony of the marital bonds. What none of them has revolutionized, however, is hetero-reality—the societal "given" that male-female relationships are the "really real" ones for women. In any society, revolutionary or traditional, hetero-relations are the only bonds that receive social, political, and economic sanction for women. In hetero-reality, female friendship is regarded as second-rate, insignificant, and often preliminary to hetero-maturity.

It is important to understand that I do not use the terms *hetero-relations* and *hetero-reality* to be synonymous with *heterosexuality*. Many Lesbian feminists have pointed to heterosexism as the paradigmatic model for the oppression of women in a patriarchal society. While I agree that we are living in a heterosexist society, I think the wider problem is that we live in a hetero-relational society where most of women's personal, social, political, professional, and economic relations are defined by the ideology that woman is for man. Hetero-relations name more accurately the ways in which Gyn/affection is obscured and eclipsed for all women, even for women who are lesbians.

Hetero-relations give men constant access to women and have consistently transformed the worlds of women into hetero-reality. For example, the takeover of the female world of birth and midwifery by men is a blatant example of this transformation, demonstrating among other things the hetero-relational imperative that men must have access to women in all circumstances. What was traditionally and primarily a woman-centered event between mothers, midwives, and female kin and friends has become a hetero-relational drama with, once again, the man (doctor) on top in the hospital-based obstetrical script. Even the new so-called natural childbirth scenarios give primary emphasis to male inclusion rather than to restoring the tradition of birth as an event that brings women together.

Mary Catherine Bateson, in her memoir of her mother, Margaret Mead, tells how Mead "was leery of the father's presence in the delivery room, feeling that this role belonged to another woman, one who had experience of childbirth, a grandmother or perhaps, as among the New Guinea Arapesh, the woman who has most recently given birth."[16] Unfortunately, many women succumb to the hetero-relational rhetoric of making men "equal" and "active" participants in the birthing process, and the traditional bonding of women at this event is obscured and forgotten.[17]

I am concerned in this work with the unchallenged proclamations that promote hetero-relations for women. Many of the statements in *The Second Sex* (a work to which I and many women owe much and which was very significant in our feminist evolution) are examples of hetero-relational dogma. "Women . . . have never composed a separate group set up *on its own account* over against the male grouping."[18] Such hetero-relational doctrines erase and ignore the historical and cultural diversity of women's associations with each other. The net effect of such statements is devastating to the feminist quest for the vital and original knowledge of female friendship. These declarations proclaim that our memories are short, that the desire to remember is not important, and that, ultimately, as de Beauvoir again puts it, "man can think of himself without woman. She cannot think of herself without man."[19] Such assertions confine the history of female friendship to the realm of the necrologist.

On a more philosophical level, hetero-reality and hetero-relations are built on the myth of androgyny. "Thou as a woman must bond with a man" to fulfill the supposed cosmic purpose of reunifying that which was mythically separated into male and female. Arguments supporting the primacy and prevalence of hetero-relations are in some way based on a cosmic male-female polarity in which the so-called lost halves seek to be rejoined. In a hetero-relational world view, the overcoming of such polarity requires the infusion of all of life with the comings-together of the separated halves. All of life's relations are then imbued with an androgynous energy and attraction that seeks to reunite the selves divided from each other, forever paired in cosmic complementarity. All of life becomes a metaphor for marriage. Every social relation demands its other half, its cosmic complement. The two—female and male—must become one, whether in the bedroom or the board room.

Hetero-relational complementarity becomes the "stuff of the cosmos."

Ultimately, the power of hetero-relations derives from their idealization. Like the idealization of slavery, hetero-relations have become the dominant structure of a social system by their benign presentation. The more domesticated hetero-reality becomes, the more "benefits" it seems to offer to women, and the more entrenched it is as a social system.

Perhaps the way in which hetero-relations have become most appealingly idealized is by their liberating or revolutionary image. Hetero-relations, or androgyny, often seem liberating as opposed to the dominance of homo-relations in a masculinist culture. This obscures the far greater liberating potential of Gyn/affection where women turn to their Selves and others like their Selves for empowerment rather than once more seeking help from men.

Hetero-relations have also affected theories and realities of feminism by defining feminism as the equality of women with men rather than the autonomy, independence, and love of the female Self in affinity with others like her Self —her sisters. This definition places feminism at a false starting point, that is, woman in relation to man rather than woman in relation to woman.

Feminism to me, has never meant the equality of women with men. It has meant the equality of women with our Selves—being equal to those women who have been for women, those who have lived for women's freedom and those who have died for it; those who have fought for women and survived by women's strength; those who have loved women and who have realized that without the consciousness and conviction that women are primary in each other's lives, nothing else is in perspective. Hetero-relational feminism, like hetero-relational humanism, obscures the necessity of female friendship as a foundation for and a consequence of feminism.

The imperative of female friendship is that women be equal to our vital "womanist"[20] Selves, equal to the task of creating a woman-centered existence. This is one of the most important distinctions between radical feminism and liberal and Marxist feminisms—their starting points. Radical feminism starts "among the women." Liberal and Marxist feminisms begin among and with the men, in tangential relation to men as a group, whether they be men as oppressors or men as oppressed "brothers." Liberal and Marxist feminisms investigate and locate women mainly in relation to male persons, history, and culture.

Men have been perceived as the ultimate mediators of reality, so that reality has almost become synonymous with hetero-reality. Gyn/ affection assures that feminism will be less and less mediated by men and male definitions of equality.

Gyn/Affection and Lesbianism

The question might be asked at this point whether the term *Gyn/affection* is equated with Lesbianism.[21] If Gyn/affection embraces the totality of a woman's existence with and for her Self and other women, if Gyn/affection means putting one's vital Self and other women first, and if Gyn/affection is movement toward other women, then many women would expect that women who are Gyn/affectionate and Gyn/affective would be Lesbians. Yet there are different ways in which women acknowledge and live out female friendship. I do not wish to simplify these differences or to restrict the reality of Gyn/affection to Lesbian existence. While respecting these differences, however, I do not pretend to understand all of them. In particular, I do not understand why Gyn/affection does not translate into Lesbian love for many women.

I also do not wish to romanticize the power of Lesbian existence. Hetero-relations can function quite smoothly in the lives of lesbians who merely "commit" lesbian sex acts or in the lives of women who make of lesbianism a lifestyle. Hetero-relations can function, more specifically, in lesbian role-playing, in lesbian S&M, in the lesbian objectification of other women, or in the lives of lesbians who act in a woman-identified way in Lesbian circles but who, in their work or social lives, for example, act the part of the hetero-relational woman.

To be a Lesbian means to extend what has been called a "sexual preference" beyond the realm and reality of a sexual category to a state of social and political existence. In this way, Lesbian existence can provide certain patterns that can be used by other women to break the stranglehold of hetero-relations. This does not mean that all women will become Lesbians. However, it may mean that many more women would consider Lesbian existence as at least a possibility and at most a real choice. Contrary to popular stereotype and pseudo-biological theories, women are not born Lesbians. Women become Lesbians out of choice.

More than any other group of women, Lesbian feminists have shrunk the power of hetero-reality and have expanded the range and reality of what has been perceived as a sexual category—lesbian sexuality—far beyond the physical body to a social and political reality. For all women, this not only raises the question of Lesbianism but also pushes women to define female friendship beyond the intimacy of a personal relationship to a politically affective state of being. As long as any group of women continuously embodies and externalizes Gyn/affection, that reality must serve as a powerful incentive for other women. Because women may choose to express affection for women in different ways, my use of the term *Gyn/affection* expresses a *continuum* of female friendship. The distinction between Lesbian existence and Gyn/affection is often not easy to make, but obviously it has been made in the lives of some women.

Many persons, however, would not distinguish between Gyn/ affection and lesbianism. Many perceive any intense relationship between women as lesbian. The ultimate threat to men generated by any act of female intimacy is the threat of lesbianism. In fact, many men perceive any act of female authority as lesbian. Professional women, female athletes, women who engage in political activism, women who dare to speak authoritatively on any subject are often deprecatingly called "dykes."

When men use the term *dyke* in a pejorative way to label women, they are betraying several attitudes. First, they are saying that any act of affection between women is perceived by them as an act of female authority. And any act of female authority conjures up increased bonding and affection between women from which men feel excluded. Women who dare to authorize themselves and their own reality somehow raise for men the specter of those women being accompanied and supported by "an army of [female] lovers." The woman who is strong enough to "authorize" herself is viewed not only as taking power from men but as taking women from men. And the woman who dares to authorize her love for other women is perceived as seizing power from men. The disparaging epithet "dyke" heightens the fact that men perceive female friendship as a profoundly political act and makes clear that men see female authority as an intensely personal and relational woman-identified act.

From a different and positive perspective, many Lesbian feminists have equated Gyn/affection with Lesbian Be-ing. They maintain that literature and lives in which women become primary for and central to each other, while not acknowledging outright lesbian affection and attraction, are in some way Lesbian-defined. For example, Barbara Smith in her essay "Toward a Black Feminist Criticism" analyzes Toni Morrison's *The Bluest Eye* and *Sula* as lesbian novels. Using Bertha Harris's definition of lesbian literature, Smith recognizes that Morrison did not intend her female characters' relationships as "inherently lesbian" but that they are, "not because women are 'lovers,' but because they are the central figures, are positively portrayed and have pivotal relationships with one another."[22]

More recently, Adrienne Rich has made this same point in her essay "Compulsive Heterosexuality and Lesbian Existence." She uses the term *lesbian existence* "to include a range—through each woman's life and throughout history—of woman-identified experience; not simply the fact that a woman has had or consciously desired genital sexual experience with another woman."[23] For Rich the term *lesbian* must be widened "to embrace many more forms of primary intensity between and among women, including the sharing of a rich inner life, the bonding against male tyranny, the giving and receiving of practical and political support."[24] Blanche Wiesen Cook's point in her article "Female Support Networks" is similar: "Women who love women, who choose women to nurture and support and to create a living environment in which to work creatively and independently, are lesbians."[25]

While my Lesbian feminist sensibility wants to affirm any woman's womanist existence and affection for other women as Lesbian, my philosophical and ethical faculties say otherwise.[26] Philosophically, I have the gnawing intuition that this affirmation is logically incorrect, morally shortchanging to women who are Lesbians, and patronizing to women who are not Lesbians.

We need to be clear about the meaning of Lesbian as contrasted with Gyn/affection. One woman expressed the difference in the following manner.

I have always been aware of loving women more deeply than men— girlfriends in childhood, friends in high school and college, and I attended woman's college for this reason. I instinctively identified with my mother when my parents fought. With great secrecy and guilt, I had an intensely close and physically affectionate relationship with my best friend through high school. Not until I was discovered in another relationship of this nature at age eighteen and punished for my attraction to women did I realize the price a woman pays for loving women. Confused and afraid of this price, I buried for nearly a decade what I thought was an aberrant tendency in myself. The rest is familiar history. With the rise of feminism and especially Lesbian feminism, I found a new reality context in which to affirm my Lesbianism. During the period that I buried my Lesbianism, all of my work life, political activities, and best friendships were with women. Sexually, however, I related to men. I was a woman-identified woman in all senses, except for being a Lesbian. But I was not a Lesbian and there exists, for me, a critical disjunction between Lesbian existence and the world of female friendship or Gyn/affection that I moved in. To call my prior existence Lesbian would have been false and somehow shortcutting the journey that I finally had to make to acknowledge and affirm my own Lesbian Be-ing.[27]

Pat Hynes used a mathematical model to explain the difference between Lesbian existence and Gyn/affection. Reacting critically to the phrase *Lesbian continuum,* she drew a graph of a mathematical function.

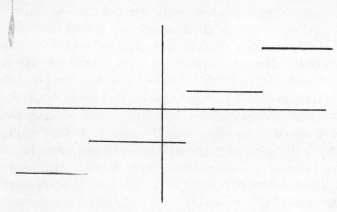

Hynes explained her graph:

> In mathematics, there can be points of discontinuity in an otherwise continuous function that demonstrate that a unique change has taken place. The graph illustrates that concept. Likewise, in the lives of Lesbians as distinguished from women who may be woman-identified in many ways, there are these points of disjunction with past and present lives— radical leaps and changes that separate Lesbians even from their own former Gyn/affectionate existence. Another way of explaining this is to note the difference between going along on a continuum of friendship with women and with one's self and, at some point, taking a leap even *off the continuum.* That leap pushes you beyond continuing with yourself and instead impels you into a different Self, helping you to move into a new context of woman-identification.[28]

In a certain way it is extremely difficult to characterize the content of this leap. However, I believe both women, in making the distinction between Gyn/affection and Lesbian Be-ing in their own lives, were pointing out that Lesbians have taken a particular journey involving an acknowledgment to their Selves and to others of their Lesbian Be-ing. This acknowledgment involved and involves a deliberate choice, the exercising of a particular kind of courage and the taking of certain risks.

Woman-identified women who are not Lesbians, while showing courage in the midst of a woman-hating society and taking other risks, have not taken the specific risk of choosing and acknowledging Lesbian Be-ing. Indeed, some lesbians have not chosen or acknowledged Lesbian Be-ing. Lesbian Be-ing is therefore not reductionistically defined by sexual/genital contact between women, although for most Lesbians it includes sexual relations.

From a different vantage point, while many Lesbian feminists may wish to include women who live a Gyn/affective and Gyn/affectionate existence as Lesbian, many of these women would not wish to be described as such. I do not think that, in all cases, Lesbian feminists can regard this as Lesbophobia. We must assume that some female friends know and live their own truth and have consciously chosen their own paths. To do otherwise is both patronizing and pretentious—patronizing to women who have consciously chosen men in some ways, no matter how much some of us may disagree with that choice, and pretentious in the sense of claiming to know these women better than they know themselves. Some women have viewed with honesty the layers of hetero-relational coercion in their own lives. Nonetheless, they may choose to relate sexually, or in some primary way, with men.

The word *Lesbian,* in this work, connotes a knowledge of and will to affirm Lesbian living. Many women do not choose to live Lesbian lives (including some lesbians). They may move in the world of female friendship, and their affinity and struggles for women may be often characterized by intense Gyn/affection. However, to use the word *Lesbian* in these cases is false inclusion. Women who are Lesbian must have a history of perceiving their Selves as such and must have the will to assume responsibility for Lesbian acts, erotic and political.

The use of the term *Gyn/affection* throughout this work is an attempt to be logical, honest, and truly inclusive of all women who put each other first in some or in all ways. It is meant to include Lesbians as well as women who, while they are intensely Gyn/affectionate, would not define themselves as Lesbians. Gyn/affection is intended to make honest and honorable distinctions while at the same time avoiding a simplistic and sentimental inclusiveness. My use of the terms *Gyn/affection* and *female friendship* is intended to affirm the vast range, the degrees, and the manifestations of Gyn/affection. In a woman-hating society, the whole range of female friendships and Gyn/affective acts is taboo. More is encoded in this taboo than the male fear of Lesbian sexuality and eroticism. In my opinion, men's ultimate fear is the threat posed by all dimensions, degrees, and manifestations of women's personal and political movement toward and for each other.

The Title of This Book

The subject matter of this book—female friendship—is considered from the particular vantage point of *philosophy*. As a philosophy of female affection—of Gyn/affection—this work has several purposes.

Initially, this is a philosophical work in the more familiar sense of philosophy. It is concerned with ideas about women's friendships. It is also concerned with critical discussion and speculation, two honorable philosophical methods. There is a long tradition in classical male philosophy—from Plato through Emerson—of philosophical ideas on friendship. Of course, the esteemed philosophers were almost exclusively concerned with friendships between men. Most of them felt that friendships between women were nonexistent.

This book attempts to distill some of the ideas that women have had about female friendship while also constructing new ideas. These ideas have been scattered in both the work and the lives of many different women throughout the ages. And because they have been so scattered and have gone unrecognized and unacknowledged as ideas, they have never had the legitimacy of being accepted as a philosophical tradition, nor have they been credited with communicating a philosophical depth of thinking. Here I refer to ideas about female friendship contained in the poetry of Sappho as well as those expressed in the letters and lives of women, known and unknown, who wrote about and lived female friendship and whose work and existence have never been praised for the philosophical wisdom that they so obviously contain.

My work is concerned with recognizing these lived ideas, but it is also concerned with generating more ideas about female friendship. Much philosophy has been devoted to analyzing the ideas of others. It is my hope to *do* philosophy as well.

Philosophy, by definition, is a love of wisdom. All of us would choose to be lovers of wisdom if only we knew how. But wisdom is often hard to pursue. Good friends are also hard to come by. Yet if we can recognize where friendship dwells and how to sustain it, we will have acquired both wisdom and friendship.

The history of philosophy is the history of men's reflection about the scheme of things and the relations between things. This has included establishing relations between persons, events, and things; analyzing systematically what has passed for reality; and challenging established values and ideals by generating others. The history of philosphy, in a limited sense, is the history of discernment. Most philosophy has been animated by the search for meaning. Unlike science, which avoids critical judgment, philosophy has never been able to escape it.

A philosophy of female friendship is an unacknowledged part of the history of philosophy. It seeks to analyze the relation between women and our world. It examines systematically what passes for reality—that is, hetero-reality—and it challenges hetero-values and ideals by generating those of female friendship. A philosophy of female friendship is one part of the history of feminist discernment. It is animated by women's search for meaning.

A philosophy of female affection is thus no neutral endeavor. It is concerned with generating ideals and values from the real matter of women's lives. It is not an objective, value-free theory, but rather is invested with a certain passion, belief in, and commitment to female friendship. At the same time, it is not separated from the objective material facts of women's affinities for each other. This work seeks to drive no wedge between well-documented and well-researched scholarship about women's friendship on the one hand and passionate inquiry on the other hand. They must come together. Thus, this book is part of a critical idealist and critical materialist feminist tradition of philosophy (see Chapter V).

Feminist philosophies, especially those which assert the history of, necessity for, but especially the vitality of women's relationships with each other, seem to bring forth charges of "romanticizing" or "essentializing" the bonding of women. Women who write about women with passion, belief, or commitment are often subjected to attacks of "sentimentalizing" women and our various activities.

It is not my intention to essentialize, romanticize, sentimentalize, or glorify female friendship. It *is* my intention, however, to represent part of the history and vitality of women's friendships and to speculate about the power of friendship in women's lives. Portraying the passion for, belief in, and commitment to friendship that many different women have had and the necessity of continued passion for, belief in, and commitment to female friendship should not be reduced to romanticizing or essentializing women's friendships.

In 1949, Simone de Beauvoir wrote of woman as "the other." De Beauvoir's female "other" was a negative construct/type that she used to sum up the ways in which woman is fabricated by man as the relative being—relative to himself as the norm. Much feminist theory since *The Second Sex* has delineated just how destructive these many forms of male-constructed "otherness" have been for women. Much more rarely has female "otherness" been used as a positive construct or typology, drawing on qualities that women have possessed to present the positive dimensions of women's history or culture. Unfortunately, when "female otherness" has been treated as positive, it has sometimes been grounded in female biology by both conservative and radical feminists.

It is my contention that the positive dimensions of women's "otherness" are grounded in the culture that women have constructed with and for each other throughout history and in all cultures. I would base women's "otherness" specifically in the culture of female friendship—a culture that has a vitality, élan, and power of its own but that resides in no essentialist female nature. Women have no biological edge on the more humane qualities of human existence, nor does women's uniqueness proceed from any biological differences from men. Rather, just as any cultural context distinguishes one group from another, women's "otherness" proceeds from women's culture.

This book is grounded in the culture of female friendship. It would be simplifying the complexity of that culture to see female friendship as the result of some essentialist capability of women to bond with each other. The culture of female friendship is depicted in this book not as some pure and unalloyed state of bliss uncomplicated by many obstacles. At the same time, however, my work does attempt to portray female friendship in all of its cultural vitality and empowering dimensions.

The culture of female friendship is not an uninterrupted chronicle of wondrous happenings, nor is it a mournful tale of failure and disruption. It is an ongoing testament and testimony of women as acting subjects who, in relation to their vital Selves and each other, have created passion, purpose, and politics. This tradition of female friendship and its ongoing life in the present needs to be thought about, lived, and celebrated.

Thus, as a philosophy of female friendship, this work is a critical yet committed vision of Gyn/affection. Female friendship is not a given category that resides in some female nature or in some female reality-as-such. It is formed in the cultural commitments that women have made to their Selves and each other in the face of repeated assaults of hetero-reality to be "essentially" and " by nature" for men. Indeed, it is hetero-reality, the world view that woman is for man, that has grounded itself in a biologically determined and essentialist view of the natures of women and men.

Those who would attack philosophies of female friendship as glorifying women's capacities to bond with each other miss the point. They indulge in a reductionism that has often served as a foil to attack any radical feminist thinking that extols or celebrates women's affection as vital and empowering. They confuse passionate inquiry with romantic or sentimental thinking.

As philosophy, this book is also meant to be a contribution to the growing body of literature known as feminist theory. We are at a point in the history of feminist thought where we need a systematic theory of female friendship—what I also call Gyn/affection—and its opposite, hetero-relations.

In developing a theory of hetero-relations, I seek to represent the structure of the world as men have created it for women. In developing a theory of female friendship, I seek to represent the world as women imagine it could be. Much feminist theory to date has sought to account for women's oppression by analyzing specific systems of oppression. It is important, in this investigation, to consider the force of hetero-relations as an overriding theory of oppression.

There has been a dearth of feminist theory that has moved beyond theories of women's oppression to theories of women's empowerment. Feminist theory must take into account the forces maintaining the survival of women as well as those forces maintaining the subordination of women. A theory of female friendship is meant to give form and expression to the ways in which women have been for our Selves and each other.

Feminists have "fought the good fight" against patriarchy, but we may also have let the struggle against women's oppression define too much of our theoretical agenda. It is time to think more spaciously about the purpose of feminism and its role in bringing women together. The range of feminist theory needs to be expanded beyond women's subordinate relation to men to include women's sustaining relations with women.

Important feminist work has been done on the history and theory of women's oppression. We need only read Andrea Dworkin's *Pornography: Men Possessing Women*, Florence Rush's *The Best Kept Secret: The Sexual Abuse of Children*, and Kathleen Barry's *Female Sexual Slavery*, among others, to learn more fully the critical truth and utter brutality of women's oppression. Mary Daly has made important connections and has established patterns between the atrocities of Chinese footbinding, African genital mutilation, Indian suttee, European witch-burnings, and American gynecology and psychotherapy.

The importance of understanding and acting on the full picture of female oppression is crucial to a feminist life. However, my work focuses on the fact that it is ultimately impossible to emerge from the effects of the "State of Atrocity" (to use Mary Daly's term), if not the atrocity itself, without pivotal bonds between women. For some women, this means finding their Selves, their original friend; for other women, it includes in addition finding the affection, strength, and empowerment of other women. The history of Gyn/affection, Gyn/authority, and female friendship must be told with the history of women as abused, battered, and killed. Behind many apparently colonized women have been women of strength and fortitude who encouraged their Selves and each other.

The lack of Gyn/affection has perpetuated the "State of Atrocity." For example, the mother who refuses to acknowledge and stop her husband's sexual abuse of her own daughter keeps her daughter in that atrocious state. The female relative or acquaintance who becomes the instrument of genital mutilation or who binds a young girl's feet participates in continuing the tradition of female atrocity. Women, albeit as "token torturers," have kept women enslaved on many levels while claiming and believing that they were giving other women the tools of survival in a world in which survival meant woman for man. The atrocity behind all atrocities is the priming by women—through mutilation, abuse, and neglect—of woman for man.

In addition to the other horrendous effects of the "State of Atrocity," one of its most devastating consequences is to make women *not lovable* to their Selves and to other women, causing women to identify with other women out of a shared pain and not out of a shared strength. When a woman sees a sister brutalized throughout history, throughout her own life, and in almost every culture; when a woman sees the endless variations this brutality takes and how few women really survive, Gyn/affection is erased from memory, and women are not affected by other women. The "State of Atrocity" reinforces the absence of women to their Selves and to each other.

Likewise, one-dimensional emphasis on the "State of Atrocity" in feminist literature, in feminist organizing, and in women's sharing of experiences can inadvertently impress women with the fact, almost like reinforcing a painful ancestral memory, that woman is for man—no matter how she might have to be forced to do his bidding—and that only man can sustain and protect. In this context, I am deeply concerned that the constant description of female atrocities, which need to be faced and fought, not lend a prescriptive force to the claimed necessity for men in women's lives. The history of Gyn/affection is a vital counterpart to the history of women's oppression.

Unless Gyn/affection becomes an intrinsic part of the feminist political platform, feminism will not fulfill its most basic goals of obliterating the mechanics, institutions, and effects of female colonization in all its forms. Women must ask not only what we are fighting against but also what we are fighting for. The destruction of all systems of female oppression and the development of female friendship go hand in hand.

The Method of This Book: Genealogy

The history of Gyn/affection is the history of a particular group of women. That history has not been charted, and one aim of scholarship on female friendship should be to trace selected lines of descent between and among women who have been/are/can be friends, that is, to do a genealogy of female friendship.[29]

Genealogy, in its most common meaning, traces a line of descent. Although we have come to think of genealogies as related to families, there are genealogies of groups and races as well. In charting a genealogy of female friendship, it is necessary to trace the lines of contact between various groups of female friends to show that we have a common ancestry.

One way to do this is to seek resemblance in diversity. A genealogical method, while demonstrating the differences between and among those who are related, establishes lines of likenesses between and among groups of women in different periods of history and in disparate cultures who are apparently dissimilar. As Dale Spender writes:

> I *know* that the experience of women today is not identical to the experience of women in the past; I *know* that time, colour, class, culture, sexual preference, age, disability, all make significant and undeniable differences to women's position in and perception of the world . . .
>
> Given these limitations, I am still inclined to the view that as women we do have a common experience which can be described and explained: it is the experience of being women in a men's world . . . We share the experience of oppression by men; we share our exclusion from the male frame of reference, our lack of knowledge of a past, our invisibility, our deviancy, our wrongness.[30]

In addition to our common experience of oppression, many women also have a common experience of empowering women, that is, of being for women.

Because the intent of a genealogical tracing is to establish the lines of contact between and among diverse groups of women, it challenges a cultural or historical relativism whose effect is to divide women from their Selves and each other. This genealogical tree, however, does not chart unbroken, linear, and undiversified lines. It is rather like a tree whose spreading branches display the interstitial, undiscovered, and unrecorded whereabouts of Gyn/affection.

An important tool of genealogy in this book is looking into the background of hetero-theory, hetero-explanations of woman-identified phenomena, and the "disciplines" of hetero-relations. For example, hetero-explanations for the existence of the marriage resisters in China rationalize their "deviance" by portraying this group of women as coming together out of economic necessity or because of a dearth of males in the particular period and culture rather than as independent women who resisted hetero-confinement and chose to spend much of their lives with women. One who searches for the genealogy of female friendship can utilize these kinds of hetero-explanations by looking into the background of what they really mean and what is not said and raising these background dimensions to the foreground.

When we examine the "disciplines" of hetero-relations with eyes that search for evidence or clues of Gyn/affection, we break through the restraints that hetero-relational theories have imposed on a woman-identified search for knowledge. We find not only that such theories have "disciplined" the memory of Gyn/affection out of academic and social existence but that, in doing so, they disclose many unacknowledged fears and subtle threats that men have always perceived in women's affinities for each other. For example, the measures men have taken to suppress Gyn/affection of any form and intensity often says more about the perceived power of female friendship than about its actual suppression.

As one specific illustration, the extent to which Lesbians have been caricatured as mannish, as imitating men, is an indicator of the degree to which men perceive Lesbians as "real" women, that is, as not man-made. Also, the ways in which men have described Lesbians as afraid of relationships with men is an indication of men's acute but unacknowledged recognition of the fearlessness of Lesbians, that is, Lesbian ability and strength to defy conventional hetero-relationships and standards.

Looking into the background of hetero-explanations and the disciplines of hetero-relations creates a *counter-memory*.[31] Counter-memory is able to glimpse that which arises in opposition to the prevailing memories of a subject or event. For example, the history, biology, and psychology of hetero-relations tell us that woman has always been "naturally" attracted to man. If this is true, counter-memory questions why hetero-relations for women have to be enforced by the myriad prohibitions against Gyn/affection, ranging from the brutalities of clitoridectomy, woman-battering, and sexual slavery to so-called soft-core pornography, which keep women "in line" with one man in particular or with men in general.

Counter-memory raises the question of why, according to Freudian theory, woman has to transfer her initial attraction for the first woman in her life (her mother) to a man if, as Freud acknowledges, Gyn/affection was her aboriginal attraction. For years, psychoanalytic thought has postulated that what is required for mature female sexuality is a shift in woman's erotic allegiance away from her first love, a woman, to a man. This is often referred to as the oedipal conflict in women. Feminist counter-memory, in its quest for the origins of Gyn/affection, must learn to detect what lies in back of such assertions.

Michel Foucault has remarked that "genealogy . . . operates on a field of entangled and confused parchments, on documents that have been scratched over and recopied many times."[32] Using the word *documentation* in its widest sense, we must note that much of the documentation about Gyn/affection is scarce and entangled, already having been subject to hetero-revision. We see this revision at work in our own time, as in Doris Faber's book *The Life of Lorena Hickok, E.R.'s Friend.* It is as American as "hetero-pie" that Franklin Roosevelt had his mistress. Yet the devoted friendship and, most probably, the lover relationship that existed between Eleanor Roosevelt and Lorena Hickok is perceived by Faber as an aberration that the author must rationalize, soften, transmute into something else, and apologize for. Faber tells readers how aghast she was when she discovered the content of many of the hitherto unexamined and unrevealed letters that passed between E.R. and Lorena. In fact, Faber was so upset about the extraordinary emotional revelations in the correspondence that she tried to persuade the director of the F.D.R. Library to postpone, and thus suppress, the disclosure of the letters. Unable to accomplish this, Faber takes great pains throughout her book to set the record "straight," as it were, to lend a "contexual" perspective to some of the more emotionally intense letters, and to portray Eleanor Roosevelt as the "great" woman and Lorena Hickok as the partner victimized irrevocably by a childhood hardship, flavored by a hint of sexual abuse, who inevitably played on E.R.'s sympathy for the downtrodden.

Much of the documentation about women and Gyn/affection has also been destroyed, erased, and made insignificant. Vera Brittain, in her *Testament of Friendship,* noted that "the friendships of men have enjoyed glory and acclamation, but the friendships of women . . . have usually been not merely unsung, but mocked, belittled, and falsely interpreted."[33] Elizabeth Gould Davis points out that the library at

Alexandria, which contained much of the documentation on woman-centered societies, was burned.[34] The feminist scholar who searches for library and research information on women's history is confounded by the ways in which data on women have been catalogued or not catalogued. Early and recent feminist books go out of print. Feminist scholars always seem to be starting over because the work of our foresisters has been buried or erased.

Finally, genealogy is not reticent to excavate the ruins. A genealogical method does not idealize Gyn/affection or romanticize its possibilities. It takes account of the ruptures, betrayals, and dishonor that have existed in the midst of the world of female friendships. Much can be learned from the dissensions and disappointments that friends have experienced, and this too forms part of the genealogy of Gyn/affection. Like women in general, female friends have been divided from our Selves and have, at times, become discontinuous with our own ideals. We have made historical mistakes and sustained great losses. I look for evidence of descent in those places (and non-places) where Gyn/affection has been lost or let go as well as in those situations where it has been enhanced.

My method of genealogy is not concerned with defining relations of causation, the exact positioning of each clue or fragment vis-à-vis another, overall laws of symmetry between different groups of female friends, or even key periodization points. What I want to establish is a *way* of tracing genealogy rather than an exhaustive account of the genealogy of female friendship. I hope that this method of genealogy—using the tools of tracing lines of contact, seeking resemblance in diversity, looking into the background of hetero-explanations and the disciplines of hetero-relations, establishing a counter-memory, untangling confused documents, and excavating the ruins—will disclose some of the content as well as a method of the genealogy of female friendship.

The Political Is Personal

Emphasis on the political aspects of feminism, expressed in the early adage "The personal is political," has kept many from recognizing that a complete feminist vision must also turn these words around. By politicizing areas of female life, feminism cannot ignore or erode the affective bonds that hold women together. Women must pay as much attention to these human bonds—to our ways of loving and living—as we do to our feminist politics. A purely political definition of the word *feminist* that accents oppression, struggle, conflict, and resistance is circumscribed and limited. It is as absurd as the Marxist interpretation of the person primarily as worker.

Feminists have talked much about the ideals and realities of community and sisterhood. Many different schools of feminism have stressed the political nature of feminism and feminist action in the world. I would suggest that such discussions have lacked a certain vitality and vision because they have not considered friendship as a basis for such community. Thus, what often emerges in feminist theory is a formal, and often derivative, characterization of feminist community based on leftist egalitarian and collective theories of association that lack a deeper and inner meaning. Friendship invests the idea and reality of feminist community with a "moreness." It augments the notion of community defined as an "association" of persons who interact in the more positivistic regions of due proportion, egalitarianism, and concern for the common welfare, thereby infusing feminist community with an energy or vital force of affection—in its widest meaning of Gyn/affection. Friendship gives sisterhood the capacity to become Gyn/affective. It imbues sisterhood with spirit.

A slogan that became popular in the current wave of feminism is "Sisterhood is powerful." (In Robin Morgan's most recent book, which includes writings from women around the world, we see also a confirmation that "Sisterhood is global.")[35] The necessity for sisterhood arose out of the recognition that women were and are oppressed in all cultures throughout all periods of history. In sisterhood, feminists began to struggle against all forms of tyranny over women—rape, pornography, battering, international sexual slavery, and so on—and to realize that women had much in common. Sisterhood became a way of expressing the spirit of women's resistance to the common global reality of women's oppression. The slogan "Sisterhood is powerful" signaled a coming together of women formerly separated from each other. Ideals of sisterhood became materialized in feminist literature, theory, and action. Different schools of feminism all stressed the necessity to build a strong solidarity of sisterhood.

Over the past two decades, we have seen that, indeed, sisterhood is powerful. There have emerged rape crisis centers, battered women's shelters, feminist bookstores, women's health clinics, feminist journals and magazines, Women's Studies programs, and all sorts of women's conferences. All of these ventures generated a sisterly solidarity, but many of them also failed because, in my opinion, there was nothing to hold them together beyond what I call the communion of resistance. Unfortunately, sisterhood that was created in the struggle against all forms of male tyranny did not mean that women became friends, that they shared a common world beyond the struggle. Sisterhood did not automatically create a private and public space where female friendship could occur. Many women who fought so hard and who believed that the sisterhood of struggle against male tyranny would give them more than it did with each other got burnt out or disillusioned with women.

Sustained emphasis on female oppression, the "State of Atrocity," and the communion of resistance can have the unintended effect of making the female experience or situation synonymous with the colonization experience. *Feminist* must mean something different— not only women in struggle and conflict with men and male supremacy, but women in concert with our Selves and each other. Feminists must also be defined by the reality of female friendship in our lives. As feminists, women must be for each other. Female friendship gives depth and spirit to a political vision of feminism and is itself a profoundly political act. Without Gyn/affection, our politics and political struggles remain superficial and more easily short-circuited. Change may occur, but perhaps only for a limited time and only on levels that do not really shake the foundations of hetero-reality. When women assert their power of absence to all forms of hetero-relations, we assert a power of presence to our Selves. This is indeed empowering.

It is not enough for feminists to dissect the corpse of patriarchal pathologies. It is not enough for women to depict the state of hetero-reality. Women have not always been for men. We need to know the genealogy of women who did not and who do not exist for men or in pivotal relation to them. And we need to create a vision of Gyn/affection. What women search for can be as important as what we find.

I
Origins of
Female Friendship:
In the Beginning
Was Woman

What a woman thinks of women is the test of her
nature.

> George Meredith,
> *Diana of the Crossways*

I am due to have this friendship with Ethel Waters,
because I worked for it...I am her friend, and her
tongue is in my mouth. I can speak her sentiments for
her, though Ethel Waters can do very well indeed in
speaking for herself.

> Zora Neale Hurston,
> *Dust Tracks on a Road*

Jezebel, that flighty forthright, used to spend much
of her Time in angling from her Window and crying
"Uoo Hoo!" to the Kings that way wending to War
and to Death. And some turned in at her Door, and
others went on, though not a many 'tis true. Thus was
Jezebel employed, when the Queen of Sheba passed
beneath her Window, and Jezebel leaning outward
called "Uoo Hoo!"
And that was Jezebel's last "Uoo Hoo!"

> Djuna Barnes,
> *Ladies Almanack*

According to Man

Men have always realized that it is important to begin at the beginning. Male scholars have developed elaborate theories of origins, creation myths, and evolutionary schemas that claim to account for the unfolding of the human race. In all these scenarios, man and woman evolve to be for each other. According to man, woman is not for woman. Within hetero-reality, Gyn/affection has no original status.

Before woman, there was man. All the male chroniclers of human origins, ignoring or disdaining biological evidence, put man at the beginning and the begetting points of human existence. The Hebrew Bible recounts:

Yahweh God fashioned man of dust from the soil . . . Yahweh God said, "It is not good that the man should be alone. I will make him a helpmate . . ." So Yahweh God made the man fall into a deep sleep. And while he slept, he took one of his ribs and enclosed it in flesh. Yahweh God built the rib he had taken from a man into a woman, and brought her to the man. The man exclaimed. This at last is bone from my bones, and flesh from my flesh! This is to be called woman, for this was taken from man." (Gen. 2.10-24)

This passage has been interpreted as mythical proof that man is the primordial human. It also casts the primordial human relationship as that of male with female.

The Genesis narrative unwittingly suggests the barrenness of the earlier homo-relational coexistence between a male god and a male human. It would seem that their "man-to-man" interval was bleak since, in the biblical account, woman becomes the being who evolves to remedy man's loneliness. Since then, men have pronounced that the original human relationship is hetero-relational while erasing the evidence of their homo-relational bonds. Thus, normal and normative love acts and feelings are supposed to exist only between males and females.

According to man, the original society consists of men and women in concert and consort with one another. The concerting and consorting are built on a theory of social evolution that rigidifies roles of sexual and social behavior. Durkheim, for example, links the evolution of society, with its transformation from mechanical to organic solidarity, to the evolution of "conjugal solidarity" in marriage and to the "evolution" of differentiation between the sexes. Earlier social groupings, in which women's functions were not clearly differentiated from men's and which did not impose conjugal constrictions, are faulted as weak societies. Real society evolved with the division of labor and its attendant submersion of women in the family and its projection of men into the public realm. The role of the division of labor "is not simply to embellish or ameliorate existing societies but to render societies possible which, without it, would not exist."[1] For Durkheim and all male functionalists, real society did not come to pass until patriarchal or, in their euphemistic wording, organic society. The primordial social group is hetero-relational, that is, based on original social arrangements and behaviors between men and women.

According to man, the construction of civilization is produced as a hetero-relational drama. Man assumed the task of world-building because man is the original actor/activist. In the Freudian evolutionary script, man is the initiator of civilization because of his higher libido. Since woman has very low sexual drive, according to Freud, and since the birth of culture involves the sublimation of sexuality, a sexuality that only men possess, woman cannot conceive civilized life. Woman's hetero-relational role has been as supporting actress in man's cultural productions.

According to man, the origins of consciousness begin in the hetero-relational academy of male mentor and female student. It is man who introduces woman to a consciousness of herself and of the cosmos. Within this hetero-relational school, man awakens himself and woman to the consciousness of self, others, sexuality and, later, language and ideas. In the Hebrew Bible it is when man becomes aware of the cattle, the wild beasts, the birds of heaven, and the creation of his rib, woman, that he names them, thus giving them existence. Male consciousness confers existence because it is man who first becomes conscious of his own existence. Woman is awakened to life and made aware of that life by man.

Woman *is* because man accepted his evolutionary role as the natural sexual initiator (fucker). One of the more blatant misogynists and anti-Semites, writer Otto Weininger, attributes the very existence of woman to man's recognition and acceptance of his sexuality.

When man became sexual he formed woman. That woman is at all has happened simply because man has accepted his sexuality. Woman is merely the result of this affirmation; she is sexuality itself. Woman's existence is dependent on man; when man, as man, in contradistinction to woman, is sexual, he is giving woman form, calling her into existence.[2]

This is one of the most arrogant justifications for the naturalness and primacy of hetero-relations. According to Weininger, and less blatant in others, not only woman but her entire affective existence was called forth by man. Therefore, man has been and always will be her destiny. For women, the original love affair is between a man and a woman. The natural relationship that men have prescribed for women is woman for man.

Man has named hetero-affection as the primordial relationship for women. It is primordial because man, as the original person, is the original initiator. This confers on him the right to call into existence creatures and things for himself. According to man, woman is the primordial receptacle. She is not the original person and thus she cannot originate. Her origins and her original affinities are bound by man. "Your yearning shall be for your husband, yet he will lord it over you" (Gen. 3:16). Male origins confer originality only on man. Since man sees himself as the original being, only he can originate.

According to Woman: The Origins of Gyn/Affection

A genealogy of female friendship—the lineage of women who have been and are primary to each other—tells a different story. It is the lineage of women who have been and are primary to each other. I use the word *primary* in both its descriptive and measured sense. In its descriptive sense, *primary* means momentous, prominent, remarkable, never to be forgotten, stirring, critical, vital, and essential. It characterizes friendships that are original and independent as well as fundamental and radical.

The genealogy of female friendship is also the story of women who have interpreted the word *primary* in a more measured sense; that is, the friendships of women are marked by a judgment of due proportion, what is due to women. In this measured sense, women who are primary to one another put each other first: first in the order of importance; first in claims of attention, affection, and activity; first in not allowing men to interfere with or encroach on female friendship; first meaning first-rate, or that which shapes the finest fabric of female existence; and first in the sense of re-possessing the memory of an original attraction to women that belongs to the initial state of Gyn/affective growth and development.

The ways in which women have put each other first are quite diverse. Repeatedly, however, many women have made their Selves and other women primary, whether they are lesbians, heterosexual, or celibate. This primariness is exemplified in the existence of black women's clubs, founded in the nineteenth century. The black women's clubs, particularly in their initial generation of club members, were composed of "race women" whose primary commitment was to end racial oppression through a strong, black, woman-identified commitment. *The Woman's Era,* a nineteenth-century black women's publication, made this remarkable statement in 1894 about the clubs: "Clubs will make girls think seriously of their future lives, and not make women think their only alternative is to marry."[3] One-quarter of the 108 club women profiled in Paula Giddings's study on the impact of black women on race and sex in America never married. Many of the most dynamic club members married relatively late, among them Mary Church Terrell and Ida Wells-Barnett. And only a quarter of the women profiled in Giddings's study had children.

There have been several interpretations of why, for example, the club women married late. Giddings suggests that because some of them held traditional views of marriage, they believed that women should "never neglect home and husband and children to enter professional life or to further any public cause, however worthy."[4] Thus they put off marriage until they could give their undivided attention to their duties as wives and mothers and to what society expected of them as women. However, one could put a different twist on this interpretation by saying that they married late *because* they put women first in the chronology and commitment of their life span. Thus they married only after they had accomplished their chosen work for women. Their women's work came first, in order of both age and their priorities.

Further, some club women, such as Ida Wells-Barnett, after stating their intentions to retire from club work to devote full time to families, lasted only several months in marital "retirement." Even some of the more socially and politically conservative club women, such as Margaret Murray Washington, were skeptical about the "joys of motherhood."[5] Of greater significance is the fact that over one-fourth of the women in Giddings's study exercised their freedom never to marry.

Another example of women who put each other first is the phenomenon of "professional lineage" set up by some of the first generation of women scientists in the United States.[6] In her book *Women Scientists in America,* Margaret Rossiter chronicles a system established by female scientists at women's colleges through which they served as mentors to particular women students, supervised their selection of graduate schools, followed their progress closely, and arranged to have their own colleges hire them as junior colleagues. In time, the protégées would assume the status of faculty mentors and follow the same process of identifying and promoting other female successors.

Some of these "protégée chains" lasted for several generations and helped establish a national reputation for the science department involved. They also influenced many undergraduate women to study science. For example, until 1932, the professors of astronomy at Vassar College were all students and "grandstudents" of Maria Mitchell, the astronomer, who had been appointed at Vassar in 1865. Susan Bowen and Cornelia Clapp originated a line of zoologists at Mt. Holyoke College that lasted from 1870 until at least 1961.

In completing her portrayal of this "professional lineage," Rossiter describes how the senior scientist, confident in her successor, would retire to a cottage on campus with a sister or another colleague. A hall or laboratory would be named for her, and when she died her protégée would write her obituary.[7]

The origins of female friendship are in female freedom, an important aspect of which is the freedom to be for women. It is important to a genealogy of female friendship that women claim this freedom to be primary to our Selves and each other in some way. The ways in which these primary aspects are increased and intensified enhance the originality of female friendship. A genealogy of female friendship reveals the many ways in which women have been primary to our Selves and other women.

The origins of female friendship are also in female culture. Female culture is past, present, and ongoing, and thus the origins of female friendship are not confined to any static original state, or golden age, of Gyn/affection. As I noted in the Introduction, the vitality of women's "otherness" is grounded in the culture that women have created with and for each other throughout history and in all cultures.

The word *culture* has several senses—social, intellectual, and artistic. Etymologically, it comes from the Latin *cultura,* meaning to cultivate the soil. From prehistory, women were the original cultivators of soil,[8] and this is an apt metaphor for representing many of women's cultural pursuits and products. Thus we have women also as the cultivators of the social group, that is, of society, as hypothesized in some of the theories about early matriarchies that credit women with bringing people together into groups;[9] women as cultivators of the mind, spawning a female culture of thinking that included early science, mathematics, and philosophy;[10] and women as cultivators of the arts of weaving, pottery, and painting.[11] Ultimately, in the evolution of its usage and in its modern development, culture came to mean "the whole way of life, material, intellectual, and spiritual, of a given society."[12]

The origins of female friendship are to be found in "the whole way of life, material, intellectual, and spiritual," that women have cultivated with each other. A genealogy of Gyn/affection lays claim to this "whole way of life" which, for many women, has represented an attempt to think in new ways about women's social, moral, and intellectual life. As the modern meaning of culture has given high valuation to a particular people's specific traditions, so too does a genealogy of female friendship. It puts a premium on women's cultural specificity—that is, women's commonalities and women's distinctive ways of being for each other—across a diversity of ethnic, racial, and national boundaries.[13] As any cultural tradition cannot be assimilated by a simple and unilinear idea of civilization, neither can the culture of female friendship be absorbed by more catholic ideas of friendship in general. The culture of female friendship has a distinctive purpose, passion, and politics. Its origins are to be found in those spheres where women were and are free to be for each other and where women provide women with a sense of difference, importance, autonomy, and affection.

In its attempts to subdue a particular people, one of the most destructive weapons of colonialism was to extinguish a group's cultural traditions. Often this was done in an abruptly violent way, as when a people's symbols, artifacts, creations, beliefs, and history were outrightly obliterated. More often, it was done over a long period of time during which this same set of cultural specifics was erased at an evolutionary pace. As women re-member and re-create the culture of Gyn/affection in our lives, we become firstborn to our Selves and each other.

One way in which men have distorted and dismembered women's origins with each other is by institutionalizing a system of primogeniture in which not only is the firstborn son considered the recognized and rewarded heir to the kingdom of the father, but the father-son relationship itself is shored up as the model for important relations between men. Patriarchal primogeniture is a strategy for bolstering the traditions of homo-relations in which all sorts of fathers bequeath to all sorts of sons the keys to their kingdoms. Patriarchal primogeniture renders invisible not only firstborn daughters but the mother-daughter relationship as well. This potentially Gyn/affective bond is deprived of its power to serve as an archetype for a succession of women's affinities with women. Instead, women are taught to disavow their affection for women. Disowned love for women is like disinherited daughters. Only men become the recognized and rewarded beneficiaries of female affection.

Men have inherited the earth and its man-made kingdoms of money, education, professional prestige, and political power. Men have also inherited, by virtue of having been born male, the "right" to women's affection. Female friendship can give back the right of primogeniture to women by establishing a firstness among our Selves. Women who are primary to our Selves and to other women are saying that we do exist, that we have a memory of our Gyn/affective origins, and that we will inherit the earth beginning with our lost affection for our original Selves and for one another.

The Meaning and Importance of the Search for Origins

The origins of female friendship are the origins of radical feminism. Until women claim and acknowledge original affection among our Selves, feminism will lack what the philosopher Henri Bergson called "an original impetus of life" (*un élan original de la vie*), that is, an original impetus of its own life—feminist vitality. When women cease believing in the primacy and primordiality of hetero-relations, they will see that the first goal of feminism is not to bring women and men together but to bring women together. Female friendship is the process by which this goal is achieved. And that process begins at the beginning, when women were proud of their relationships with women—where women still are proud.

The primary meaning of *origin* in the *Oxford English Dictionary* is "the act of arising . . . derivation . . . The fact of springing from some particular ancestor or race." In addition to a commonality of oppression, women have an ancestry of Gyn/affection, a common ancestry of survival, strength, and pride in each other.

Another definition of the word *origin* comes from mathematics, where it means "a fixed point from which motion commences" (*Oxford English Dictionary*). The origins of female friendship are also found where women have been "fixed points" for other women's movement. Women have turned to female relatives or friends, often at critical life moments, and found stable sources of strength. Very often, this strength became their encouragement to move on.

In an original and moving undergraduate senior thesis entitled "The Voices of Women Surviving: The Holocaust, Women and Resistance," Debra Seidman shows how the reality of resistance was profoundly grounded in the relationships among women in the death camps. She quotes Isabella Leitner's memoir of Auschwitz, where the author and her three blood sisters were incarcerated. Leitner describes how they enabled each other's survival:

> To have sisters still alive, not to be alone, was a blessing too, but fraught with tests daily, hourly: When this day ends, will there still be four of us? If you are sisterless, you do not have the pressure, the absolute responsibility to end the day alive. How many times did that responsibility keep us alive? I cannot tell. I can only say that many times when I was caught in a selection, I knew I had to get back to my sisters, even when I was too tired to fight my way back, when going the way of the smoke would have been easier, when I wanted to, when it almost seemed desirable. But at those times, I knew also that my sisters, aware that I was caught up in a selection, not only wanted me to get back to them, they expected me to get back. The burden to live up to that expectation was mine, and it was awesome.[14]

As the war was ending, the Nazis evacuated the camps and forced their prisoners to march through the frigid winter terrain of Germany and Poland with hardly any food or protective clothing. It was on one of these marches that one of the four sisters died. Those who saw her before she died recounted that she said, "My sisters, they have escaped. May the gods be with them and help them every step of the way."[15]

Much of Seidman's work depicts the force of such womanist bonds that existed not only among and between blood sisters but with many women who had a common ancestry of helping each other survive and who were each other's "fixed points" of existence.

> In the camps women were terrorized by having to witness other women's torture helplessly; they were meant to learn thereby not to act together in hope for success ... Accepting their limitations, women nonetheless refused to stop believing in their need to support each other altogether. It is that recognition—that they would do whatever they could, when they could, while acknowledging that they couldn't do everything, they couldn't live another woman's life for her—that characterizes female survivors.[16]

As Seidman adds, "It is not that women helped each other and men didn't,"[17] but that women's experience in the camps was inextricably bound up with the fact that they were women.

> Women could not escape their societal role as sex object in the camps, where every aspect of torture and degradation was sexualized. They clearly

had a different past and a different present set of circumstances to deal with in the camps than men did. They also faced different challenges as far as the possibilities of resistance.[18]

Elie Wiesel, who has become a spokesman for survivors, has said that after Auschwitz, literature, friendship, and hope are no longer possible. From her research on female survivors, Seidman notes that "women tell a different story."[19] Although their accounts portray the full horrors of the camp atrocities, in general,

> they are not hopeless ... For those of us living in the world after Auschwitz, our task is to re-define and re-affirm the necessity of hope, of friendship, of poetry. The accounts of women survivors tell us that these are still possible. Women speak of hope, they show us examples of their friendship, they even sing and recite poetry in Auschwitz.[20]

In her moving book *The Color Purple,* Alice Walker depicts another relationship between blood sisters in which they are fixed points for one another. Their Gyn/affection means survival for the younger sister, Nettie, and a springboard out of an oppressive situation. When the older sister, Celie, realizes that her stepfather, who has raped and forced pregnancy on her, has similar designs on her little sister Nettie, she vows to take care of her "with God help."[21] "I ast him to take me instead of Nettie."[22] Eventually, Nettie leaves the household with Celie but is forced to separate from her by Celie's husband. She then moves to Africa and helps set up a school. The letters that Nettie writes to Celie express in many ways Nettie's gratitude for Celie's gift of survival: "I miss you, Celie. I think about the time you laid yourself down for me. I love you with all my heart."[23]

The Color Purple shows the power of female friendship as drawing forth a dynamic response from another that sets free and enhances movement of all kinds. To attract is to cause a movement toward. In the mathematical sense of origin, women must be centers of movement, of genuine motion, toward each other and not merely away from oppressive situations with men.

The origins of female friendship reveal original women.* An original woman charts her own beginnings from the deepest recesses

---

*It should be clear from the entire content of this work, but to reiterate in one place and in direct terms, the phrase *original woman* is not used in any static ontological or historical sense, nor does it ground women's friendships in any biological base. Original women *create* their own originality. Such originality is a continually developing state of being, not something a woman achieves all at once in some feminist moment of truth.

of her Self and other women. She stands throughout history as the
antithesis to the man-made females of patriarchal creation. As an
original woman, she seizes the power to originate. The social
construction of reality has been "caused" by men who see themselves as
bringing female life and love into existence. The power of men to
originate all things has been a primary act of patri-genesis that has
resulted in man naming himself as the creator of woman's affections,
which he has then grounded in himself. To do this, however, man has
had to fabricate his own myths of female origins and his own creation
stories. He has had to dismember woman's memory and even her
desire to re-member her origins of her Self and her attraction to others
like her Self. Thus, as Anne Dellenbaugh has pointed out, man's
creation of woman was hardly creative. It was disintegrative, that is, it
disintegrated woman's original Selfhood and women's origins with
other women.[24]

The most disintegrating effect of man's fabrication of woman has
been the erosion of female integrity. I have written elsewhere of an
original integrity, meaning a presocialized potential for female Self-
creation unsubjected to the artifacts of sex-role stereotyping and man-
made roles—what I would now call hetero-reality. Man's "original
sin," if you will, has been the defilement of the original woman and her
origins with other women. Thus, Gyn/affection, which is an original
act, has become the most taboo of all female actions. In turn, woman's
complicity—her "original sin"—has been the denial of her origins and
the denial of her original friendship for other women.

Women must make Gyn/affection a primordial event, that is, of
prime order, in their lives. The separation of primordial into its two
constituent words sheds light on female friendship. *Prime,* meaning
first, suggests a return by women to the ways in which they have
always been primary in each other's lives. Gyn/affection, as a
continuing event of prime order, begets a genealogy of women who are
primary to each other in the many ways mentioned earlier in this work.

Prime also means the "most active, thriving, or successful stage or
period of one's life" (*Oxford English Dictionary*). Women who are
friends are thus in the prime of life, not allowing their Selves to be
primed (coached) into all sorts of hetero-relationships. Rather, these
women recognize that the prime of their lives, that which is primary,
original, active, and thriving, is to be found with other women.
Women's history and literature are replete with examples of female
friendships that have been the prime of many women's lives. For
example, Carroll Smith-Rosenberg's classic work on unearthed diaries
and letters from nineteenth-century women depicts numbers of

women who clearly preferred the company of their female friends to that of their husbands.[25]

Toni Morrison's *Sula* reveals a friendship between Nel and Sula that Nel comes to recognize as the prime of her life. "It was like getting the use of an eye back, having a cataract removed. Her old friend had come home. Sula. Who made her laugh, who made her see old things with new eyes, in whose presence she felt clever, gentle, and a little raunchy."[26] Nel's statement at the end of the novel addresses itself even more to the primacy and prime of their relationship: "'All that time, all that time, I thought I was missing Jude.' And the loss pressed down on her chest and came up into her throat. 'We was girls together,' she said as though explaining something. 'O Lord, Sula,' she cried, 'girl, girl, girlgirlgirl.'"[27]

In *Little Women* the maternal and sororal world of the March girls is the prime of their lives. This world becomes disordered and disintegrated initially by the death of Beth, which, as Nina Auerbach points out, sets the context for the marital deaths of the remaining sisters[28] and for the demise of their prime order of Gyn/affection.

In mathematics, a prime number is a positive integer that has no factor except itself and one. Among numbers, it is uniquely indivisible, capable only of being divided by itself and one. On a less literal level, one could say that it cannot be divided from itself. If we move from the context of numbers to the context of female friendship, women who are prime in each other's lives let no man divide them. This is prime order. It is a female ordering of existence done by Self order.

Under hetero-order, women have not been Self-ordered. Many women have led disordered lives, failing to put men in their proper place in relation to their Selves. Therefore, a most essential task of recovering the origins of female friendship is to restore prime order. Women must set in order an existence of our own making in which our affections are Self-directed and where we are truly prime to each other.

The question of order is irrevocably linked to the question of origins, and the question of origins raises the most important issues of searching for clues of Gyn/affection. A genealogical method looks in the most unlikely places for evidence of female friendship. Surprisingly, hetero-theory and the disciplines of hetero-reality disclose many insights into the origins of female friendship. The question of history, more specifically meta-history, is a necessary beginning point.

Meta-History and Michel Foucault

There have been various theories of history. In general, the grandiose patriarchal past has conformed its participants and nonparticipants to some underlying purpose or plan (teleological) or has used general laws or formulas (scientific evolutionism) to explain history. Even historicism, which viewed all knowledge and forms of experience in a context of historical change, promoted the belief that an adequate understanding of anything could be gained only by viewing various phenomena within a process of development. Each event was perceived in terms of a larger process of which it was a phase or in which it played a part.

More recent historiography has seen challenges to these traditional theories of history. Michel Foucault, influenced by the work of Nietzsche, has focused on a theory of history as discontinuity. It is important to examine Foucault's work because he has written about historiography and meta-history in a way that may at first seem useful for the feminist scholar in search of the origins of female friendship. His ideas on discontinuity, transgression, origins, and genealogy, considered abstractly, are attractive. Yet they cannot be divorced from his models of discontinuity, transgression, and the like.

Foucault attacks, in a style that is often elusive, the search for overall significance, totality, vast unities, and continuities that have preoccupied traditional histories and historians. Instead, he locates the method and content of history in the disorder of things.[29] Interruptions, displacements, transformations, and ruptures are the proper stuff of history, according to Foucault.

If the feminist searcher attempts to use Foucault's notion of history as discontinuity in discovering the origins of Gyn/affection, her first question must be discontinuous with whom and/or with what? Women have always been enjoined to be discontinuous with our original Selves, with a female and feminist past whose continuities we have never known. Foucault fails to recognize the unneeded and unwanted discontinuities of women for whom oppression has been continuous and who, through this continuity of oppression, have been coerced into discontinuity with the history of women in general and Gyn/affection in particular. Dale Spender has stated, with crisp directness, the historical problem of women's discontinuity with our own history:

> It is disturbing to recognise that what we today have in common with women of the past is our experience of being silenced and interrupted; our experience of becoming a member of society in which women have no visible past, no heritage, our experience of existing in a *void.*[30]

In the face of this, Foucault's adulation of discontinuity is, at best, abstract and, at worst, ignorant of the real discontinuities of women's lives. As Pat Hynes sees the solution, "Women's history is/must be discontinuous with patriarchal history but continuous with its own history."[31]

If, as Foucault says, discontinuities and disruptions are the stuff of history, then the origins of Gyn/affection are to be found in women's historical discontinuities with men. The continuity of female friendship has made possible women's interruptions and displacements of the man-made history of hetero-reality.

Foucault finds his heroes of discontinuity not "among women." His model transgressors are the Marquis de Sade and Georges Bataille. After reading Andrea Dworkin's ground-breaking work on pornography, which contains lengthy analyses of these two men and their pornographic work, one recognizes that the "philosophizing" about pornography and pornographers by such reputed scholars as Foucault covers a multitude of "transgressions" that in no way offers a new theory of history but reinforces the old. Foucault is fascinated with "the absence of God and the epidermic play of pervesity. A dead God and sodomy are the thresholds of the new metaphysical ellipse . . . Sade and Bataille."[32]

To Sade, Foucault attributes a major transformation of language and history:

> The date of this transformation is roughly indicated by the . . . appearance at the end of the eighteenth century of the works of Sade . . . It is not [his] common predilection for cruelty which concerns us here . . . these languages are constantly drawn out of themselves by the overwhelming, the unspeakable, by thrills, stupefaction, ecstasy, dumbness, pure violence, wordless gestures . . . This language's claim to tell all is not simply that of breaking prohibitions but of seeking the limits of the possible.[33]

It must be understood that "the overwhelming, the unspeakable . . . thrills, stupefaction, ecstasy, dumbness, pure violence, wordless gestures" were all accomplished over the degraded, mutilated, and often dead bodies of women who, without doubt, *were* overwhelmed, inarticulate, stupefied, and made dumb. As for "thrills and ecstasy," these experiences belong to Sade. Foucault, however, would not concern himself, or us, with Sade's "common predilection for cruelty." For cruelty is much too "common," that is, ordinary, when compared with the more lofty and intellectually weighty matter of language. Foucault transmogrifies Sade's torture and rape of women, his endless child abuse, brutality, and murder into a "transforming" language of defiance, discontinuity, and transgression.

Sade is credited not only with providing a new language but with delivering a new theory of history. For Foucault, Sade's language of transgression has immense historical weight.

> ... at the root of sexuality, of the movement that nothing can ever limit ... a singular experience is shaped: that of transgression. Perhaps one day it will seem as decisive for our culture, as much a part of its soil, as the experience of contradiction was at an earlier time for dialectical thought.[34]

This is old intellectual stuff, indeed. Claiming to offer a new language and method of history, Foucault does not challenge hetero-historical continuity—the utter abuse, degradation, and mutilation of women found in Sade and in all hetero-relations of a male-supremacist history. Foucault joins the long parade of men who, as Andrea Dworkin notes, have kept Sade's work alive for nearly two centuries "because literary, artistic, and intellectual men adore him and political thinkers of the Left claim him as an avatar of freedom."[35]

Georges Bataille is another hero of transgression and discontinuity for Foucault. Foucault's essay "A Preface to Transgression" originally appeared in "Hommage à Georges Bataille," which lauds Bataille's work *Story of the Eye*. Briefly, in this upper-crust pornographic fiction, the eye, which is the subject of immense fascination, takes the form of hard-boiled eggs whose yolks are sucked out, pissed on, and then swallowed from the bottom of toilets by the protagonists. There is also a bullfighter's eye which dangles from his head as Simone, a major female character in the story, has an orgasm. And, to illustrate the epitome of transgression as sacrilege, Bataille focuses on a murdered priest's eye that Simone gleefully inserts in her ass.

For Foucault, the eye is valued as a symbol of inner experience. It also becomes a figure of being "in the act of transgressing its own limit."[36] Foucault equates the enucleated or upturned eye with Bataille's philosophical language:

> The eye, in a philosophy of reflection, derives from its capacity to observe the power of becoming always more interior to itself ... *This inner movement is finally resolved in a nonmaterial center where the intangible forms of truth* are created and combined, in this heart of things which is the sovereign subject. [Italics mine][37]

The "sovereign subject," the male eye, can see everything except the sovereign object—woman. Foucault "philosophizes" that death is the limit that the eye ceaselessly transgresses. Meanwhile, the material and tangible forms of truth—that women are abused, maimed, and die, that intellectuals find the meaning of life in sex as death, and that force is romanticized because it leads to death—are erased and invalidated by Foucault.

Here we have fetishism as philosophy, pretending to expand inner human vision and the limits of transgression. Foucault would have us believe that an egg in a toilet is a profound symbol of transgression representing "our" inner experience. Never is it asked whose inner vision or whose limits are transgressed. His eye is most certainly not hers.

Such are the transgressions, the displacements, transformations, and discontinuities, of language and history that Foucault would have us pursue. Sade and Bataille would supposedly lead us into a new time, what Foucault later and in a different context calls "effective history." Men may revel in this "new" and "effective" history. Women who have eyes (real eyes) to see recognize it as the same old story.

In our historical searches, feminists must see the real discontinuities with, and transgressions against, hetero-history that female friends have achieved—that women have not, are not, and will not always be in relation to or in relationships with men, by choice and not by default, because of strength and not because of weakness, because of attraction to women and not because of victimization by men. The explanation for Gyn/affection is not hetero-relational deprivation, as the psychologists have theorized; it is the independent wealth and attractiveness of female friendship.

As women regain our autonomous history with each other, we must also realize that hetero-history is the real discontinuity and transgression in women's lives and friendships with each other. Male bonding and the male bondage of women have disrupted the course and current of the history and culture of Gyn/affection. The academic fields of hetero-relational knowledge have "disciplined" the memory and reality of Gyn/affection out of many women's lives.

Clues from the Disciplines of Hetero-Relations: Psychologisms

The first tenet of Freud's theory of female sexuality is that femaleness is flawed. Early in her life, the young girl realizes this ultimate female adversity—that she lacks a penis—and this has ramifications for all areas of female existence in the world. It is a supposed tragedy that will haunt the young girl all her life.

> They notice the penis of a brother or playmate, strikingly visible and of large proportions, at once recognize it as the superior counterpart of their own small and inconspicuous organ, and from that time forward fall a victim to envy for the penis.[38]

In this schema, one can say that the female develops not only inferiority and self-contempt but also contempt for other women. For the girl initially blames her mother "who sent her into the world so insufficiently equipped" and who is "almost always held responsible for her lack of a penis."[39]

According to Freud, the maturing female directs herself to men after she rejects her own sex in the initial person of the mother. This is the beginning of the oedipal stage in girls. Assuming that her mother has castrated her, she turns her attention to her father and, through him, to other men. For Freud, the major oedipal taks is adjustment of the young, maturing girl to heterosexual relationships. Freud makes clear that girls must be primed for these. In fact, we infer from his work that a whole scaffolding must be constructed for mature heterosexual orientation to take place. It is also important to understand in this context that the production of women's heterosexuality is part of a larger project—that of the construction of hetero-relations in general.

The major supports for this scaffolding consist of three tiers. Not only must the girl surmount her penis envy to achieve normal female heterosexuality; she must also replace her first love—mother/woman—with another, that is, father/man. Simultaneously, she must transfer her sexuality from clitoris (active) to vagina (passive). Freud defines an affinity for clitoral stimulation as "pathological regression" and as that which cripples "the sexual functions of many women."[40] Yet Freud also states that "the chief erogenous zone in the female child is the clitoris."[41] In order for the girl to become a woman, she has to "repress" clitoris sexuality during puberty.

Dorothy Dinnerstein in *The Mermaid and the Minotaur,* a work that has been used widely in Women's Studies and in feminist circles, adheres to Freud's theory of love transference from mother/woman to father/man but highlights this shift quite differently than Freud does. "The girl's original love . . . was, like the boy's, a woman. Upon this prototypic erotic image, the image of man must be superimposed."[42] Unlike Freud, Dinnerstein develops the idea that the girl's original love was a woman and that the love of a man is secondary. Even more pointedly, Dinnerstein remarks, "To realize that one is a female, destined to compete with females for the erotic resources of males, is to discover that one is doomed to renounce one's first love."[43]

There is, then, in Dinnerstein's work a sense of the actual tragedy that confronts the young girl: that she must renounce her primordial feelings of Gyn/affection in order to become a "normal" female; that she relinquishes to someone else (a man) love that rightly and originally belonged to a woman; and "that she has cut herself off from a continuity with her own early feeling, for which she now mourns."[44] What Dinnerstein fails to note is that the young girl is also cut off from her own history and culture of Gyn/affection and the possibilities for strengthening its present reality in her life.

One can interpret from Dinnerstein's analysis of the oedipal theory clues that are important for a genealogy of female friendship: that love of woman is primordial for women; that women remain angry and ambivalent at having to suppress that original Gyn/affection; and that women may spend lifetimes trying to regain that love, although often in contorted and convoluted ways. However, for all of Dinnerstein's enlightening variations on the oedipal theme, what she ultimately highlights is the absence of women's love for other women, not the presence of it. Her book is finally directed toward the improvement of prevailing "sexual arrangements," that is, "the male-female *collabora-tion* to keep history mad." [Italics mine][45]

Other Freudian commentators take a different tack. Helene Deutsch, who did even more than Freud to promulgate the theory of female masochism, nevertheless diverged from Freud's oedipal theory.

> It is erroneous to say that the little girl gives up her first mother relation in favor of the father. She only gradually draws him into the alliance, develops from the mother-child exclusiveness toward the triangular parent-child relation and continues the latter, just as she does the former, although in a weaker and less elemental form, all her life.[46]

Nancy Chodorow in *The Reproduction of Mothering,* another widely used text in Women's Studies, follows Deutsch in accenting what I call the lingering Gyn/affection of women. "For girls, then, there is no absolute change of object, nor exclusive attachment to their fathers."[47] Girls never make "final and absolute commitments to heterosexual *love,* as emotional commitment, whether or not they make final commitments of genital object-choice."[48]

Traditional psychology has focused on women's ambivalence toward women, that is, the fact that women distrust or envy their female peers. Chodorow emphasizes that many women feel profoundly ambivalent about loving women because an original and powerful attraction to women is constantly at war within women competing with a superimposed attraction to men.

> Girls cannot and do not "reject" their mother and women in favor of their father and men, but remain in a bisexual triangle throughout childhood and into puberty. They make a sexual resolution in favor of men and their father, but retain an intense emotional triangle.[49]

Of course, Chodorow omits the fact that many women do not "remain in a bisexual triangle" and that this concept does not describe the reality of those women who do not participate in such a triangular arrangement. Further, many other women who do remain in this triangle have not made a "resolution" in favor of heterosexuality but have been coerced into that "resolution" or perhaps, have resigned themselves to it.

Chodorow theorizes that a girl's transference of love from mother/woman to father/man is not completely accomplished for several reasons. Comparatively speaking, the father is not as physically or emotionally available as the mother. Like Dinnerstein, Chodorow notes that through erotic identification with a man, a woman "refuses" herself with a woman. Freud too recognized this when he said that women in heterosexual relationships look to men for "gratifications they want from a woman."[50] However, because a mother does not confer upon the girl the same kind of love that she gives a boy, the daughter looks elsewhere—to the father—for "the same confirmation of her specialness that her brother receives from her mother."[51] At the same time, a daughter seeks to escape from the mother, to develop a sense of separateness and individuality, which is also found in turning to men. "She is more able to do this because her distance means that she does not know him."[52]

Refuting the societal stereotype that women are the romantics and men the rationalists in love, Chodorow makes clear that "women have acquired a real capacity for rationality and distance in heterosexual relationships, qualities built into their earliest relationships with a man."[53] She cites clinical and sociological evidence to support this claim. "Most of these studies argue ... that women's apparent romanticism is an emotional and ideological response to their very real economic dependence."[54] In addition to economic rationalism, Chodorow might have cited other social and psychological powers that men exercise over women's lives that make women more "rational-istic" in giving an apparent primacy to hetero-relations. As Andrea Dworkin has enumerated, men, besides having the power of money, have the power of self, parasitic though it may be; the power of physical strength, used over and against women; the power to terrorize and inculcate fear; the power of naming, initially analyzed in Mary Daly's work; the power of owning women and all that issues from them; and the power of sex, that is, fucking—taking, forcing, conquering.[55]

To women's distance from men, Chodorow juxtaposes the affinities women have for each other. Women spend more time in the company of other women than men do in the company of men. Citing Wayne Booth's findings as well as writings from men's liberation groups, she states that women's friendships with each other "are affectively richer than men's."[56] In many cultures, female relatives are each other's friends. "However, deep affective relationships to women are hard to come by on a routine, daily, ongoing, basis for many women. Lesbian relationships do tend to recreate mother-daughter emotions and connections, but most women are heterosexual."[57] Although Chodorow mentions heterosexual preference, "taboos against homosexuality," and economic dependence on men as the reasons that make primary sexual bonds with other women unlikely, the phrase "most women are heterosexual" is a vast oversimplification. Adrienne Rich has stated the complexity most clearly.

> The assumption that "most women are innately heterosexual" stands as a theoretical and political stumbling block for many women. It remains a tenable assumption, partly because lesbian existence has been written out of history or catalogued under disease; partly because it has been treated as exceptional rather than as intrinsic; partly because to acknowledge that for women heterosexuality may not be a "preference" at all but something that has had to be imposed, managed, organized, propagandized, and maintained by force, is an immense step to take if you consider yourself freely and "innately" heterosexual. Yet the failure to examine hetero-sexuality as an institution is like failing to admit that the economic system called capitalism or the caste system of racism is maintained by a variety of forces, including both physical violence and false consciousness.[58]

On the level of personal relations, Chodorow does acknowledge that "women's desires for intense primary relationships tend not to be with other women, both because of internal and external taboos on homosexuality, and because of women's isolation from their primary female kin (especially mothers) and other women."[59] Further, the lack of affective response that women get in hetero-relations, what Chodorow calls "contradictions in heterosexuality," help promote these same hetero-relations as normative. To have deep affection, women seek emotional sustenance with children and are thus oriented toward family and mothering, says Chodorow. "Thus, men's lack of emotional availability and women's less exclusive heterosexual commitment help ensure women's mothering."[60]

Were not Chodorow's analysis of personal factors so emphatically psychoanalytic and her analysis of social factors so emphatically economic, she might have named as "internal and external taboos on homosexuality" all of the obstacles that are marshaled against the whole continuum of Gyn/affection in a hetero-relational culture. And she might have named women's supposed "isolation" from other women as the enforced segregation and sundering of women from each other.

Chodorow and Dinnerstein provide clues to the origins and primacy of Gyn/affection, it seems, without intending to do so. Their ultimate goal, as is apparent from the conclusions to both books, is to bolster and maintain flagging hetero-relations and failed fathers. They wish to reorganize the institution of parenting so that men take more responsibility. Both argue that the male absence from childrearing is responsible for a host of individual and social disorders. If this inequitable situation were remedied, they say, and men took an equal part in parenting, all sorts of saving graces would follow. Chodorow states:

> . . . this dependence on her [mother/woman] and this primary identification would not be created in the first place if men took primary parenting responsibilities.
>
> Children could be dependent from the outset on people of both genders and establish an individuated sense of self in relation to both.[61]

Dinnerstein states:

> When the child, once born, is as much the responsibility of man as of woman, the early vicissitudes of the flesh—our handling of which lays the basis for our later handling of mortality—will bear no special relation to gender.[62]

What both Dinnerstein and Chodorow tell us is that once more men will be the saviors. When men become equal parents, the grievances and ambivalences of childhood development that are now foisted on the mother, the blame she incurs from being primary caretaker, and the gamut of "heterosexual knots" and "sexual arrangements" will not occur.

What this finally means is that, once more, hetero-relations must be the focus of women's lives and that women should devote themselves to re-constructing new forms of hetero-relations. There is no perception, and certainly no prescription, that women need to create new forms of relations with women. Having developed some remarkable insights into original attraction of women for women and having given us some clues as to why women reorient that attraction to men, both authors fail to emphasize the importance of women's affection for each other as primary and paradigmatic.

Instead, Dinnerstein and Chodorow present an implicit and invisible exhortation for women, once more, to mother men. But this time, women must mother men to be mothers, for if women do not do so, who will? This is the unacknowledged, and perhaps unforeseen, agenda in both books.[63]

Dinnerstein and Chodorow give us in theory what movies such as *Kramer vs. Kramer* offer us in film. All three present the full-blown, "humanized," and caring father. None of them tells us where he will come from.

The major problem is not that mainly women parent. Rather, the major problem is that mainly women become the visible and immediate conduits of hetero-reality while deriving the least benefits from such a system.[64] As long as women acquiesce in the formation of what Dinnerstein and Chodorow would call the oedipal conflict in girls, and what I would name hetero-reality—the channeling of female love, power, and energy into men—nothing will change radically. Until women "mother" to love and care for other women, the system of women hetero-reality will not be transformed.

If the original woman, who experiences primary love for her mother (women) were not confronted with the mother(women) as hetero-relational and patterned into these relations herself by the mother (women), but were instead confronted with the mother as a female friend who puts women first in her life, then Gyn/affection would become a prevailing reality. The young girl would draw quite different conclusions about her feelings for her Self and other women.

It is not coparenting and the inclusion of the male in equal parenting responsibilities that will restore (among other imbalances) the lack of female friendship, because then presumably women will be free not to hate or be ambivalent about other women. Rather, coparenting under present conditions enhances male supremacy because it gives men more power than they now have, this time emotional presence and power within the family. To continue to ignore women's lack of power in all other social institutions and to prescribe male parenting as the solution to our oppressive "sexual arrangements" is a lopsided vision indeed.

Furthermore, where the male is portrayed as a sensitive and caring coparent, the mother is often displaced. What emerges is a more "humane" and "touching" version of male bonding. At least this is the cinematic message in *Ordinary People* and *Kramer vs. Kramer,* two popular films of the early 1980s that depicted the sensitive father. In the latter film, the mother is physically absent because she has left husband and son to "find her self" and her way in the world, exiting from a troubled marriage. In the former, the mother is emotionally absent from the son while remaining physically present as wife and mother. Both films contain touching, teary-eyed scenes of father-son love where father becomes not the coparent but eventually the only parent who is really present. The mythic theme of male mothering is indeed made flesh.

What Dinnerstein and Chodorow send women searching for is the "new man." But the new man is, in many ways, the old man. First, he is a man, not a woman, and women have been traditionally enjoined to seek men, albeit new and sensitized men. Second, he bonds with his own kind, even under the influence of sensitization. We see this bonding at work in the new "sensitive male" films, and we can expect a rejuvenated form of male bonding from the fulfillment of Dinnerstein's and Chodorow's visions of the male as coparent. Women are oriented to new forms of hetero-relations here. And what is not discussed is that men will be encouraged to create new forms of male bonding because leeway for increased intimacy between men will be established under the influence of sensitization. Male intimacy, added to the present male solidarity based on male money, power, and physical prowess, will result in the further institutionalization of homo-relations. Women's relationships with each other will remain ever secondary to the imperative to create new forms of hetero-relations. Any such bonds which occur among women within this "new" hetero-relational context will, as in the old hetero-relational context, be secondborn. They too will not be lived as primary.

For both women and men, love for women will continue to be kept in its proper place, not allowed to interfere with the vital ties between men. Men, having been "freed up" to express emotion, will be able to manifest their love for men in different ways than before. Women, having been reoriented to new forms of hetero-relations, will also be directed to men again and will be much more confined and constrained in manifesting Gyn/affection.

In the final analysis, Dinnerstein and Chodorow's theories maintain the present system of hetero-reality. They even give it a new boost, although there is no conscious intent, and certainly no articulated prescription, to do this. However, male bonding will persist and thrive in the wake of new forms of hetero-relations since homo-relations can only be strengthened in the absence of any focus on the primary importance of women's relations with each other.

There is nothing in Chodorow or Dinnerstein that sets primary store on women's relations with women. There is no ultimate and concluding prescription in their works for the enhancement of Gyn/affection that compares with their final idealizing of hetero-relations. The girl or woman is offered nothing to encourage her original attraction to women. Again, but this time more subtly, she is encouraged to be for men.

Clues from the Disciplines of Hetero-Relations: Biologisms

Arguments from biology have proved very powerful in maintaining hetero-relations and, therefore, in suppressing Gyn/affection. Among the most commonly accepted biological arguments for the primacy of hetero-relations have been theories of biological complementarity. These contend that nature ordained woman for man as evidenced by the obvious anatomical correspondence of the respective sexual organs —in more reductionistic language, "the vagina was created for the penis" or, its crasser version, "the hole was created for the pole." This "argument," in "expanded" form, maintains that the logical extension of biological heterosexual complementarity is hetero-relational complementarity in all spheres. Thus, the anatomical construction of the genitalia, according to this way of reasoning, points to the "natural" necessity for hetero-relations.

There is, of course, no sheer natural fact of heterosexuality or of its expanded version, hetero-relations, that can be argued from the vantage point of biological complementarity. It may be "significant" to some people and for some purposes that the penis may "fit" the vagina, as it is significant to some people and for some purposes that it also "fits" elsewhere! It is not necessary that every penis "fits" every vagina, nor is it "fitting" that hetero-relations govern personal and social existence. Hetero-relations, which derive their logic from such biologisms, equate significance with necessity. From a Gyn/affective perspective, it is equally significant that the testimony of many women's initial and continued heterosexual intercourse establishes the "fact" that on an anatomical level itself, many penises do not "fit" so neatly and nicely into many vaginas and that what is claimed as "natural" is often accomplished through repeated pain and trauma to the women involved. Heterosexuality, in this view, is most unnatural in the sense that it is learned and often forced.

In her chapter "Sexual Initiation" in *The Second Sex,* Simone de Beauvoir relates many cases of sexual initiation for girls and women where "defloration was a kind of rape . . . it can be painful even when quite voluntary."[65] De Beauvoir quotes Isadora Duncan:

> "I confess that my first impressions were a horrible fright and an atrocious pain, as if someone had torn out several of my teeth at once . . . Next day what was at that time no more than a painful experience for me continued amidst my martyred cries and tears. I felt as if I were being mangled."[66]

De Beauvoir comments: "Before long she came to enjoy, first with this lover, then with others, the rapture she lyrically describes."[67] Heterosexual relations, from the first description, hardly seem natural, that is, ordained by nature, unless repeated pain is also natural and ordained by nature. Further, like everything else in the developmental process of man-made femininity, the supposed "rapture" of heterosexuality and hetero-relations is learned. For many women, it is never experienced; others fake it.

Such an unlikely source as Bruno Bettelheim captures well the developmental process by which disgust and pain are changed into rapture and pleasure, in his interpretation of the fairy tale "The Frog King."

> The fairy tale by agreeing with the child that the frog (or whatever animal it might be) is disgusting, gains the child's confidence and thus can create in him [*sic*] the firm belief that . . . in due time the disgusting frog will reveal himself as life's most charming companion. And this message is delivered without ever directly mentioning anything sexual.[68]

Unfortunately, Bettelheim chose a frog to represent a "disgusting" animal to the child. Animals are always singled out for negative caricatures, as opposed to "handsome" human kings or princes in the fairy tales of hetero-storytelling. Having said this, however, Bettelheim's interpretation is an apt paradigm for the institutionalization of hetero-relations, that is, for all the processes by which women's originality becomes obliterated and hetero-reality becomes consolidated.

Phyllis Chesler offers a different kind of evidence exposing the lie of natural and rapturous heterosexuality:

> Clinical case histories, psychological and sociological surveys and studies—and our own lives—have documented the extent to which most twentieth-century women have not been having orgasms; or not having the "right" kind of orgasms; or not having *any* kind of orgasms very frequently or very easily; or having orgasms only under conditions of romantic monogamy, legal prostitution, or self-degradation; or only after much purposeful "learning."[69]

The Hite Report is another testimony to the lack of sexual and emotional fulfillment of women in heterosexual relations and also to the fact that there is nothing "natural" about the whole gamut of hetero-relations.[70] And most recently, Ann Landers reports that 60,000 women have written letters to say that sex is not fulfilling, "that they far prefer being hugged and treated tenderly by men to having sexual intercourse with them."[71] Many of these women, 40 percent of them under the age of forty, wrote emphatic three- or four-page letters when Landers's poll asked only for a yes or no answer, "Many of them have written over the years to say they've had it, because it's a burden, a bore, no satisfaction . . . nothing comes back to them."[72]

The "natural" argument persists for heterosexuality and for hetero-relations because heterosexual intercourse often issues in the reproduction of the species. Thus the genital complementarity argument is bolstered by the potential or actual product of penis-vagina relations. Not only heterosexuality but an extended range of hetero-relations, such as traditional family roles, sexual division of labor, and gender-defined childrearing and education, are rationalized as necessary for the continued preservation and maintenance of the human race.

Reproduction can be accomplished in several ways, however, without ordaining heterosexuality as normative, natural, and not to be deviated from, and without orchestrating hetero-relations as the inevitable accompaniment to this supposed biological fact. Reproduction can occur through "normal" male-female intercourse in a variety of contexts that do not presume continued heterosexuality or hetero-relations outside the reproductive relation. Artificial insemination is possible, although its use in the medical domain has been widely restricted to heterosexual and married women. In these cases, hetero-relations, specifically those within the confines of marriage, are used to naturalize and normalize artificial methods of reproduction, *not* repro-duction that naturalizes and normalizes hetero-relations. The new reproductive technologies are another form of procreation that defy the biological "facticity" of natural heterosexual reproduction, although proponents who wish to justify the use of such technologies have argued that these methods, such as *in vitro* fertilization and embryo transfer, be confined to married couples. Such proponents have gone further in stating that these technologies may even stabilize faltering marriages on the verge of disintegration because of infertility.[73]

Finally, if the complementarity of male-female organs and the complementary reproductive capacity of both sexes are the main biological arguments for the maintenance and support of hetero-relations, the question must be asked why so many physically abusive actions have been necessary to enforce the "natural" state of hetero-relations. Something that is so natural should never have to be coerced for so many women.

The prohibitions against birth control and abortion are examples of enforced motherhood, a state that has also been promoted through the historical enslavement of women as "barefoot and pregnant." Clitori-dectomy and surgical oophorectomy were both measures enforced to restrain so-called unbridled female sexuality. Clitoridectomy is still performed for this reason today in many countries. Although women's sexuality is generally understood to be the unleashed and promiscuous sexuality of women with men in general, or with certain men, one must delve further into the background of such prohibitions and maiming abuses to see that an unacknowledged fear behind such coercion and mutilation is the potential undoing of hetero-relations. The medical performance of oophorectomy in this country was employed to control so-called deviant women.

Biological arguments have also been used to justify rape as natural. If the natural heterosexual woman won't "put out" for the natural hete-rosexual man, then aggressive sexual violence toward women is often rationalized as part of the "natural man"—a component of his ever-to-be-satisfied, innate sexual drive. As Andrea Dworkin noted in analyz-ing Kinsey, who was a proponent of this viewpoint:

> The sense of Kinsey's view is that rape to the extent that it does exist (mostly illusory), would not exist if females would comply, which they would do were they not twisted. It is the female who refuses and then accuses, destroying the natural man who just wants to function in harmony with his authentic sexuality.[74]

The same kind of rationalization for the biological innateness of the male sex drive has been and still is used to argue for the legalization of prostitution. William Acton, a nineteenth-century British physician renowned for his work on sexuality, pronounced that it was impossible to exaggerate the force of the male sex drive and that any constraints on this drive would reduce man to a pitiable condition. Thus, Acton argued, men would find it necessary to use prostitutes, especially in societies that delayed marriage.

What is important for our analysis of Gyn/affection is that it takes an enormous amount of coercive activity to create the so-called natural woman who is ever ready to satisfy the natural man. In fact, what the natural man constantly requires is the "unnatural woman," the woman who is man-made. To become man-made natural women, that is, unnatural women, women have to break with their originality and their origins with their original Selves and other women. This rupture, symbolized in the act of heterosexual intercourse and in all the disjunctions of hetero-relations, tears the young woman out of an original and potentially future world of women and throws her into the world of men. Hetero-relations are built on the conquest of the real natural woman, she who is her woman-defined Self.

Female friendship means the arousal of the original, or the wild, Self in each woman. Friendship for women is basically "the call of the wild." It is a contagious cry from another like the Self to arise from a tamed and domesticated existence. It inspires a woman, again and again, to return to an original state of female existence not tamed by man.

"The Call of the Wild"

Mary Daly has pointed out that dictionary definitions of both *wild* and *tame* give us clues to the original woman.* The stories of women who are tamed by men are a standard stereotype in literature and in movies. No less a classical source than Shakespeare depicted such a woman in *The Taming of the Shrew.* In Louisa May Alcott's *Good Wives,* the strong-willed Jo begins to fall in love with her future husband when he reproaches her severely for some blunder. Television and movies consistently portray wild women tamed by the "wholesome brutality"

Wild means "living in a state of nature," "growing or produced without the aid of man." *Wild* also means "deviating from a natural or expected course." *Tame* means "made tractable and useful to man," "domesticated," "maintained or displayed to serve the purposes of another." Mary Daly, *Gyn/Ecology: The Metaethics of Radical Feminism* (Boston: Beacon Press, 1978), p. 343.

of a husband or lover, flavored by a slap or two, a good spanking, or a seduction laden with violence.

In hetero-reality, women and Gyn/affection are often tamed at a young age. In many cultures, women are married young. A significant part of this taming is that the young woman is wrenched out of the world of women. In western societies, young girls at puberty are taught to leave behind what for many has been a gynosocial and Gyn/affectionate world of learning with female teachers and best girlhood friends for the more "mature" world of hetero-relations. The original woman and the world of female friendship often die early. Not without reason did George Eliot have her heroine, Maggie, in *The Mill on the Floss,* die young. Diderot, in a letter to Sophie Volland, said, "You all die at fifteen." If not literally, many girls die to their original Selves and to other women in adolescence. And, for many girls, this kind of dying is happening much sooner as they are swept into the pseudo-maturity of hetero-reality at an increasingly earlier age.

Some women do grow to adulthood fired by the Gyn/affection of an earlier time in their lives. In spite of the obstacles to female friendship, such women still remember the original woman and her origins of Gyn/affection. This wild or original woman often finds herself friends with the world of physical Nature, for it is here that she finds a sense of unlimited be-ing that she doesn't find in the world of hetero-reality. The quest for Self in much literature written by women has been intimately bound up with Nature. In forest or meadow, on mountain or shore, there is the smell and color of life for women which has been diminished in hetero-reality. Sensation makes real. Existence here is wild and transcendent, unfettered by the constraints of hetero-relations. Beyond the man-made woman of hetero-reality, even beyond Nature, woman seeks a Self so near and yet so far.

One thinks of Emily Brontë and *Wuthering Heights.* The landscape of the novel defines the illimitable boundaries of the major character's original Self. Cathy's wild Self is that which many women surely have yearned to actualize. The wildness of the moors becomes almost interchangeable with this wild Self. Barbara Deming has suggested that we read *Wuthering Heights* "as though Heathcliff were not literally a separate person but were simply—as Cathy herself speaks of him-herself."[75] Deming asserts that Emily Brontë used unconsciously, though with profound insight, the device of imagining the lost Self as a separate character.

The passionate self-identification of Cathy and Heathcliff ("I cannot live without my life! I cannot live without my soul!") takes on a different dimension beyond its personal power if one sees in its vision of love "the call of the wild" Self of woman to woman. If we remember that Cathy and Heathcliff are one and the same person, we can interpret Heathcliff's return to Thrushcross Grange and Wuthering Heights years after his childhood exile as symbolizing the return of Cathy's original and wild Self. It is this homecoming that resurrects the tamed and married Mrs. Linton (Cathy) from domesticated oblivion. And it is the death struggle between the tame and the wild that Cathy cannot reconcile and that causes her bodily end. Death, however, does not suppress her wild Self, for her spirit lingers after death.

If Heathcliff is indeed Cathy's other Self, then it is Cathy who in the person of Heathcliff gives notice of her continued existence on this earth by dashing Heathcliff's head against the knotted trunk of a tree and howling like a "savage beast being goaded to death with knives and spears." At this point, the persona of Heathcliff no longer represents Cathy's wild Self. Cathy finds her own complete Self, no longer domesticated in life and no longer bound by the constant conflict between the tame (Edgar) and the wild (Heathcliff). This is evident from Brontë's portrayal of Heathcliff throughout the rest of the book. Without Cathy, Heathcliff utterly decays. He becomes mean and vengeful and finally dies.

Some will object that this is a traditional theme—that women must die to regain their Selves. I would suggest, however, that Emily Brontë writes of Cathy's death as the entrance to a new life. In other works where major female characters die, they are no longer heard from in death. They are released, through death, from the suffering of a this-worldly existence into the tamed and oblivious state of an other-worldly existence. Not so with Cathy. She remains in this world and inhabits it on her own terms. Her presence haunts Wuthering Heights. She comes and goes at her will.

Barbara Deming asserts that Heathcliff "is a figure created out of the very depths of a woman's being."[76] Those who know about the lives of the Brontë sisters are aware that Emily Brontë saw her mother and two of her sisters die before her. It is possible that Emily may have been writing not only of her lost Self in *Wuthering Heights* but of her lost sisters. *Wuthering Heights* was a means of consecrating their sisterhood which, in childhood, had been expressed in their imaginary play world of kingdoms and revolutions, passionate intrigues, and adventurous escapades on the moors of Haworth. Emily Brontë perhaps re-created this sisterhood in the persons of Cathy and Heathcliff, endowing them with a similar passion, adventure, wildness, and love of Nature.

That she certainly, in her immersion in and depiction of the wild-

ness of Nature, re-created her original Self is evident from Charlotte
Brontë's words about her sister:

> My sister Emily loved the moors. Flowers brighter than the rose bloomed
> in the blackest of heath for her . . . She found in the bleak solitude many and
> dear delights; and not the least and best loved was—liberty. Liberty was the
> breath of Emily's nostrils; without it, she perished.[77]

Later she added, "I have never seen [Emily's] parallel in anything.
Stronger than a man, simpler than a child, her nature stood alone."[78]

The wildness of original women is not to be confused with sexual
promiscuity. Under the latter guise, many women have settled for new
patterns of conformity. The sexually liberated woman, described in the
hip literature of the 1960s, is "with it" by hetero-relational standards
but is without Gyn/affection—featureless, passive, and nonoriginal.
Sexual promiscuity, in this context, often becomes the model for total
promiscuity, a promiscuity not only of sexuality but of thinking, values,
and commitments.

However, many men and women do confuse wildness with promiscuity. For men, any free and independent woman signals a "loose
woman." The freedom of women is equated with whoredom. A woman
"on her own" is regarded as "free for men." Looseness is reduced to
lewdness. Freedom is transformed from a positive state where women
are free of all men (for example, celibates or lesbians) or even where
women are free of some men (unmarried heterosexually active
women, prostitutes), to a negative state. In hetero-reality, such women
are "free" to be tamed (which often means raped).

Virginity, for example, is attractive to men because it presents the
lure of untamed womanhood. More than this, virginity also signals a
woman who still resides in the world of women. She is thus fresh and
ripe for the world as men have made it. When a man deflowers a
woman, he takes her out of the world of women while also depriving
her of a future with and for women. He is taking her Gyn/affective
power for himself. The virgin symbolizes the woman intact in all her
past and potential Gyn/affective wildness and originality.

De Beauvoir has observed that, for men, "virginity has this erotic
attraction only if it is in alliance with youth . . . Many men of today feel a
sexual repugnance in the presence of maidenhood too prolonged."[79]
De Beauvoir attributes this repugnance to man's fear that old women
have escaped his power and have too much power of their own.
Another possible interpretation specifies the source of such womanly
power—the fact that older virgins have lived a long time in the world

of women or have escaped the sexual and relational constraints of hetero-reality. Whether actualized or not, their potential attraction for their womanist Selves and other women has not been deflowered.

Furthermore, many old women do return literally to the worlds of women. In old age, women are each other's most constant companions. For many, it is the first time in their lives when they do not have to "relate to" or take care of men and children. Margaret Mead spoke of "post-menopausal zest,' of the energies and social roles of women whose child bearing years are past and who then move more freely in society without the constraints that being a woman puts on them . . . rich in knowledge and tradition."[80] For many other old women, it is the time of their lives when they return to their original vital Selves. Barbara Macdonald's work *Look Me in the Eye: Old Women, Aging, and Ageism* speaks eloquently to this point:

"I like growing old," I say to myself with surprise. I had not thought it could be like this. There are days of excitement when I feel almost a kind of high with the changes taking place in my body, even though I know the inevitable course my body is taking will lead to debilitation and death . . . I never grew old before; never died before. I don't really know how it's done. And then I realize, lesbian or straight, I belong to all the women who carried my cells for generations and my body remembers how for each generation this matter of ending is done.[81]

Old women, in general, are not as submerged in the world of hetero-reality as are younger women. In particular, old virgins, female friends, and lesbians have escaped many of the stifling strangleholds of hetero-relations.

Within hetero-reality older women in general and older virgins, lesbians, and/or intimate female friends in particular are perceived as ruined for men. In addition, their feared and mysterious power, to which de Beauvoir refers, may also derive from the threat they pose of ruining young girls for men. Thus the stereotypes of the old hag, the elderly sorceress, and the ancient witch may have an entirely different Gyn/affective power than has been attributed to them thus far in feminist writings. Any woman-identified and autonomous woman, but especially one who has lived a long lifetime in the worlds of women, is perceived as not only spoiled for men but as spoiling other women for men. Gyn/affection is contagious.

Man wants to give woman the world—as he defines it for her—and here are loose women taking it for themselves. The independence and wildness of the loose woman—the virgin, the lesbian, the old woman—conjures up the vision that women not only will take power from men but will take women from men too.

> That two women could mean a great deal to each other while they awaited men to lead them to marriage and the real business of life is negligible; that they could believe that the real business of life is in meaning a great deal to each other and that men are only incidental to their lives—is of course frightening.[82]

A Genealogy of "Loose Women": The Prostitute and the Lesbian

We know very little of the history of loose women. Or rather we know very little about the real history of loose women. In hetero-history, the loose woman is the lewd woman—the harlot, the wanton woman, the degenerate, the woman who engages in all manner of illicit intercourse. I contend that the original loose woman is the free woman—loose and free from bonds and bondage to men. The loose woman is the unattached woman. And because she resisted attachment to men, she became deprived not only of patriarchal protection but of patriarchal repute.

In fact, many women who have not resisted attachment to men but who are perceived as "manless" women, women who are not visibly allied to men, are labeled prostitutes. News accounts from Zimbabwe in mid-November 1983 reported that several thousand women had been arrested in military street sweeps. The government's explanation for arresting these women—most of whom were Black and poor, although the sweeps also reached out to students, nurses, industrial workers, domestic workers, and women working in ministries—was that they wanted to "clean up" prostitution in Zimbabwe. Rudo Gaidzanwa, a native of Zimbabwe and sociologist at the university there, reported that

> ... most women were presumed to be prostitutes until proved otherwise ... During the detentions, women had to produce marriage certificates in the streets. This posed problems for Black women, most of whom are married customarily. Women also needed men to vouch for them at police stations and detention centers so they could be considered non-prostitutes.[83]

This happened in a country which views itself in transition to socialism, and yet the socialist progressivist ethic, as far as thousands of women are concerned, is still oppressively hetero-relational. Women who cannot prove attachment to men are considered prostitutes.

The history of loose women is the history of Gyn/affection, and that history can be found in several places. One starting point is the etymology of the word *hetairā* (or *hetaera*), which originally meant companion, most often companion to other women and only later sexual companion to men. The history of loose women is also related to the history of prostitution. And, finally, it can be found in the woman-identified culture produced by Sappho and her companions on Lesbos.

Kenneth Dover, in *Greek Homosexuality,* acknowledges that *hetairā* in its earliest usage meant companion: "a woman could refer to a female friend of hers as 'my hetairā.'"[84] Sappho in her poetry called her female students *hetairai* (plural), close companions or friends. How the female companion to other women (the original *hetairā*) became the prostitute or the sexual companion of men (the hetero-revisionist *hetairā*) is one starting point for the history of loose women.

In this hetero-revision of women's history, we find an early lesson in how the history of Gyn/affection becomes transmogrified into the history of hetero-relations. Like all historically independent and deviant female acts, woman-identified looseness came to be defined solely in hetero-relational terms and captured by hetero-relational standards. For example, men have consistently appropriated female independence by defining it in heterosexual terms that signify either the presence of illicit heterosexuality (prostitute, whore) or the absence of approved heterosexuality (frigid, old maid). Loose women who repudiate containment by men frustrate the traditional categories of hetero-reality (wife, mother, mistress, and so on). The only way of bringing such women back into the fold of hetero-reality is to assign them hetero-relational labels (prostitutes, lonely or frustrated women, "women who can't catch men").

The word *hetairā* is also associated with lesbianism.[85] One reference, found in Aristophanes and thought to be the first such association between the two words, "derives *hetairistriai* from that category of original double beings who were all female."[86] Dover emphasizes that this word clearly means a homosexual relationship between two women, "and it may acquire a derogatory nuance from *laikastria,* 'whore.'"[87] Aristophanes provides one of the earliest references documenting the change of female companion of other women (and/or lesbian) to prostitute.

This same transformation—from female companion to prostitute—is at work in the demeaning of the historical Sappho. It began with the

Athenian comic poets. In their work we find Sappho's Gyn/affection and lesbianism equated with prostitution. In fourth-century B.C. Athens, when these poets were writing, women had no political or economic power, no legal rights as adult persons, and no choice in marriage. The Greek Demosthenes had divided women into three categories: "Hetaerae [courtesans] we keep for the sake of pleasure; concubines [female slaves] for the daily care of our persons; wives, to bear us legitimate children and to be the trusted guardians of our households."[88] Thus, when the Athenian comic poets wrote of Sappho and her companions, they were befuddled. How could they portray such loose women who encouraged others like their Selves to live a loose and undefinable existence? Sappho did not fit into any of Demosthenes' accepted categories. As Dolores Klaich phrases it: "She hadn't been a wife. She hadn't been a slave. That left only courtesans, and accordingly, without facts, the Athenian comic poets, those who wrote what we call Middle Comedy, treated Sappho as a joke in their plays, portraying her as a prostitute, something she had never been."[89] Sappho's independent Gyn/affection was transformed into the mirror opposite of what it actually was. "Her free-wheeling, nondomestic, nonappendage life, and the fact that she had spoken openly of this life, set her apart from the silenced Athenian women—that is, enough apart from the then cultural average—to warrant ridicule."[90]

Thus a loose woman who cannot be circumscribed by hetero-categories for women goes down in history as a woman ready for any kind of sexual behavior, that is, a prostitute. This perception is also in keeping with a secondary definition of prostitute in the *Oxford English Dictionary:* "a person given over to infamous practices of any kind." The Athenian humorists held up Sappho and her companions as examples of "shameless and uninhibited sexuality" and credited them "with all such genital acts as the inventive pursuit of a piquant variety of pleasure can devise, including homosexual practices together with fellation, cunnilinctus, threesomes, copulation in unusual positions and the use of olisboi."[91]

The loose woman—the female companion of other women—and the lesbian were later consolidated as prostitutes in the work of the Roman satirists. Writing later, in the second century A.D., they subject Sappho and her companions to ridicule and censure, outrightly associating lesbians with heterosexual prostitutes. For example, in *Dialogue of the Courtesans,* Lucian has one prostitute say to another:

> "We've been hearing queer things about you, Leaena. They say Philippa, that millionaire lady from Lesbos, feels about you the way a man does and

that the two of you have been making love, doing Lord knows what to each other. What's this—blushing? Tell me, is it true?"

"Yes, Clonarium. But I'm so ashamed of myself! It's all so unnatural!"[92]

This passage initiates, among other things, "the practice of lumping lesbians with whores in an atmosphere of general debauchery."[93] To this insight I would add that this passage begins a trend that persists to this day of transforming woman-identified affection and love into hetero-relational sex "acts." We will see this same changeover at work, in different ways, in the labeling of other groups of women who maintain strong Gyn/affective ties. Among groups like the marriage resisters and nuns, for example, Gyn/affection is attributed to hetero-sexual deprivation or hetero-relational failure, when it is not turned into promiscuous heterosexuality. The roots of converting Gyn/affection or woman-centered living into a hetero-relational sexual ethos are found in many disparate places.

In the winter of 1979, I traveled to the Yucatán in Mexico. One of my destinations was the Isla Mujeres, "Island of Women." Before going, I researched where the name had originated. Most of the guidebooks reported that the island had been so named because sailors had formerly kept prostitutes there for their return after long voyages. Upon further and less superficial investigation, I learned that the Spanish called it the Isla Mujeres because they had found numerous statues of female figures there, which they construed to be evidence of a goddess-worshiping culture largely populated by women and in which women were held in high esteem. The popular guidebooks had transformed a woman-centered milieu into an island of prostitution.

The same phenomenon is at work in David Reuben's *Everything You Always Wanted to Know About Sex*. Here he treats lesbianism and prostitution in the same chapter. The parallel placement is self-explanatory. Reuben, however, is merely one of a long list of writers who have consistently and without evidence lumped lesbians together with prostitutes. Zola, Daudet, and de Maupassant are only a few of the authors who collapse lesbians into prostitutes and vice versa.

This equating of lesbianism with prostitution proclaims that lesbianism is one of the most degenerate vices comparable to what is regarded as the sludge of prostitution. As the highest of virtues for women is defined in hetero-relational terms (for example, marriage), so too is the lowliest of vices. In this equation, the evil, and in more recent times the sickness, of lesbianism cannot be adequately portrayed unless it is framed in heterosexual terms. The so-called moral corruption of loose women can be gauged only by hetero-relational standards.

Once again, the woman-identified deviant from hetero-relations—the loose woman—becomes known and encompassed by the very hetero-relations that she is defying. Hetero-*reductio ad absurdum* (loose woman equated with lewd woman) reminds us of de Beauvoir's words: "He tries to get possession of the woman even in her resistance; he pursues her in the very liberty though which she escapes him."[94]

The reduction of lesbian and/or female companion to prostitute has not been a mere literary construction. Some lesbians have been prostitutes, or some prostitutes have been lesbians, depending on how you choose to frame your sentence. This fact has not been overlooked in many histories and psychologies of prostitution. Havelock Ellis and John Addington Symonds, in their study *Sexual Inversion,* noted "the frequency of homosexual practices" among prostitutes in all parts of the world.[95] The thesis that "prostitutes are lesbians in disguise" has been advanced by many men who have "studied" both lesbianism and prostitution—among them Lombroso, Moll, Carlier, Martineau, and others.[96] Harold Greenwald, in *The Call Girl: A Social and Psychoanalytic Study,* writes of "reaction formation" in prostitutes, a so-called defense mechanism in which there is "an attempt to express in overt behavior the exaggerated opposite of their original impulse."[97] He continues:

> Being homosexual, they tried to act heterosexually . . . One tries to act out the exact opposite in order to *deny the original impulse* . . . because the defenses of the girls were so weak and spotty, one would frequently find reaction formations existing side by side with the direct expression of the impulse they were designed to suppress. [Italics mine][98]

Lest one miss the point in this tangle of psychoanalytic jargon, Greenwald means that the behavior of a prostitute was acted out at the same time that she carried on lesbian relationships. What is more important, however, is that in this same knot of psychoanalytic reasoning, we find an acknowledgment that lesbianism is the "original impulse" for such traditionally heterosexually defined women.

I do not mean to hold up as authoritative sources such as Havelock Ellis, Frank Caprio, or Harold Greenwald. They are all notoriously ignorant on the subjects of prostitution and lesbianism. What is instructive in the passages cited is the testimony that prostitution, seemingly the most promiscuous of heterosexual acts, is pseudo-heterosexuality and a flight from lesbianism. If prostitution is the oldest profession, then women loving women may well be the oldest and most truly affective relationship!

Most histories of prostitution begin with the chronicling of sexual acts engaged in by women that were reputedly carried out in sacred temples. These women have come down to us labeled as sacred prostitutes. We know, however, that the women who inhabited the most ancient temples were sacred virgins. Only later did the phenomenon of temple prostitute arise. I maintain that the sacred virgin becomes transformed into the sacred prostitute in much the same way that the lesbian or female companion has been changed into a prostitute: by male definition, to contain female independence and to heterosexualize loose women. Anthropologists have cited the prevalence of certain rituals of sacred virgins from which men and even male dogs were excluded.[99] They have named these "female homosexual" rites. Wherever women are joined in affinity with each other, men have often felt left out and have felt compelled to invade such woman-space. In fact, there were direct and physically assaultive male invasions of such rites—rapes. Under such siege, many women probably were forced into prostitution in exact opposition to their "original impulse."

Anthropologist Fernando Henriques's work *Prostitution and Society* gives evidence of this forced prostitution under the most extreme conditions. Henriques speaks of ancient Phoenicia, where "their virgins also were presented for prostitution to the strangers who resorted there."[100] He describes a particularly barbaric account of the atrocities perpetrated against the sacred virgins of Heliopolis when Constantine abolished the "custom" of giving over sacred virgins to prostitution:

> They stripped the holy virgins who had never been looked upon by the multitude, of their garments, and exposed them in a state of nudity, as public objects of insult and derision. After numerous other inflictions, they shaved them, ripped them open, and placed inside them the food usually given to pigs; and the animals thus devoured these human entrails in conjunction with their ordinary food. I am convinced that the citizens perpetrated this barbarity against the holy virgins from motives of revenge, on account of the abolition of the ancient custom of yielding up virgins to prostitution.[101]

At this time in history, c. the fourth century A.D., as well as in other periods, and in various parts of the Mediterranean as documented by Henriques, many young women spent a part of their lives acting as sacred prostitutes. These women were required to be virgins, their virginity being sacrificed as a ritual offering. If we see virginity in a more woman-defined sense of female integrity—as a woman who is unto her Self, independent from men—we can also understand how men would perceive such integrity as necessary to contain and control. Thus the sacred virgin becomes the sacred prostitute who later becomes the secular prostitute.

The christianized version of the sacred virgin has been the nun. As with her sisters, the lesbian and the prostitute, the nun was categorized, contained, raped, and martyred for being a loose woman. Chapter II chronicles the long, proud, and sometimes ambivalent history of the nun as loose woman.[102]

II

Varieties of Female Friendship: The Nun As Loose Woman

The female possessed of masculine ideas of independence, the viragint who would sit in the public highways and lift up her pseudo-virile voice, proclaiming her sole right to decide questions of war or religion, or the value of celibacy and the curse of woman's impurity, and that disgusting anti-social being, the female sexual pervert, are simply different degrees of the same class—degenerates.

> William Lee Howard
> *The Perverts*

I am independent!
    I can live alone
and I love to work.

> Mary Cassatt

The most holy bond of society is friendship.

> Mary Wollstonecraft

I am not talking to you now through the medium of custom, conventionalities . . . It is my spirit that addresses your spirit . . . equal,—as we are!

> Charlotte Brontë,
> *Jane Eyre*

Among the many attacks on convents and nuns, especially during the Protestant Reformation, the charge of loose woman recurs frequently. Lust, carnal attachments, harlotry—all vices reputed to reside in convents from the very beginning of their existence—were said to derive from the loose condition of religious women, that is, their state of being independent and unattached to men. The supposed "unnaturalness" of nuns living apart from men, vowed to virginity and engaging in activities denied to women of their time, was a convenient explanation in which to ground their status as "fallen women."

Martin Luther, in one of his letters, gave the following hetero-rationale for why nuns were supposedly abandoning their cloisters during the Reformation:

> Women are ashamed to admit this, but Scripture and life reveal that only one woman in thousands has been endowed with the God-given aptitude to live in chastity and virginity. *A woman is not fully the master of herself.* God fashioned her body so that she should be with a man, to have and to rear children.[1] [Italics mine.]

From a Gyn/affective perspective, these words can be interpreted in quite a different way. In the background of many similar attacks on virginity is a perception that virginity represents female independence from men and a woman-centered integrity. If we rephrase the quotation from Luther in the following way, we have a clearer idea of what all the attacks were directed at:

> The thousands of women living in chastity and virginity are not capable of doing so because women *should not* be the masters of their Selves. Too many women have become the masters of their Selves, spurning men, and refusing to breed men's children, thus violating their "God-given" and "natural" purpose, as evidenced by the way in which their bodies are fashioned. Since the majority of women *should not* live an unattached existence, the large numbers of women now doing so must be living a loose, that is, an unchaste and wanton, life.

Not only Luther but the many attackers who followed and preceded him were fearful that too many women were indeed becoming the "masters of themselves." The attacks on virginity specifically betray that the detractors understood virginity in much more than sexual terms. As a consecrated state that legitimated an "unhusbanded life,". virginity carried the germ of female independence, integrity, and intimacy that would give women freedom from men and male dictates. It was a state of "single blessedness."

For years, Catholic clerics and critics had attacked the independent lives of nuns. The Protestant Reformation grounded these attacks in the virginity of nuns, seeing this as the ultimate symbol of their looseness. It used the age-old hetero-relational tactic of transmogrifying the virgin—she who is untouched by men—into the prostitute, she who is despoiled, conquered, and constantly handled by men. In this view, all women who were unmarried were immoral. Once more, the female companion of other women was represented as the sexual companion of men *(hetairā)*. A loose woman who resides in a female world that is free from direct bonds with men becomes a loose woman who is put in constant bondage to men and male desires. Women who are unattached to men become immoral.

The Reformers, however, reinforced and created new grounds for assaulting a tradition of female monasticism that Lina Eckenstein has characterized as heir to the independent spirit and activity that existed among women, much earlier, in "outgoing heathendom, that is, in pre-Christian times," Eckenstein connects the development of religious communities of women in early Christianity, particularly among the Germanic peoples, with pre-Christian goddess traditions.

> Reminiscences of an independence belonging to them in the past, coupled with the desire for leadership, made many women loth to conform to life inside the family as wives and mothers under conditions formulated by men. *Tendencies surviving from the earlier period, and still unsubdued,* made the advantages [*sic*] of married life weigh light in the balance against a loss of liberty. *To conceive the force of these tendencies is to gain an insight into the elements which the convent forthwith absorbs.* [Italics mine][2]

With the advent of Christianity and the demise of what Eckenstein calls "heathendom," commanding female figures all but disappeared. Women ceased to have significant intellectual, political, and social power. The convent thus became the refuge of many women who still craved this power and independence. It offered opportunities undreamed of an unactualized by most women during these times. As Eileen Power notes, monasticism "made use of their [nuns'] powers of organization in the government of a community, and in the management of household and estates; it allowed nuns an education which was for long better than that enjoyed by men and women alike outside the cloister."[3]

The nun carried on the tradition of the loose woman, that is, the independent woman, associated with a pagan and ungodly period. Therefore, female autonomy and detachment from men were regarded as pagan and ungodly. The male hierarchy was always in conflict with the independent spirit which had drawn many women to convent living initially. Eckenstein notes that the good/bad woman distinction arose prior to the introduction of Christianity.

> It arose as the father-age gained on the mother-age, when appropriated women were more and more absorbed into domesticity, while those women outside, who either resented or escaped subjection, found their position surrounded by increasing difficulties, and aspersions more and more cast on their independence.[4]

Christianity, however, accepted and reinvigorated this distinction and attempted to force women to live within its parameters. Consistently, it cast "aspersions" on women's independence. It domesticated the earlier traditions of loose women, which attracted women to convents, by gradually regulating the Rule and the living conditions of nuns along with their ability to move freely in the world at large. It also transformed the Gyn/affective integrity of the pre-Christian loose woman by symbolically heterosexualizing the nun as the "bride of Christ" in its liturgy and traditions of prayer.

The taming of nuns must be placed alongside the circumscribing of all unhusbanded women, as a class, in Christianity. Large numbers of loose women abounded particularly in the late Middle Ages. Tax records indicate that considerable numbers of unattached women were on the tax rolls: "a door-to-door survey in Frankfurt between the years 1354 and 1463 showed that independent, that is, unmarried women comprised one-sixth to one-fourth of all taxpayers."[5] Many loose women played a role in the life of the court and the town. Others emerged into the labor force, though not without considerable opposition from men.[6] Many earned their living by selling in the marketplace. Some set up house together, leading to cooperative arrangements and female organizations.

The Beguines, in particular, are a Gyn/affective testimony to the history of loose women. They gathered themselves into communal settlements throughout Europe, especially in Flanders, where many of their remarkable dwellings still stand.[7] Dayton Phillips estimates that in Strasbourg, the community of Beguines and the unattached women who gathered around them constituted at least 10 percent of the city.[8] Despite disapproval from church authorities, the Beguines continued to grow. The movement spread "like contagion." In the thirteenth century, Matthew Paris said that the rapid progress of the movement was one of the wonders of the age.[9] By the middle of the century, there were societies of Beguines in almost every urban area of Europe.

As a religious group without vows and outside the established religious orders of women, the Beguines posed an immense threat to the Church hierarchy. They often held meetings of women at which theology and spirituality were discussed without the counsel of priests. Hostile churchmen denounced their thirst for theological knowledge, saying that the study of theology should be restricted to clerics. Beguines sought no church approval for their lives but called themselves religious women.

The Beguine movement differed from all earlier female religious groups in that "it was basically a women's movement, not simply a feminine appendix to a movement which owed its impetus, direction, and main support to men."[10] It had no Rule of life. It sought no authorization from Rome and no benefits or patrons. The majority of its members came from the lower classes and lived by the toil of their own hands.

Many people in the towns where they lived disapproved of the liberty that Beguine women enjoyed. R.W. Southern, a Church historian, puts it this way: "Parish priests who lost parishioners to the friars, fathers who lost daughters, men who resented the women who got away, were all the enemies of the beguines."[11] And bishops felt that women became Beguines to escape obedience to priests and "the coercion of the marital bonds."[12]

The commitment of the Beguines to each other was not sealed by the irrevocable promises of religious vows. Their commitment was evident, however, in the ways in which they cared for each other. Dayton Phillips, who examined the wills and addresses of the Beguines in Strasbourg, reveals that a whole section of town was inhabited by women who shared houses, rented to other women, bequeathed property to their Beguine friends, and ensured that other Beguines could become tenants after the present residents moved on or died. Often Beguines became the center for larger groups of loose women.

As with all loose women, the Church acted to curtail their independence. The General Council of Vienne in 1311 condemned the Beguine way of life. Shortly thereafter, many cities acted to dissolve the Beguine houses, or Beguinages, but this was not really accomplished until the beginning of the fifteenth century. Some of these women continued to live in a modified Beguine style until the end of the eighteenth century. Others went into established religious orders. Many others, according to Rufus Jones, who "were deprived of their Beguinage and turned adrift without means of support, and forbidden to beg, were compelled to die of want, or to find husbands, or to sink to a life of prostitution."[13]

By its intolerance of independent women such as the Beguines, the Church created the climate in which some women were forced into actual prostitution. This was the ultimate consolidation of the Church's definition of all loose women as lewd, that is, as prostitutes. Eckenstein addresses this:

> The loose or unattached women of the past are of many kinds and many types; to apply the term prostitute to them raises a false idea of their position as compared with women in other walks of life. If we would deal with them as a class at all, it is only this they have in common,—that they are indifferent to the ties of family.[14]

Some loose women were prostitutes, but many more were not. Most were single women, unattached to men. However, since the good woman was either the wife/mother or eventually the domesticated nun, the unhusbanded woman was consigned to the category of whore.

Nuns are also associated with prostitution in etymologies of the word *nun*. The *Oxford English Dictionary* gives as one definition of *nun* "a courtesan" and informs us that this is its "transferred sense." Interestingly, as an example of this usage, it also gives the following: "1776 Foote, Lame Lover I. Wks. 1799, II. 60. An abbess, well known about town, with a smart little nun in her suite."

More interestingly, the historian Friedrich, investigating the beginning of convent living in Augsburg, Germany, cites the settlement of Afra and her companions. These women, converted to Christianity in the early part of the fourth century A.D., became nuns and established a foundation in Augsburg for women of like-minded religious conviction. However, prior to her conversion, Afra is said to have "kept a house of ill fame with three companions."[15] Some time after their conversion, Afra and her three companions were martyred for their faith, and Afra was canonized as a Christian saint. As with all saints, she became the patron of a particular cause or lifestyle. In Afra's case, she was entitled the patron saint of hetairism,[16] probably because in the mind of the Church she would then become an example for the numbers of loose women, who were all lumped together as prostitutes and whom the Church wished to bring under its control in convents.

The Church used the Empress Theodora who, "mindful of her own early lot," gathered more than five hundred harlots together in an effort to bring them to a different life in what were called "convents of repentance."[17] Such churchly labors continued well into the late Middle Ages. "Many efforts were made to rescue the prostitutes who abounded in the Middle Ages. In the thirteenth century an Order of St. Mary Magdalene existed for them, and in the fourteenth century numbers of cities contained houses of *sorores de penitentia* (literally translated as houses of penitential sisters).[18] Women who did not join these orders permanently were encouraged to remain for a respectable time of "conversion."

> As an incentive to get these converted women back into the marriage market (and as a further indication that incentives for men were needed), it was ordered that any man who married one of the women was to suffer no slights to his honor nor any damage to his rights as a guild member. Further, if his new wife returned to her errant ways, she was to be drowned.[19]

Since any unattached woman was labeled a prostitute, however, the category is ultimately meaningless. For those loose women who entered convents and remained, the Church failed to realize that many of them carried their traditions of looseness into the monastery. And often, in the convent, the revised *hetairā* (the so-called prostitute) found her "original impulse" toward hetairism in the sisterhood of her female companions. For example, it should be noted in the case of Afra that although she relinquished her supposed life of "ill fame," she did not give up her companions. Many loose women, in converting to Christianity and taking up residence in "convents of repentance," did so with scores of women whom they had known "in another life." By doing this, they re-created the meaning and reality of hetairism, restoring its most original and woman-identified sense. They established in their convents a hetaerocracy, or Rule of companions.

The history of nuns and convent living is, I maintain, a hetaerocracy, a Rule of companions. It has not been a smooth and unalloyed history of female friendship. Nonetheless, it is a history that deserves recognition in the genealogy of Gyn/affection.

The convent is also a primary locus for the long-term institutionalization of female friendship under the aegis of sisterhood, a situation in which women spent their lives primarily with women, gave to women the largesse of their energy and attention, and formed powerful affective ties with each other—so powerful that this Gyn/affection became effective in the world outside the convent. Today,

> they are the largest group of "professional" women Christians in the world; there are over a million of them—mostly Roman Catholic, but a substantial number who are Orthodox or Anglican. They are a genuinely international group; with the possible exception of China (whence there is no evidence) they can be found in every country in the world.[20]

The aim of this genealogy is not to romanticize nuns as models of female friendship. Having spent twelve years of my life in a religious community of women and having experienced at first hand the ambivalences and complications of Gyn/affection within this context—on these grounds alone, it would be difficult for me to glorify female friendship in convents. What I did experience there, however, was a richness of friendship. And it is this that I contend can serve as an empowering example for the Searcher of female friendship—in spite of all its mixed messages.

The Rule of Companions

Men have always been portrayed as comrades-in-tasks, male bonding being the supposed result of a shared and manly commitment to similar work. Yet women have always come together over common tasks—the tending of children, quilt making, establishing the female guilds in the Middle Ages, and supervising the marketplaces of various cultures. It has long been ignored that women "find love where they work." It took Havelock Ellis, noting the connection between feminism and lesbianism, to publicize that one often leads to the other.

> . . . having been taught independence of men and disdain for the old theory which placed women in the moated grange of the home to sigh for a man who never comes, a tendency develops for women to carry this independence further and to find love where they work.[21]

The Rule of companions was based on a notion of spiritual friendship that expanded the meaning of affection. It moved, acted upon, influenced, and impressed women with the spirit of other women. Nuns affected each other in the wider sense of Gyn/affection. They affected the course and the history of Christianity, political affairs, education, culture, and society in general.

In attempting to suppress a whole class of loose women, Christianity tried to create a controlled place for them in monasteries and convents. Women in convents were regarded as subject to an "honorable independence." Almost from the very beginning of convent living, male clerics attempted to define and limit what was regarded as "dishonorable freedom," euphemistically referred to as female "immodesty" or as "usurping the prerogatives of men." Initially, this control was not as direct as it became in later years. The seventh through twelfth centuries especially saw a flowering of female monasteries and an emerging power of nuns and abbesses in the intellectual, political, and spiritual realms. For almost five centuries, the power and achievements of many nuns demonstrated that a woman-willed, woman-defined independence could not be squelched. These early nuns, indeed, reclaimed the prerogatives of earlier independent women.

Initially many married women left their husbands to establish and direct settlements of women. A large number came from the royal and aristocratic classes and brought with them the wealth needed to subsidize such undertakings. Many were accompanied by other women—daughters, sisters, nieces, and friends—who populated the communities they founded.

Much has been made of the fact that convents were convenient places for royalty to dispose of daughters who could not be married off because of unattractiveness, sickness, or even politics. It has also been generally assumed that large numbers of women were forced into convents and confined there unwillingly, often for a lifetime. A variety of writings, including Reformation literature, later reinforced this perspective, a perspective often accompanied by the ever-present representation of nuns as embittered, sexless, sick, and despondent women. "[The convent] is above all the haven of broken lives, the almost obligatory asylum of women suffering from small-pox, a malady all but forgotten to-day, but one which disfigured a good quarter of the women of that time."[22]

More scholarly explanations attribute the large numbers of women entering convents, especially during the Middle Ages, to the "low sex ratio" in Europe (females outnumbering males in the late Middle Ages by margins of ninety-two in many areas to eighty-three in others).[23] Hetero-scholarship portrays these women as male-deprived. John McNeill represents this viewpoint: "the crusades had called many young men abroad so that many women were left widows or *doomed to spinsterhood*." [Italics mine][24] The "surplus" of women, it would seem, found a natural place within the established religious orders for women and, when needed, created new communities for the growing numbers of women wishing to join.

These explanations ignore several facts. In the late Middle Ages, large numbers of women clamored to join convents.[25] But convents were few in number, and many remained exclusive. Many women demanded new female communities, initially attaching themselves to established male orders but gradually seeking recognition of their own separate female orders. In reaction to these demands, the Fourth Lateran Council in 1215 issued a decree that there would be no more orders and that any new religious community had to be set up within the Rule of an approved order.

> Some historians believe that the Beguines were a natural consequence of the reluctance of the men's religious orders in the twelfth and thirteenth centuries to run convents for women. According to this thesis, the Beguines were *not women who could not marry, but who could not get into convents.*[Italics mine][26]

Convents were therefore attractive places for many women. The student of female monasticism is forced to recognize that the prime impetus to this attraction was the independence and wealth of intellectual, spiritual, and political offerings that convents held out to women who had no access to them in the world outside the convent. "The career open to the inmates of convents both in England and on the continent was greater than any ever thrown open to women in the course of modern European history."[27]

The age was a violent one. Women were treated badly, especially during the late Middle Ages. Domestic violence, as well as political violence, abounded. Wife-beating was legitimated by the Church. Many women who had pride and self-respect could not be attracted to marriage. The convent allowed this pride and self-respect to be exercised in the pursuit of a higher good—God and what was viewed as "the work of God."

While men were doing battle against women, they were also waging war in general. Constantly engaged in fighting, many men remained coarse and uneducated. It was not considered a disgrace for even aristocratic men to be illiterate as long as they were skilled in the "arts" of war. Culture and learning became more and more the province of women in monasteries. Noblewomen were confined to their homes, cut off from any interaction with women of their age and standing and from possibilities of intellectual development. In such a context, convents held an immense and independent attraction for women.

The convent also was one of the few female institutions in which older women became tutors and out-of-the-ordinary mentors for younger women who were drawn to their companionship of living and learning. Many such girls came to convents at an early age. Some of them left in later life, but many stayed on to become permanent members of communities.

Most important, female monasteries offered a "companionship of equals." Here women dedicated to learning and the arts resided in permanent companionship. The presence of women for each other, committed to the same tasks and legitimated by godly motives, created a rich community life. Spurred on by spiritual friendship, women cultivated the life of the spirit, the life of the mind, and even the life of the *polis.*

It is this element of independent attraction to women and woman-defined contexts that is constantly left unexamined in hetero-explanations of separate women's communities. Indeed there was a dearth of males in the late Middle Ages, as measured by normative sex ratio patterns. However, this dearth can be interpreted in a much more woman-enriching way than the "deprived women" theories that accent "surpluses" of "unmarriageable" women. Instead it can be understood as a major factor that helped create the conditions for women's independence and affinity for each other.

> In low sex ratio societies, women themselves question the value of mar-
> riage—as well they might, when the ugliness of competition, their social
> and economic disadvantages in marriage and the reluctance and misogyny
> of men all add to its repugnance ... In these societies, some women try,
> using whatever means possible within the cultural context, to gain an
> economic, social and sexual existence for themselves outside the traditional
> roles of wife and mother. This puts them into direct competition with men,
> a competition which men heartily dislike and which adds to male mis-
> ogyny. As women seek to define new roles for themselves, their conflicts
> and struggle are reflected in speech and writing. Spokeswomen arise;
> women are no longer silent.[28]

These words still do not give enough emphasis to women's independent attraction for each other, but they do recognize, from those preoccupied with sex ratio patterns, a more women-centered analysis.

Large numbers of women were attracted to convents for their own woman-defined reasons. During the early history of female monasteries, such women were mainly from the upper and aristocratic classes. Their lives, some of which were recorded, give evidence of a personal and social rejection of the lifestyle of their class. Many chose to deny their aristocratic backgrounds, finding their treasure in the vow of poverty. For many, this was a revolutionary gesture. Since religion was central to everyday life at this time, women would understandably struggle for independence and liberation in relation to it.

Later, however, the same reasons that propelled upper-class women into convents attracted women from the lower classes. Women who were not attracted to marriage, who were drawn by the independence and companionship of women, and who wanted an outlet for talents and work not available to them in the secular world found in convents a natural habitat. It was the demand from large numbers of lower-class women that created the crisis over expanding the number of female orders for women and ultimately precipitated the 1215 decree forbidding new foundations.

There was a strong anti-female reaction in other orders against the large numbers of women who wished to join them. "It was thought that women inevitably contributed to indiscipline . . . Women were also considered to be receptive to all forms of religious prophecy and to be completely unrestrained in relationships with their leaders or patrons."[29]

More specifically, what were the spiritual, intellectual, and political attractions of convent living? The range of subjects taught in Saxon convents, for example, was extensive. It included religious and classical literature, spinning, and weaving. Reference is also made to the study of law, which a Princess Sophie mastered so well that she entered into disputation with learned men and successfully opposed them. Many of the better-known monasteries for women—particularly Herford, Gandersheim, and Quedlinburg—became centers of culture and learning.

Roswitha (Hrotsvith), a nun in the Saxon monastery of Gandersheim, made the monastery famous for its brilliant learning and drama. She occupies a unique place in the history of women in monasticism and is recognized for her exceptional literary genius. She wrote legends, and her work in this area is said to be the earliest account in verse of a pact with the devil. As such, it is a precursor to the many versions of the legend of Faust.[30] However, she is most renowned for her dramatic compositions, originally composed for her companions in the monastery. In fact, between the comedies of classical times and the medieval miracle plays, no other drama except Roswitha's was composed.[31] Roswitha modeled her plays on those of the classical dramatist

Terence but deliberately reversed his antifeminist themes. Where the plays of Terence portray the seductiveness and frailty of women, Roswitha depicted the stamina of women, particularly their moral stability and resistance to evil.

Women's religious settlements also became centers of art and the art industry. The design and ornamentation of books was cultivated there. Manuscripts were transcribed, and convents became centers of culture in proportion to their wealth in books. Women attained great proficiency as calligraphers and miniaturists. According to art and Church historian F. Bock, "It is in the nunnery that the art of design as well as the technique of weaving were brought to highest perfection."[32] The weaving of church hangings and the embroidery of altar cloths, vestments, and coverings for church furniture were the work of nuns. Besides being Spinsters in the sense of unattached, independent women, nuns were also Spinsters in the primary sense of that word— "a woman whose occupation is to spin."[33]

One of the earliest abbesses who wielded both intellectual and political might was Hilde (Hild) of Whitby in Britain. She and the abbesses who followed her were ranked only after bishops in dignity and importance. Some of these abbesses also acted as representatives of the emperor in times of his absence. Kings and princes sought their counsel. As independent landowners who held jurisdiction over large parcels of land and the people who worked on them, they were peers and employers. In an age when the feudal system was harsh and oppressive, the territories that abbesses ruled were noted for their just treatment of tenants and workers. Abbesses owned home-farms like any other lords of the manor, but they did not act like typical feudal lords.

Whitby was a double monastery where both women and men resided in separate quarters. Hilde presided over the entire complex. The origins of the double monastery are unclear. Despite their portrayal by the later Protestant Reformers as hotbeds of heterosexual lust and immorality, they were probably set up for protection [34] or to assist the nuns in the heavy task of farming the fields as well as to provide priestly services for the nuns.[35] Many of these monasteries, especially in Anglo-Saxon England during the seventh and eighth centuries, were led by women. Historian Eleanor McLaughlin notes that "this female leadership was not perceived as unusual by witnesses such as Bede." [36]

Hilde was the most prominent of the English abbesses. It was during her rule that the renowned scholarly and artistic period of Celtic monasticism, which produced the Lindisfarne Gospels and the Book of Kells, occurred. She herself was a great scholar who trained both women and men, although she is more famous because of her male pupils who rose to scholarly and administrative positions not open to women. Hilde is also rememberd for translating many biblical stories from Latin into the vernacular, recognizing that people needed to learn in a language that was their own.

The female monasteries and the abbesses who governed them exercised enormous political power.

> . . . in England in the tenth century four abbesses sat in Parliament as peers. The authority of such persons was enormous. As feudal lords they had the right of ban, sent their contingents of armed knights to the field, gave judgment in courts, and in Germany (as in England) were summoned to the imperial diet. Certain German abbesses had even the right to mint coin.[37]

As a temporal ruler of large areas of land, the abbess's rights of overseeing encompassed many miles. She had the duties and privileges of a baron who held her or his property from the king. Thus the abbess was not dependent on any other political figure.

During the early medieval period, abbesses had ecclesiastical prerogatives that were later reserved for male clerics. Some abbesses, notably those of St. Cecilia in Cologne, had juridical and suspension power over male clerics. When newly consecrated, the abbesses of Conversano, in Italy, are reported to have had the traditional homage ceremony paid to them by each member of the clergy in their respective districts. In this ceremony men were required to prostrate themselves before the abbess and kiss her hand.[38] Originally the power of many of these abbesses extended to giving licenses for preaching, confessing, entering religious life, and convoking synods.[39] Some abbesses retained these powers as late as the fifteenth century.[40]

What do all these intellectual, political, and spiritual powers have to do with Gyn/affection? If Gyn/affection, in its expanded sense, is "the state of influencing, acting upon, moving, and impressing and of being influenced, acted upon, moved, and impressed by other women," the intellectual, political, and spiritual activities of these early nuns must have created a climate in which women, in the company of their female companions, could grow and develop. We have seen that in the male tradition of ancient Greece, politics, art, and philosophy all constituted the basis of and emerged from friendship. In the convent, intellectual pursuits, spiritual contemplation, and temporal power became both the foundation for and the effect of a "companionship of equals." Friendship here was much more than the personal movement of one woman toward another.

The genre of spiritual friendship that developed in convents and monasteries certainly included a profound attraction for others who, like the Self, were engaged in the quest for transcendence. However, it did not stop there, nor was such friendship oriented only to a world that existed within convent walls. Early nuns had a profound impact on the world around them.

Many sources acknowledge the intellectual, political, and ecclesiastical power of early nuns with a disapproving tone and even with a bias toward explaining away or diluting these powers. Thus much hetero-research does not detail the influence convents had on the milieu in which they existed. What we do know, however, is that "the monastery was, in those days, anything but an isolated and strictly meditative community. It was a busy and active unit of society with its own economy and definitely an outward thrust of service to the community."[41] It was a context in which women could do great things. It was a community of spiritual friends.

Spiritual Friendship

The companionship that developed in religious communities of women was based on spiritual friendship. This constitutes a unique genre in the history of ideas about friendship and must be examined as such. Spiritual friendship has a language and style of its own within which a deep Gyn/affection was embodied. Nuns expressed commitment to each other in a mode of communication that is peculiar to spiritual friendship, along with a highly pietistic tone that is typical of this "companionship of souls."

To examine spiritual friendship among nuns, we must look at the monastic tradition as a whole and its literature on friendship, most of which has been preserved from male authors. The classic work in this area is *Spiritual Friendship,* written by Aelred of Rievaulx in the twelfth century. Aelred's treatise on friendship was the classic text that influenced the friendships of both nuns and monks of this period. It was read and distributed widely. Even outside the monastery, it enjoyed much popularity. In both style and content, it influenced the direction of spiritual friendship for many years.

The monastic literature up to the ninth century communicates a general distrust of human affection. Early monastics were ambivalent about heartfelt friendship among their members. There is some discussion of friendship as a Christian virtue, a form of charity, and a symbol of the relationship that existed in the Trinity. However, in general, the monastic attitude, as represented by Augustine, is that since all mortal life perishes, the spiritual person is better off not becoming too attached to anything or anyone except God. Aelred, in contrast, held that to become a saint, one does not have to reject or distrust human affections.

The beginning of the twelfth century saw the proliferation of new orders of women as well as monks and canons, "whose fervor and enthusiasm were far beyond the respectable if slightly tepid, monasticism common in older Benedictine houses. This new fire could not help but encourage and spread the devotion to spiritual friendship."[42] Monks and nuns of the twelfth century were not satisfied with the "dry prudence of earlier authors, and they boldly explored the most shocking metaphors of the Song of Songs to express the energy of their passionate love."[43] The book that was most frequently read and commented on in the medieval monastery was the Old Testament's Song of Songs, [44] which uses the language of erotic symbols and metaphors to speak about the desire for and the pursuit of God's love. It was in this context that Aelred's treatise on *Spiritual Friendship* was written.

Aelred insisted that friendship is part of a good and sacred life.

> ...scarcely any happiness whatever can exist among mankind without friendship ... He is entirely alone who is without a friend.
>
> But what happiness, what security, what joy to have someone to whom you dare to speak on terms of equality as to another self; one to whom you can unblushingly make known what progress you have made in the spiritual life; one to whom you can entrust all the secrets of your heart ... What, therefore, is more pleasant than so to unite to oneself the spirit of another and of two to form one.[45]

Furthermore, Aelred held that friendship is "natural" and that "God is friendship." In doing so, he elevated the love of friendship to the love of charity, a revolutionary equation at that time.

Aelred placed great emphasis on a very particular notion of friendship, an emphasis that was much distrusted in later religious Rules and communities.

> And yet, not all whom we love should be received into friendship, for not all are worthy of it. For since *your friend is the companion of your soul*... you wish to become one instead of two... you should... surely choose one who is considered fitted for all this. Then he is to be tried, and so finally admitted. [Italics mine] [46]

This was also a revolutionary concept in the history of spiritual friendship, especially in the context of monasticism's previous aversion to particular friendship. This emphasis on particularity is reinforced by the dialogue in which *Spiritual Friendship* is written. One passage—a discussion between three of the monks, Walter, Gratian, and Aelred—contains very pointed comments about the paricularity of Aelred's choice of friends.

> ... that friend of yours, whom many think you prefer to all of us ... said and did something that everyone could see displeased you ... when we speak together, you will not neglect anything that pleases him no matter how trivial it may be.[47]

In Aelred's concept of particular friendship, there is also discretion in intimacy. Friendship, while it proceeds from affection, must also proceed from reason: "the love is pure because of reason and sweet because of affection."[48] In this notion of reason, as well as in other elements of his development of a theology of friendship, Aelred follows the classical philosophers of friendship, most notably Aristotle and Cicero.

Order is also important to the fullness of spiritual friendship.

> ... the beginnings of spiritual friendship ought to possess, first of all, purity of intention, the direction of reason and the restraint of moderation; and thus the very desire for such friendship, so sweet as it comes upon us, will presently make friendship itself a delight to experience, so that it will never cease to be properly ordered.[49]

It was order and discretion in intimacy that kept a spiritual friendship from becoming "carnal."

The stylized language contained in Aelred's treatise is present in other monastic authors who wrote about friendship. Where commentary exists on these works, their language of love and friendship has been interpreted as camouflaging a lack of content. R. W. Southern, for example, writing on Anselm, another male monastic, sums up Anselm's quite passionate prose on the subject of friendship as a language "enormously overdone for us who are accustomed to read quite different meanings than he intended into the words he uses."[50]

Anselm had written a letter to two young aspirants to the monastic life: "My eyes eagerly long to see your face, most beloved; my arms stretch out to your embraces. My lips long for your kisses; whatever remains of my life deserves your company, so that my soul's joy may be full in time to come."[51] In his commentary on this passage, Southern explains that these expressions of passion, this effusive style, does not convey the depth of intimacy or the felt intensity that these words have today.

> These expressions are not expressions of friendship as we understand it. But still less are they expressions of the passionate love which such words now suggest . . . We are still in a period when love was essentially an intellectual concept. No doubt these words were written under the impulse of a strong emotion . . . This, then, was not a private letter intended for no other eyes than those of the recipient. It had a wider application, and it was intended ultimately to reach a large public.[52]

To Southern, I would respond yes and no. Yes, such letters were written for a wider public. However, this does not nullify their passionate content since, in a religious community, one could be passionate with many individuals. Indeed, spiritual friendship was encouraged with more than one person. No, to the notion that love was "an intellectual concept" in this age of troubadour love poetry. Love, in fact, was becoming highly sensualized. Anyone who reads Anselm's "Prayer for Friends" will find that his notion of love was hardly intellectual. Southern's argument has been used by like minded commentators to dismiss the passionate and heartfelt intimate friendships of other monks and nuns.

It is patronizing to see such friendships as mere language conventions of an age, devoid of content. It is also patronizing to judge this genre empty of passion and intense emotion. Because the hetero-reality of the modern age reserves these feelings, and this language, for lovers, it cannot understand that the spiritual friendships of monks and nuns were just as heartfelt. They were exemplars of Aelred's words "your friend is the companion of your soul." What Lillian Faderman says of romantic friends applies to spiritual friends:

> Their language and behavior are incredible today. Thus such friendships are usually diminished by attributing them to the facile sentimentality of other centuries, or by explaining them in neat terms such as "lesbian" meaning sexual proclivity. *We have learned to deny such a depth of feeling toward anyone but a prospective or an actual mate.* Other societies did not demand this kind of suppression. What these women felt, they were able to say; and what they said, they were able to demonstrate. [Italics mine][53]

Many patterns recur in the journey of women in search of the "companions of their souls." Faderman lists many of these patterns in

a different context in her book *Surpassing the Love of Men*. She notes
that it was the fondest dream of many romantic friends to live together. Initially, this same attraction drew many women to convent
living, for the convent was an all-female physical space where women
shared their lives with other women whose goals and aspirations were
the same. The convent provided proximity to women, freedom from
economic worry, and, later, liberation from the social stigma of being
labeled a lesbian, loose woman, or even old maid. Nuns belonged to a
spiritual community of women who vanquished evil and did so for a
larger goal—the love of God and the world.

Nuns saw themselves as able to change the world, as having a
spiritual, social, and intellectual mission to the secular world. Although
they would have used such words as "service to God and Church,"
"apostolate," and "ministry" (and still do), a prime attraction of
convents was a way of life which gave women, who would otherwise
have had no such possibilities, an access to effect change, a prominent
and active role—in short, a vocation in the world. Sisterhood was seen
as a great undertaking in the service of an active and enthusiastic faith.
This sisterhood, this companionship of souls, was developed and held
fast by a cosmic purpose. Spiritual friendship sustained these women
emotionally and socially. It helped them to engage in a battle that few
women had fought—the battle for souls. In a masculinist world and
church, a convent community in which women were encouraged to be
worthy of each other's and God's love was a powerful motivation for
the many achievements that nuns have wrought from the early monastic period to the present.

Aelred's phrase "companion of the soul" had a profound meaning
for religious women. They delighted in the union of souls and expressed this in the literature of mysticism, in their theology, and in
their poetry. Teresa of Avila, Catherine of Siena, and Juana Inez de la
Cruz are only a few of the prominent women in whose work can be
found expressions of this companionship. Christianity assured nuns
that what they loved so passionately in each other was the soul.
Therefore, it was irrelevant that the friend was of the same sex. The
union of souls was foremost.

An intensely erotic physical affection, of course, could accompany
this spiritual friendship. However, the Rule tried to keep the physical,
and indeed the particular, nature of friendship within boundaries of
moderation. The fact that these boundaries were assailed is attested to
by the prohibitions against particular friendship and the expressions
of what were called "undue intimacies."

Aelred had distinguished between carnal and spiritual friendship, a conscious and experienced distinction on his part. Before he had entered the monastery, Aelred was a rising and successful member of the court of Scotland. During his last period at the Scottish court, he spoke of an inner distress that he describes only in vague terms but that prompted him to leave the court. Aelred's biographers attribute this distress to a relationship formed at this point that caused him great concern.

> ... it is at least possible to interpret his relationship of great intimacy and youthful passion in the light of the remarks about "carnal" friendships in the *Spiritual Friendship*. There may well have been a homosexual component to his youthful friendship which he found disturbing, even if he was not fully aware of its implications. In this case, his conversion to the monastic life might have been, to at least some degree, a method of escaping a potentially sexual situation of which he could not morally approve ... The close and emotional friendships which he was able to enjoy in the monastery prove that a negative reaction to his own youthful crush on a member of the court of Scotland did not inhibit his emotional freedom in later life ... Aelred, unlike some other abbots, was not scandalized by demonstrations of affection, such as holding hands, by his monks.[54]

Unfortunately, other and later religious men and women were scandalized by close and intimate attraction and affection within religious communities, that is, by "the scandal of the particular."

Particular Friendship

In every religious community of women, there have been strong particular friendships. And in every community there have been written and enforced prohibitions against particular friendships. The past Rule of the Sisters of Mercy is representative of such proscriptions:

> As the love and union of religious persons should be founded not on flesh and blood, or on any human motive, but on God alone ... the Sisters shall not admit any inordinate particular friendships, attachments, or affections among them.[55]

The curious coexistence of particular friendship and its interdiction can be partly explained by the presence—over centuries—of a strong tradition of spiritual friendship which, while cautioning against "inordinate" preferential love, also sacralized particular preferences.

For example, Teresa of Avila warned her sisters:

> If our will becomes inclined more to one person than to another ... we must exercise a firm restraint on ourselves and not allow ourselves to be conquered by our affection ... In checking these preferences we must be strictly on the alert from the moment that such a friendship begins and we must proceed diligently and lovingly rather than severely. One effective precaution against this is that the sisters should not be together except at the prescribed hours, and that they should follow our present custom in not talking with one another, or being alone together, as is laid down in the Rule.[56]

On the other hand, however, Teresa described her vision of spiritual friendship in very particular terms.

> It is strange to see how impassioned this love is; how many tears, penances and prayers it costs; how careful is the loving soul to commend the object of its affection to all who it thinks may prevail with God and ask them to intercede with Him for it; and how constant is its longing, so that it cannot be happy unless it sees that its loved one is making progress. If that soul seems to have advanced, and is then seen to fall some way back, her friend seems to have no more pleasure in life: she neither eats nor sleeps, is never free from this fear and is always afraid that the soul whom she loves so much may be lost, and that the two may be parted for ever.[57]

The coexistence of particular friendship and its prohibition was not an easy one, for the claims of the spiritual were very often pitted against the claims of the particular.

Spiritual caveats against particular friendships fell into two categories. The first was offenses against the virtue of charity. "An inordinate particular friendship is one based on purely natural motives that may be foolish, sentimental, or even sensual in character. It leads those Sisters concerned to violate silence and charity."[58] It was feared that particular friendships would be harmful to the spirit of community living, would create factions, and, ultimately, would be injurious to the love of all in the community. As early as the Rule of St. Benedict in the sixth century A.D., it was intimated that particular friendships led to the formation of factions that would disturb and destroy the cohesiveness of the group. Again, Teresa of Avila says of particular friendships:

> One result of it is that all the nuns do not love each other equally: some injury done to a friend is resented; a nun desires to have something to give to her friend and tries to make time for talking to her, and often her object in doing this is to tell her how fond she is of her, and other irrelevant

things, rather than how much she loves God. These intimate friendships are seldom calculated to make for the love of God; I am more inclined to believe that the devil initiates them so as to create factions within religious Orders.[59]

Preferential, that is, particular, love was seen as tending toward exclusive love, and exclusive love was regarded as initiating the demise of religious life.

The second spiritual claim brought against particular friendship was that it violated the vow of chastity. In taking the vow of chastity nuns promised to "avoid undue familiarities, to guard modesty in all their actions, to mortify the senses."[60] Chastity was often interpreted as refraining from illicit intimacy with the opposite sex. However, within the community itself, chastity was always emphasized in the context of avoiding undue intimacy with the same sex. Suzanne Campbell-Jones, in her 1978 study of working nuns, writes: "When the nuns talked to me about chastity they did not refer to relations with the opposite sex, they referred mostly to relations with their own sex, to their own sensuality and sexuality. Indeed the constraints of the chastity vow were felt most strongly within the community itself."[61] Behind all this is the fear of lesbianism, the fear that Gyn/affection would become carnal, unduly intimate, and surpass the boundaries of moderation. For this reason, also, particular friendships were actively discouraged.

Almost every woman who entered a convent prior to Vatican Council II, in the early 1960s, has memories of herself or others being censured for developing what was judged an undue intimacy with another woman, whether with a sister in training or an older professed sister. Often such censure was traumatic because a woman was made to feel that by singling out another in friendship, by wanting to spend time with another, and by demonstrating affection, she was doing something that was an "occasion of sin" or, worse in the emerging age of pastoral psychology, that she was engaged in an abnormal act. Occasionally, and very frequently in some communities, the novice mistress would give daily lectures to young sisters-in-training and would hint at the dangers of homosexual feeling (the word *lesbian* was never used). She would intimate, but never fully explain, that young women at this vulnerable age (usually seventeen to twenty-five) would, if they were "in the world," be "normally and naturally" engaged in hetero-relational friendships, dating, and intimacy. The all-female world of the convent was presented as abnormal, and because of this the young sister was cautioned not to "substitute" inordinate particular friendships with women for what, in a "normal" context, would be lawful hetero-relations. Novices were warned against possible homosexuality, latent or overt.

I remember that during my training period I read monthly notices placed on the bulletin board in strategic locations which informed us that certain members of our group had left the convent that day. Later I learned that many of these women had been asked to leave because they had engaged in "particular acts" of friendship that were "unduly intimate."

My own experience of being censured for forming a particular friendship was an outgrowth of a walk in the woods with another novice during the course of a rare "free day," that is, a day on which convent duties and obligations were reduced to allow free time for prayer, study, and walks out of doors. We had interrupted our walk to sit down on a large boulder, at which point we admired the trees coming into spring life, spoke about our common passion for writing and its relationship to the spiritual life, and briefly—in the ecstasy of being at one with God, the cosmos, and each other—held hands! One of our peers, who evidently saw us engaged in this rather innocuous act of "pressing the flesh," felt it her spiritual duty to report us. That evening, in the refectory, we were both publicly chastised and berated for endangering these rare days of freedom for the rest of our sisters because we had passed the boundaries of permissibility. In private, after the public exposure, my companion was browbeaten by the novice mistress into "confessing" her "illicit affection" for me. The novice mistress attempted to elicit a similar confession from me, but I was not to be intimidated by her representation of our holding hands as simulating intercourse! For this willfulness, I was told that "pride goeth before the fall." My friend, who was traumatized by the censuring and the innuendos of abnormality, inwardly confused about her own feelings, and certainly not helped by my own disdainful judgment that she had allowed herself to be overwhelmed by the novice mistress, left the community a year later.

The fear of homosexuality has been present in religious communities from the beginning. Several early male monastic works and other secondary sources acknowledge this phobia. Derwas Chitty, in his study of early monasticism, cites the dangers to chastity that monks warned against in allowing young boys to join a monastery. He quotes Isaac, Priest of the Cells, who said: "Don't bring boys here: for four Ecclesiae have become desolate in Scetis because of boys."[62] This obscurely worded passage refers to a period of so-called monastic decadence around A.D. 407–08 in which "homosexual carnality" played a major part.

The earliest Rule for religious, the Rule of St. Pachomius, also contains strict injunctions against physical contact between monks.[63] In addition, some early monastic authors had been ambivalent about the value of friendship in the monastic community, citing it as a danger to the spiritual life which leads to a loss of community. They placed the love of friendship in opposition to the necessity for an exclusive love of God.

Although there is very little explicit discussion of the subject of homosexuality in this literature, both the penitentials of the early Middle Ages and the moral literature of the later Middle Ages testify that homosexuality was regarded as a serious sin.[64] In addition, Eleanor McLaughlin, in her article on women in medieval theology, makes the fleeting suggestion that "homosexuality was more of a daily threat to the chastity of the monk than seduction at the hands of a beautiful woman. Could the frequent outcries against the dangerous female be a projection of that fear of the implications of friendship among the brothers?"[65]

The later Middle Ages and the Counter-Reformation shared a similar distrust of particular friendships among religious men and women. Friendships of any sort were almost banned, and the most ordinary of personal contacts were viewed with great suspicion. This distrust, as Cistercian writer M. Basil Pennington points out, bordered "on the neurotic."[66]

We see an explicit reference to the existence of lesbianism in convents in the *Colloquies* of Erasmus, which contain many anti-convent and antimonastic barbs. Specifically in his colloquy entitled "The Girl with No Interest in Marriage," Erasmus concocts a dialogue between two characters, Eubulus and Catharine. Eubulus, a would-be suitor of Catharine, is trying to dissuade her from entering a convent. Primary among the various reasons he offers for not joining is the following:

> Eub: What's more, not everything's virginal among these virgins in other respects, either.
> Cath: No? Why not, if you please?
> Eub: Because there are more who copy Sappho's behavior than share her talent.[67]

These remarks must be viewed within the context of the general antagonism toward immorality within religious communities during the period of the Dissolution of monasteries and convents in the sixteenth century. However, the words of Erasmus do indicate that the suspicion of lesbianism among nuns, if not its reality, must have been talked about during this period.

Vita Sackville-West, in her book on Teresa of Avila, notes that in Spain Teresa's name was associated with that of Sappho. Teresa, like Aelred before her, had alluded in her autobiography to the past occurrence of an intimate relationship between herself and a girl cousin plus "another who was given to the same kind of pastimes." Teresa's parents greatly distrusted this particular cousin and were distressed by their daughter's friendship with her. Teresa, however, continued to enjoy the cousin's company in spite of her parents' disapproval and was led into "wrongdoing." Sackville-West states:

> This is where it becomes difficult to determine what Teresa really did. It is clear that she blames herself bitterly for something; she uses strong words, "mortal sin," "blinded by passion;" and insists that the fear of God had utterly departed from her though the fear of dishonour remained, a torment in all she did.[68]

Sackville-West maintains that such words would not be used in referring to a boy-girl flirtation or to the "salacious conversation" of girls.

It is thought that Teresa's experience with her cousin, as vaguely as she describes it, influenced her later written opinions about "illicit affections." In the context of a lecture given to her nuns on the difference between spiritual and "ill-starred earthly affections," Teresa wrote:

> These last affections are a very hell . . . for the least of the evils which they bring are terrible beyond exaggeration. There is no need for us ever to take such things upon our lips, sisters, or even to think of them, or to remember that they exist anywhere in the world; you must never listen to anyone speaking of such affections, either in jest or in earnest, nor allow them to be mentioned or discussed in your presence.[69]

Within the last twenty-five years many articles in spiritual journals whose readership is largely religious women have attempted to negate the traditional distrust of particular friendship. Jane Becker, a nun, writes: "When I hear someone criticizing friendships my first reaction is suspicion of her. I suspect that she is the last of the great witchhunters of pre-Vatican days, still out stalking the infamous 'particular friendship.'"[70] Many others follow similar lines. They try to reconcile celibacy with close and intimate friendship; to distinguish between healthy friendships and dependent and exclusive relationships; to establish guidelines for good friendships; and to speak openly about sexual feelings as well as about the subject of lesbianism.

Becker writes further:

> ... while only a minority of women may be lesbian, homosexual feelings are possible in all of us; homosexual feelings are not "queer." Most of us have so strongly repressed these feelings that we never become aware of them, but as the larger culture encourages more acceptance along these lines, then consciousness of these feelings is more likely to arise.[71]

In addition, she warns nuns that because they feel deeply about friends of the same sex, this need not mean that they are homosexual. "Sexual feelings tend to make themselves felt when we care deeply about someone; their arousal seems to be a natural part of intimacy."[72] For Becker, the celibate, in this age of the media treatment of homosexuality, may believe that these feelings indicate that she is homosexual, even if she doesn't act on them. She may remember that she had crushes on girls in high school, that she was once a tomboy, that she might have wanted to be a boy, and that she has no sexual interest in men. Becker notes that "even" many heterosexual women have had the same experiences and, therefore, such feelings do not prove homosexuality. However, a nun should confront questions of feared homosexuality directly, even though she is "most likely to find her questioning unfounded in the end."[73] A good spiritual director or counselor should not be too quick to reassure her but rather should explore all such questions honestly. "Homophobia ... is a far more dangerous feeling than homosexual desires."[74]

Finally, even if a woman is oriented in a "homosexual way," such an individual is capable of living a religiously celibate life. Celibate lesbians are in a situation analogous to celibate heterosexuals.

> The critical variables here are not one's sexual orientation but one's ability to maintain celibate friendships and one's commitment to this lifestyle. Research with lesbians suggests that this choice of celibacy is even more possible for females than for males since even active lesbians are less interested in the physical aspects of their relationships (and more interested in psychological intimacy) than are their male counterparts.[75]

The article indeed contains mixed messages. On the positive side, Becker stresses that particular friendships need not be an impediment to community, that sexual feelings "even" of a lesbian nature can coexist with celibacy, and that intimacy and intensity of feelings are to be affirmed. Thus, as her subtitle declares, "friendship is good."

To be evaluated less positively is her assumption that only a minority of women are lesbian, although she herself states clearly that many so-called heterosexual women have experienced sexual feelings for women, role-defying behavior as young girls, and little sexual interest in men. Evidently, these feelings are not equated with being lesbian. In addition, Becker pits physical intimacy against psychological intimacy. She accepts too easily the facile stereotype that lesbians are less interested in physical intimacy than their gay male counterparts. Becker also jumps too quickly to the conclusion that nuns who face sexual feelings of intimacy for other women will "most likely" find their concerns "unfounded in the end." Although one might not wish to judge this attitude homophobic, a fear which Becker herself denounces, it is at best a subtle put-down of the prevalence of lesbian existence.

In the end, however, the final message of Becker's article is one of Gyn/affection. Her writing is more representative of a recent spate of articles on the subject of friendship in convent communities, advocating that nuns should not fear intimacy and even intensity of feeling with other women. Particular friendship, they say, should "come out of the closet" in religious communties of women.

Suppression of Loose Religious Women

The particular friendships of religious women were confined historically by much more than the Rules of their respective communities. Wherever convent Gyn/affection has been lived out, in its more expanded sense of nuns being affective in the social, intellectual, spiritual, and political realms, it has been suppressed—either internally by Roman Catholic male church authorities or externally as in the Dissolution of convents in England and on the continent during the sixteenth century. The Dissolution and the Protestant Reformation were responsible for driving many former nuns into marriage by promulgating "new" religious values demeaning the worth of sacred virginity and by forcing the closing of convents all over Europe.

Internal Suppression: Canonical Restraints
and the Rule of Enclosure

As early as the tenth and eleventh centuries, the suppression of religious women can be seen in the decline of the double monasteries. Abbesses forfeited all their previous authority. The great female abbeys were relegated, by Church decree, to the status of priories— smaller houses under the governance of a larger house. Most of the newly established priories were made subject to male abbots, and their

female superiors were demoted to the rank of prioress. The power of
the abbess of Las Huelgas in Spain, who in 1210 refused to relinquish
her sacerdotal functions, is an exceptional exercise of female monastic
power during this time. However, the abbess was excommunicated in
1260 when she refused to receive and subject herself to the male abbot
of Citeaux. That other nuns did not passively relinquish such spiritual
powers is attested to by thirteenth-century attacks on religious women
who continued to officiate at divine services.

In commentaries on female monasticism, the major reason given for
this loss of power was the necessity to reform religious houses of the
time. Reformation and purification are frequently equated with the
removal of power from the hands of women. The Protestant Reformation, in the person of John Calvin, expressed this equation quite
directly in affirming that leadership by a woman was a sign of cosmic
disorder and a punishment of God that must be endured until God
removes it.[76] Catholic churchmen saw themselves performing the
work of God in removing nuns from authoritative positions. Of course,
the disorder, luxurious lifestyle, and sexual immorality that are often
cited as reasons for reform were just as, if not more, prevalent in male
religious houses. Yet it was the independence of nuns that was curbed
by the reforms. It was nuns who bore the brunt of canonical legislation
which restricted their freedom of movement and previous powers. It
was nuns who were scapegoated in the name of religious renewal.

Some scholars date the decline of nuns to the reform movement
which began at Cluny, in France, during the tenth and eleventh centuries and which was masculinist in substance and style.[77] Male communities, such as the Cistercians, were rejecting the large numbers of
women who tried to establish foundations for women in conjunction
with some of the older religious orders of men. Thus a wave of new
orders began to emerge throughout Europe to accommodate the
increasing numbers of women wishing to enter religious houses.

Most of these women came from the lower classes, and Eckenstein
reports that the Church "encountered certain difficulties" in dealing
with them. The primary problem seemed "the disorderly tendencies
which had become apparent in connection with *loose women*." [Italics
mine][78] Eckenstein notes further that the class of loose women, attracted to the new orders, included "women of loose life *as well as those
who held aloof from men*." [Italics mine][79] One way of restraining
these women and their "disorderly tendencies" was the rule of enclosure.

The notion that religious women should refrain from contact with
the outside world was incipient in early Christianity. The idea gained

solid ground during the twelfth century when female religious activity became confined within convent walls. "The nuns remained inside the monastery, and were removed from contact with the world, while the [male] canons were but little restricted in their movements."[80] In 1289, Pope Boniface VIII made the rule of enclosure mandatory for all women who wished to live a canonically approved religious life. The Council of Trent reaffirmed Boniface's ruling, and Pope Pius V later issued decrees that all nuns must accept this imposed cloistering. The rulings of cloister and enclosure were not enforced within religious communities of men.

Further antifeminist legislation restrained the freedom of nuns. The wearing of a distinctive habit of clothing was imposed on nuns, greatly restricting their physical mobility. This habit usually enshrouded their bodies and became a kind of clothing cloister that encumbered all sorts of physical activities. Men were not required to wear the awkward and uncomfortable headgear that enclosed nuns for centuries. This headpiece was rationalized as fulfilling Paul's injunction that women should keep their heads covered, especially in church, so as not to distract or seduce (presumably men).

The freedom to engage in an active ministry was also removed from women's communities and became a male religious prerogative. Using another antifeminist standard of reasoning, Church authorities promulgated that women could best "save their souls" by not assuming active "masculine" tasks, by modestly withdrawing from the world, and by helping other women to live a life of silent prayer and domesticity. This legislation camouflaged a clerical distrust of female competence and morality while reserving an active spiritual role for men.

Self-governance was also curtailed. Canon law later regulated the election of superiors of women's communities and decreed that bishops and/or papal clerical representatives preside over these elections. Male religious communities were not subjected to the same restraints. For example, Canon 506.1 allowed male institutes to carry out their own election of superiors, but Canon 506.2 required that the local bishop was to be informed of the day and hour of the election of superiors of female institutes. Henceforth, according to the new canonical legislation, men could be superiors of religious orders of women, but women could not be superiors of religious orders of men.

The former intellectual achievements of nuns were also brought into decline. More and more, convent life centered on the domestic. In settlements where women's and men's houses continued to coexist in the same location, nuns prepared the meals and made clothes. The domestication of convent life, combined with the development of an artisan system outside the cloister in the towns, gave over the arts of writing, decorating, bookbinding, and weaving to secular workers. Especially during the fourteenth and fifteenth centuries, convents relinquished their artistic pursuits.

Another factor contributing to the decline of intellectual life in convents was a growing indifference to the education of women. With the surge of intellectual humanism, which promoted education and centered it in the universities during the thirteenth century, women were excluded. "The development of Universities (in which the existence of women was ignored) resulted in a serious lowering of the educational standard of the convent."[81] Nuns were cut off from secular learning, and thus their creative outlets were stifled. Due to the rule of enclosure and the shrinking contact of nuns with the world of learning, the literature that became prevalent in convents was devotional—divine service books, legends of the saints, some scripture and theology of the spiritual life, and books that emphasized piety, modesty and good manners. The rule of enclosure cloistered more than the physical space and mobility of religious women. It also circumscribed their minds.

Another side to the rule of enclosure, however, must be viewed from a more womanist perspective. Pat Hynes has suggested that this rule must be seen not only as something that was imposed by men to keep women in line. Religious orders of women may also have accepted enclosure to ward off male intrusion and invasion, both secular and ecclesiastical. In this interpretation, the rule of enclosure may have been perceived by nuns at this time as one means of Self-preservation and control within a convent milieu that was becoming literally penetrated by men.[82]

More terrifying than male juridical interference in the internal affairs of religious women was the increasing frequency of forcible male entry. There are many examples of the seizure of individual nuns carried off by rapaciously intruding men. As early as the eleventh century, "the Danish earl of Swegen . . . took away . . . the abbess Eadgifu of Leominster in Herefordshire in 1048, and kept her with him for a whole year as his wife."[83] This action must be named for what it is —kidnapping, assault, and rape. Several years after their abbess was seized, Eadgifu's settlement of nuns ceased to exist. A similar seizure and rape befell the convent at Berkley-on-Severn, despite the heroic resistance of the abbess. "The story is told . . . how it was attacked and plundered at the instigation of Earl Godwin (1053) and how in spite of the stand made by the abbess, a 'strong and determined' woman, the men who took possession of it turned it into a 'pantheon, a very temple

of harlotry.' Berkley also ceased to exist."[84] In Italy, Pico della Miran-
dola speaks of the barbarity inflicted on religious women as late as
1513.

> Were god-vowed virgins, at the (recent) plunder of Brescia, torn from their
> most religious temples, as a prey to the soldiery . . . At the sack of Prato,
> were maidens formerly noted for their holiness given over to prostitution?
> . . . . that in many cities the precincts formerly dedicated to virgins had been
> changed into brothels and dens of obscurity.[85]

Threatened with forcible rape, seizure, and the extermination of
their communities, religious women may well have accepted, and even
welcomed, the rule of enclosure in the interests of Self-preservation
and as a desperate attempt to keep men literally out of their environs.
Seen in this light, the acceptance of enclosure becomes a Self-directed,
though ineffective, means of conserving some pittance of the independent existence of loose women.

The rule of enclosure was a double-edged sword. Whichever way
nuns turned, their Self-definition, freedom, and ultimately their physical well-being and integrity were under siege. If they did not submit to
the so-called reform measures, they were subject to male invasions of all
sorts. They were easy targets for assault and rape and could not count
on any protection from church authorities. If they did submit to the
"reforms," they had a relative amount of protection from the local
ecclesiastical authorities, but they abdicated freedom of movement,
independent decision making, and the right of Self-governance. At
best, acceptance of such "reforms" gave nuns a modicum of separation
from men and a cloistered sphere of sisters. Most religious communities of women chose the crumbs of Self-preservation.

Nuns' acceptance of the rule of enclosure has generally been interpreted as their internalization of male-defined images of female impurity. The renewed emphasis on chastity and virginity in religious
orders of women that accompanied this ruling has also been defined as
antisexual, in a puritanical sense, rather than as antiheterosexual and as a
revulsive reaction to the prevalent male promiscuity and ravaging of
convents. The defense of chastity that attended the rule of enclosure
must be viewed from a Gyn/affective perspective rather than in a
simplistic hetero-relational and antisexual sense as defined by men.
Women reacted to male abuses of their integrity by defending that
integrity in the way that was available to them—through their vow of
chastity.

Attacks on nuns as loose women still continued, however, and once
more virginity or chastity became the issue. Cloistered nuns were still

portrayed as man-haters. Nigel Wirecker, a monk, wrote that nuns "as a means of preserving chastity... systematically enjoin hatred of men."[86] As Lillian Faderman has written, "Occasionally male hysteria about increasing female freedom was not even hidden by pretense of reasoned arguments about female passivity and male superiority. Irrational fear that the male sex was breathing its last was openly expressed."[87] In this case, even though the freedom of nuns was decreasing, male irrationality still prevailed.

Satires on monks and nuns proliferated, highlighting their supposed joint lewd behavior. "The Land of Cockayne" is one poetic satire that has received special attention. It pictures nuns and monks bathing in a river, frolicking together, and throwing off all restraints with each other.

The satiric genre was most skillfully developed by Erasmus. A monk himself who had left the monastery but not the priesthood, Erasmus had a great antipathy to religious life. His *Colloquies* make frequent mention of the lack of purpose in monastic life. Monks and nuns are equally immoral, and all sorts of abuses are portrayed. Yet Erasmus reserved his most stringent condemnation for independent women. He noted the proliferation of loose or unmarried women and, as mentioned earlier, he hints at lesbianism in convents.

Many of the titles of his *Colloquies* are indicative of his disdain for unattached women—"The Penitent Virgin," "The Virgin Averse to Matrimony," "The Uneasy Wife," for example. He lumps together the conversion of convents into brothels with the willfulness of independent nuns and sees both as equal indicators of the general debauchery into which women's and men's orders had sunk. But he does not attack men for asserting their independence or for refusing to subject themselves to women.

Thus Erasmus prefigures the Protestant Reformation's emphasis on the high value of married life for women, the scorn for unhusbanded women, the necessity for women to cultivate domestic qualities, and the domestication of women in general.

External Suppression: The Dissolution and the Protestant Reformation

"The decline of monasticism was inevitable as soon as the idea that virginity was in itself pleasing to God ceased to be in the foreground of moral consciousness."[88] The Reformers attacked nothing so forcefully as the state of religiously vowed virginity, which they saw as generating the moral corruption of nuns and priests. Again, their reform measures—marriage and motherhood—were directed mostly at women.

They preached that women's vocation was henceforth in the home. For example, the well-known statements of Martin Luther emphasized that a virtuous women is a wife. She remains at home, sits still, keeps house, and bears and rears children.

The vocation of woman as wife and mother was also a fact for Calvin. Like Luther, Calvin emphasized the role of woman as helpmate to man. He exhorted women to recognize that "this is my husband who is my chief: he has authority over me, and God compels me."[89]

The superiority of marriage and the vocational emphasis for women on wifehood and motherhood "was in part the effect and in part the cause of the decline in female education."[90] At the same time, the Reformation undermined any display of female leadership in the world. John Knox's *First Blast of the Trumpet Against the Monstrous Regiment of Women* is representative of the Protestant attack on women who would govern. Knox decried the two queens of Scotland and England whose reigns, he said, were indications of God's dissatisfaction with and punishment of mankind.

These ideas prepared the way for the Dissolution of nunneries. The Dissolution materialized the theology of the Protestant Reformation. It smashed devotion to the mother goddess, Mary, and her incarnation in groups of nuns living together. Its strident attack on virginity was accompanied by contentions that nuns broke up family bonds, were unwilling to engage in the natural duties of marriage and motherhood, and wanted to escape the bonds of marriage only so as to lead loose lives. Women who were not married were abused and feared in an emerging social climate that placed marriage and motherhood at the top of the moral ladder to God.

One of the more infamous pamphlets attacking unattached women was written by Simon Fisk around 1592. Called "Supplication for Beggars," it depicted the poverty of people who had been robbed by the Roman Catholic Church, the immorality of those who had made religious vows, and the lewdness of loose women. It advocated the confiscation of monastic property and provided a rationale for Henry VIII's rupture with Rome and his suppression of religious houses. A short time later, John Geiler, a contemporary of Luther, said from the pulpit of the Strasbourg Cathedral that "he would rather his sister should become a prostitute than that she should be thrust into a nunnery of lax life or should be made abbess of a community of wanton canonesses."[91]

It is difficult to grasp the logic of this statement in light of the fact that most of the Protestant Reformers, and indeed many Catholics, regarded nuns as prostitutes anyway. Jean Gerson, who was esteemed as a "great" French Catholic, wrote in his *Compendious Declaration of the Defects of Ecclesiastics,* "Open your eyes again, and see whether nowadays the cloisters of nuns have become as it were brothels of harlots."[92]

The Protestants, however, solidified this view of nuns. In equating virginity with prostitution and nunneries with brothels, they were reiterating one of the earliest transformations of the female companion to the female prostitute. They proclaimed that the sacred virgin was the profane prostitute. The Reformation was bent on drawing a clear line between married and unattached women. It stamped and stigmatized all loose women. The Reformers "maintained that marriage was the most acceptable state before God and that a woman had no claim to consideration except in her capacity as wife and mother."[93] As is the case with all movements that regard themselves as progressive, the Reformation branded certain states as regressive. The vocation of the nun was seen as violating the spirit of reform and progress.

The words of the Reformation regarding unmarried women "were made flesh" in the Dissolution of convents, beginning on a large scale in sixteenth-century England. "The fact is noteworthy that wherever the property of women was appropriated, it was appropriated to the use of man."[94] Many convents were turned into male colleges of higher education. For example, the nunnery of St. Radegund's was changed into Jesus College, Cambridge.

The Reformers distributed propaganda stating that the closing of convents, which they initiated, was done with the voluntary cooperation and even at the pleas of the inhabitants. They were fond of quoting statements that ex-nuns had signed after the Dissolution of their convents: "Not compelled by fear or dread, nor circumvented by guile or deceit, out of my own free will, for certain just and lawful reasons (I) do resign and renounce with all my right, title, interest and possession that I have had and now have in the aforesaid monastery."[95] Many of the charges of immorality brought against such houses were spurious, but convents were dissolved, one after another, supposedly with the consent of those suppressed. Geoffrey Baskerville, in his often sarcastic, anti-Catholic, and antiwoman book *English Monks and the Suppression of the Monasteries,* nevertheless admits that "the reports of the royal commissioners who were carrying out the suppression of the smaller houses in 1536, show that ... The great majority [of the inhabitants] were, however, in favor of continuance."[96] Thus, consent was hardly as widespread as the Reformers claimed.

What happened to the nuns who were "freed"? Those who took dispensations were given a small sum of money to tide them over until they presumably "settled down" and got married. Many women were simply "set free" to drift and fend for themselves. These women had led secluded lives and were discharged into a world where they would never really belong. Henceforth, they were obviously endangered. And, once again, the Church—this time Protestant—created the very class of loose women against which it inveighed.

Some convents did not submit to the Dissolution passively. For example, Florence Bannerman, abbess of Amesbury, refused every bribe and forceful measure to make her surrender. "Considering the helpless position in which religious houses were placed, it seems a matter for wonder that any opposition was made."[97]

In Germany, the same thing happened on the outbreak of the Lutheran agitation in the sixteenth century. The memoir of Charitas Pirckheimer, the abbess of a convent at Nürnberg, gives a rare insider's insight into conditions there. She describes the abolition of Catholic religious ceremonies, the nullification of vows and rules of religion, the enforced closure of convents, the exit of nuns and priests, and the marriages they entered into.

Charitas and her nuns held out against the suppression after repeated attempts to close their convent by violent measures. In her supplication to the town council refuting the charges of immorality brought against the convent, Charitas denies that she despises the married state and retains nuns by force. "But as we compel no one, so too we claim not to be compelled, and to remain free in mind as well as in body. But this cannot be if we are given over to strange priests, which would be destruction to our community."[98] During many stormy encounters, the Reformers came to Charitas's convent to demand that the house be closed. But their force was matched by the unyielding protest and opposition of Charitas and her sisters. Informed by a town council member that her opposition was inciting other convents to resist the Lutheran reforms, she was charged with promoting bloodshed. However, Charitas was not dissuaded, and her nuns, in the face of stoning, physical violence, and obscenities, refused to disband.

After repeated attempts to close this convent, the parents of three of the younger nuns tried to take their daughters away. The three young nuns hid, seeking refuge in the convent chapel.

> ... the young women besought her [Charitas] to protect them ... their parents and others abused and reviled them ... in spite of their protests, their indignation and their tears, their relations at last resorted to violence.

Four persons seized each nun and dragged and pushed her out of the chapel, while the women present shouted approval, and once outside their convent clothes were torn off and others substituted in their stead . . . they were carried to a chariot waiting outside and conveyed away.[99]

Charitas reported that this catapulted her and the other nuns into utter grief and despair, but they persisted even after such an invasion. The memoir of Charitas ends in 1528, and from other sources we learn that she remained unmolested and passed the last of her days in peace with her sisters.

In the emerging Protestant perspective, convents were seen as destructive to the family. Attacks on unmarried women who took religious vows continued well after the first days of the Reformation. When the Catholic Church was allowed to reestablish its hierarchy in England in 1850, rabid anti-Catholicism followed. Many of the attacks on the Church included propaganda against the reestablishment of convents. The Protestant Truth Society published salacious titles such as "Revelations of a Convent" and " The Ruin of Girls in Convent Schools." Among the chief objectives of this society, as outlined in its own literature, were the following:

1. To obtain and circulate reliable information concerning the Conventual system.
2. To aid those who escape from convents and those who desire to do so.
3. To exercise just and lawful means to deter persons from entering Convents or taking Conventual vows.
4. To influence parents against sending their children to Covent schools.
5. To use such means as are best calculated to promote legislation for the:

   (a) Inspection of all Conventual Institutions
   (b) Registration and protection of all inmates of such institutions
   (c) Special registration of births and deaths that occur therein
   (d) Reform of the burial laws in their application to convents
   (e) The eventual suppression of all institutions where the inmates are bound by Monastic or Religious vows.[100]

These objectives codified the then-prevalent perception of convents as centers of heterosexual immorality in which unwilling women had babies, easily disposed of their infants, and buried them unnoticed.

In a climate such as this where the unattached woman was regarded as immoral, where convent living was pictured as lewd, and where all kinds of suspicions were cast on religious life, many convents ceased to exist. Those that lingered survived as "mere shadows of their former brilliant selves."[101]

It was not until the nineteenth century that religious congregations of women began to grow again. New apostolic orders, dedicated to teaching and nursing, arose at a remarkable rate. In examining this more recent history, one sees that the same battles as occurred in medieval times ensued again between the male hierarchy and the emerging numbers of religious women. "The work of the apostolic nuns, busy and independent, must have seemed one more threat to the conservative elements of the church—on their guard already against the dangerous phenomenon of 'Women's Rights.'"[102]

Conclusion

There is much that female friends can learn from both the positive and negative aspects of hetaerocracy, the Rule of companions, in convents. Many of these elements are discussed at length in future chapters but some, such as order, tension between the individual and the community, and intimacy, require notice at this point.

The issue of order relates to the necessity for Self-ordering discussed in Chapter I. Women were of prime order in nuns' lives. In the evolution of convent living, order took many forms and was of primary importance for these women. When it was Self-directed, order was thoughtful and intelligent. It fostered female freedom and brought harmony to the social group. Order ensured a continuity of convent history and purpose while providing certain expectations for all. It helped religious women to immerse themselves in their chosen work, to move on with the task at hand, and to go about their own business of writing, teaching, or social activities.

In an interview with Pat Hynes and me conducted by Rosemary Curb for the anthology *Lesbian Nuns: Breaking Silence,* I remarked that order in convent community "had a lot to do with a certain sense of basic boundaries and agreed-upon rules that helped to encourage respect and caring. The failure of convent community, for many women, was a result of these boundaries and rules becoming too restrictive and dogmatic."[103] Pat Hynes added, in comparing the sisterhood in convents to that of feminism:

The convent offered the structure of community. You didn't have to create that, nor did you have to sustain it. The community financially was established. Education was guaranteed, at least in my community. You had a job. You had a place to be buried. You had older women who were mentors. You did not have to invent everything as you went along. With feminism none of the structure is there. Many early feminist institutions, women's centers, and businesses were short-lived because there were no guiding principles of organization. Disagreements often escalated into divisiveness that undid many early attempts to create feminist institutions.[104]

Within convents, order also maintained a certain balance between the individual and the group. It ensured that trivial decisions did not have to be made over and over again, as happens in many feminist collective structures, and that time and energy could be given to the more important aspects of group life. Its negative side was that decision making was often lodged in irresponsible and tyrannical individuals and transformed into arbitrary authority.

The zeal for order was often achieved at the expense of female freedom and friendship. When this happened, convent life was regulated with a mathematical precision, meticulously organized by authoritarian superiors and structures in which the individual, independent, loose woman was subordinated to the legislated well-being of the social organism. As convents became more and more defined by hetero-order and by male constraints posing as orderly rules, order became a mindless leash on female passion and purpose. Order was emphasized at the expense of female independence.

It is instructive that what male Catholic and Protestant church authorities attacked was the "disorderly" tendencies they perceived to be inherent in religious communities of loose women. Women unattached to men were labeled "out of order." Nuns were seen as "naturally disordered," because they held themselves aloof from husbands, family, and children. What was really being attacked here, of course, was the Self-ordering of religious loose women, which impelled their passion for each other and their independent, active work in the world.

The crucial lesson to be learned from the history of religious loose women, as one can learn from the history of women in general, is that order must be internally generated and established for women's purposes. It cannot be externally imposed by male authorities. When convent living functioned as a rule of equal companions, even though certain lines of internal authority were devised, it was a living testimony to the difference between uniformity and order—to the difference between being systematic and producing a system that regulates the totality of personal and social existence—and to an order that supports a creative existence. At its best, it was a thoughtful life that gave rise to a certain regularity and arrangement of priorities without imposing a final and totalistic system of living into which all loose ends and loose women fit. Work, prayer, conversation, and study were comfortably balanced to promote individual growth and community purpose. Convent order, where it was thoughtful and not a mindless yielding to external male directives, fostered friendship by balancing personal achievement with cooperative well-being.

The tension between individuality and community that existed in religious communities of women is also instructive. In the present age when many women and women's groups have uncritically assimilated the norms of collectivism or of countercultural sensitivity groups, this tension is all the more important to discuss.

At its best, the tension between individuality and community permitted the individual woman a separate existence while establishing a basis for a powerful spirit of sisterhood. It helped women to be clear about their responsibilities as individuals and the possibilities of community life. It ensured that the community was a conjunction of individuals rather than a substitute for individuality, where those who are truly individuals are limited by the insecurities of others.

The word *individual* literally comes from *indivisible*. Hetero-reality and regulations have often divided women from their original Selves and from each other. So too did/does an uncritical community ethic that destroys individuality or limits its expression in the name of community or collective values. At its worst, convent communitarianism leveled distinctions between women in the name of this false harmony. At its best, it promoted the indivisibility of women whose individuality was necessary to the integrity and strength of the community.

Within many groups that espouse collectivist values, privacy is often the first thing to go—private thoughts, private emotions, and private manifestations of both. In some women's groups, privacy has been considered almost a fault—a kind of sin—tantamount to repressiveness. The ethic instead is "let it all hang out."

Where the tension between individuality and community is kept, privacy is preserved in the midst of an intense and deep community spirit. Within communities of religious women, privacy helped individuality flourish. Where the tension was not kept, especially after the imposition of the rule of enclosure, the lives of nuns were in essence made the public property of the community by petty rules, concerns, and purposes. The private time and space needed for friendship was also limited, and a kind of communal surveillance mechanism against particular friendships was encouraged. The community became "big sister," comparable to an internal CBI (Convent Bureau of Investigation) for the monitoring of particular friendships.

With these constraints, a kind of total institutionalization of existence occurred in which religious women became enclosed within themselves, their creativity stifled or channeled into monolithic and insipid directions. Along with this total institutionalization came a sense of unreality, a posture of dissociation from the world that was debilitating to nuns' former independence and work in the world. The community became an entity unto itself, holding the power to mold opinion, pass judgment, and hold sway over everything a woman did. In the same way, feminists can learn that when a movement or women's community becomes hardened into rhetorical positions, when the language of nonthought and clichés begins to prevail, there is no genuine feminist movement.

The tension between the individual and community gave rise to certain forms of friendship in convents. I have already discussed the notions of both spiritual and particular friendship that are unique genres in the history of friendship and that influenced patterns of intimacy in the lives of religious women. In conclusion, I wish to examine the more positive dimensions of intimacy in convents, particularly because, up to this point, I have emphasized the prohibitions against such intimacy.

The notion of order had an important effect on convent friendships. It ordered intimacy. As one woman wrote of celibacy in religious communities:

> A little more discretion in our intimacies might keep our energies directed more usefully, and spare us a lot of the pain that makes casualties of us before we ever get to the battlefield ... Disordered uncentered "loving" deflects energy and postpones the Revolution.[105]

Disordered and uncentered loving promotes an ethic of relationism, discussed in Chapter IV, where women become "professional relaters"—that is, immersed in relating and relationships as the focus of their lives, whether with women or with men. At its best, particular friendship in convents helped to order and center intimacies.

Kathleen Barry has compared sexual intimacy to that which is most private and unique to individuals.

> There are those ideas or thoughts that are very private and special to me. They stem from the very depths of my being and in a sense define a very

personal part of me. I share these thoughts with only a few people, those whom I trust and who I want to know me on that level.[106]

Barry contrasts this kind of intimacy to the "nonspecific openness" shared with everyone in an age when expressiveness is the norm. One of the better legacies of convent life was a habit of discretion which taught that intimate friendship was not something to be given lightly. "Such intimacy grows and is cultivated from dignity, respect, caring, tenderness."[107]

Convent living fostered discretion in intimacy. It promoted "the rigors of discernment" (a concept of Alice Walker's that I use frequently throughout this book). It helped women to cultivate a habit of discretion in friendship and created the conditions in which to exercise that habit. Quite simply, convent living helped develop an ability, a kind of sixth sense, to discern who was a true friend and who was not.

Discretion taught that to know a person you have to grow and take time with her and that there is no such thing as instant intimacy. It cautioned against sharing intense emotions and thoughts with those with whom one is barely acquainted. And it cut through the easy rhetoric of quick recipes for breaking down barriers between people by revealing how facile friendships can set up new barriers and create new forms of alienation based on false intimacy.

Of course, the habit of discernment could not guarantee an infallible judgment and the absence of mistakes. More often than not, however, "the rigors of discernment" nourished accuracy, sustained a cultivated capacity for making friends, and bolstered a reservoir of internal judgment that could be called upon when necessary.

Audre Lorde, in writing about the erotic, suggests that the "erotic .... is an internal sense of satisfaction to which, once we have experienced it, we know we can aspire."[108] Eros is by no means always narrowly "erotic." *Intensity* is another word for conveying this expanded sense of eroticism. Indeed, nuns exemplified that all affection is not sexual/genital but is intensely affectionate. Nuns gave witness to the fact that there are intense passions of love and of friendship besides the sexual/genital. Emotional energy has many forms of intensity. Nuns also knew that the intensity of an intimate friendship is a highly fragile possession and must be allied to other forms of emotional, intellectual, social, and spiritual life if it is to survive.

By becoming affective in the world outside the convent, the Gyn/affection that existed in convents served as a distinct example of "the personal is political." Nuns had an expanded political, intellectual, and social affectiveness, as we have seen. The unique amalgam of the notions of spiritual and particular friendship enabled women to invest their friendships with a dimension of importance beyond the friendship itself. Nuns had a companionship of equals based on an equality of "being equal to the task," not only the task of building a dedicated and committed friendship but the task of building a better world. Within convent life, the rationalization for intimate friendship was religious. A particular friendship was spiritual because a third dimension — God—was present. A sense of transcendence was introduced into the relationship. Spiritual friendship was based on the common knowledge and love for something that at the same time went beyond the friendship and cemented the friendship in daily life. Its impetus could be summed up in the words of Ortega y Gasset: "people do not live together merely to be together . . . They live together to do something together."[109]

While engaged in a common task or cause, spiritual friends became aware of particular and profound affinities between them—the knowledge and experience of similar emotions, thoughts, and purposes. The same spiritual current circulated in friends, deepening and intensifying the intimacy of equals. As "they found love where they worked," they also found work where they loved.

Many ex-nuns have observed how difficult it is to sustain a former intensity with women once they have left the convent. In a study of ex-nuns, one woman said: "You can't have relations with women on the outside like you did in the convent. Things are so different and you yourself change . . . now I'm in the market, so to speak, for romance."[110] Where a continued context of woman-centered existence is absent, Gyn/affection is not sustained. In this same study, many ex-nuns commented on how secular society "activates one's sex role" by encouraging conformity to hetero-reality.

Unfortunately, many women who had been in the convent accepted their new hetero-relational status and indeed conformed to it with an attitude of inevitability or even enthusiasm. Pat Hynes and I mention more specific reasons for this conventionality. I note:

> One of the unfortunate things that happened when I left the convent was that I lost contact with many of the women with whom I'd had intense friendships . . . Almost as soon as they got out they became immersed in the heterosexual dating scene and eventually got married and are still married. Given the fact that relationships with women were primary in the convent but not the norm in the world, I suppose they were trying to normalize themselves. Maybe they looked back upon their intimate convent relationships as an adolescent stage they had to go through.[111]

In responding to these words, Pat Hynes focused on the absence of a context for ongoing Gyn/affection after women left the convent.

> I stepped from a woman-centered existence into "the world," as we called it, as if the convent were not part of the world. I had no support for continuing intense relationships with women. I remember feeling a tremendous loneliness for the community of women I had wanted to get out of. I felt that no one would understand if I kept up those relationships . . . I understand better than Jan what pushed ex-nuns into going into bars and dating and getting married very quickly. The only thing normative was heterosexuality. Frantically we tried to erase our convent experience and to ease the strangeness of the world.[112]

For those women who became feminists after leaving the convent, a real continuity was established between their new lives and the best of what convent Gyn/affection offered. Having spent a part of their lives in an all-woman context, where female friendship was the norm, many came to feminism with a heightened experience of the possibilities of Gyn/affection. In spite of the mixed messages and attempts to suppress the intensity of friendship while in the convent, the prevailing experience was one of freedom in the company of women. Where other women may have experienced more of a rampant history of male domination/victimization/oppression in past lives, many ex-nuns speak of the convent as a prime locus of "sisterhood is powerful."

In the final analysis, the power of female friendship in convents derived from the fact that friendship is by nature a spiritual communion, but that women are not and never will be pure spirits. With nuns, as with all women, friendship is mediated through and only becomes Gyn/affective in the material world.

III

More Loose Women: The Chinese Marriage Resisters

I trim my lamp, and weeping write this letter,
Seal, and send it ten thousand miles,
To tell you how wretched I am
And beg you to free my body.
Dear mother, how much is left of my bride price?

> Shao Fei-fei,
> "A Letter," seventeenth century,
> *The Orchid Boat: Women Poets of China*

I have closed the double doors,
In what corner of heaven is she?

> Wu Tsao,*
> "To the Tune 'Flowers Along
> the Path through the Field,'"
> *The Orchid Boat: Women Poets of China*

And you and I made our friendship the pledge of a
belief in eternity. We vowed it.

> Diana to Emma,
> George Meredith,
> *Diana of the Crossways*

---

*It is thought that Wu Tsao wrote about 1800. Her biographical note in *The Orchid Boat,* a special collection of writings of Chinese women poets, tells us: "She had many female friends and lovers, and wrote erotic poems to several courtesans. She was very popular in her lifetime, and her songs were sung all over China . . . She is one of the great Lesbian poets of all time . . . Wu Tsao is usually regarded as the third woman poet of China."

Where, after all, do universal human rights begin? In
small places, close to home ... Such are the places
where every man, woman, and child seeks equal justice, equal opportunity, equal dignity without discrim-
ination. Unless these rights have meaning there they
have little meaning anywhere.

Eleanor Roosevelt,
speech at the United Nations, 1958

W hen I first heard the term *marriage resister,* I felt that here at last was a phrase that adequately captured the political content of women's age-old repudiation of marriage. Here, finally, were words that took opposition to marriage out of the modern reductionistic context of psychological abnormality with its framework of "heterosexual deprivation," "single by default," and the "rejected woman syndrome." Instead, "marriage resistance" highlighted the aspect of conscious choice and, more, showed how that choice became affective in the larger context of group resistance.

From the early nineteenth to the early twentieth century, numbers of women, especially in the rural Kwangtung (in the more recent spelling, Guangdong), regions in China, refused to marry or, once ceremonially married, refused to live with their husbands. *Resistance* is an appropriate word for the actions of these women since, in a society that was family-oriented and family-bound, all women were pushed toward marriage. By Chinese tradition, any woman was a temporary member of her family of birth, and she created her permanence by entering into a family by marriage. An unmarried woman was a woman who belonged to no family.

Marriage held bitter consequences for Chinese women. As the old Chinese proverb said, "A woman married is like a pony bought — to be ridden or whipped at the master's pleasure." In contrast to other cultures, such as Muslim societies, where the segregation of females or female kin in the harem gave the newly married woman support and where "the female relatives of a man—wives, sisters, mothers, aunts, daughters—share[d] much of their time and their living space, . . . [enabling] women to have frequent and easy access to other women in their community . . . across class lines,"[1] the marital situation of Chinese women was different. Women were forced to break with their natal families at marriage and begin as strangers in their husbands' families.

A Chinese bride . . . left her natal family in the midst of a celebration designed to dramatize her permanent departure and the lasting severance of her ties with her natal family. The symbolic pouring of a cup of water over the threshold after her departing figure was token of the fact that, like the water, she could never return to her former place. Moreover, joking and informal rituals in her household prior to her wedding made it clear to her that she was about to enter enemy territory and should prepare for war.[2]

Just as a Chinese woman's security in this life was bound to her place in a family, her security in the next life was dependent on those family members who would worship her after death. "A single woman could not have a soul tablet erected at death, for her worship."[3] Francis Hsu observed that "since the role of the individual is to be a link in the great family continuum, a bachelor or spinster is socially lost. This is particularly true of the old maid because a woman has no place in life apart from marriage."[4]

From roughly 1400 to 1900, a pattern of universal marriage in Asian agrarian societies was the norm, whereas marriage was not the norm in preindustrial European societies.[5] Given this normative standard, it is a wonder that the resistance movement originated and lasted as long as it did.

Not only woman's encapsulation in marriage but her place and non-place in Chinese society were culturally and ideologically orchestrated to minimize both her social and metaphysical existence. The Chinese female was likely to be unwanted from her first days of existence. In fact, the Chinese term for a daughter is *she-pen huo*, "goods on which one loses." The devaluation of women was buttressed by a metaphysical worldview that identified women with all that was yin: negative, empty, and, in the Confucian system, ill-omened. This cosmic inferiority of women was materialized in the social world by the widespread practices of female infanticide, footbinding, the marrying off of daughters at an early age to the point of selling them into other families at infancy, the drudge work that was a woman's burden, women's lack of education, and the high rate of suicide among Chinese women.

Using her own family background, Maxine Hong Kingston elucidates how the Chinese viewed girls and women.

> When one of my parents or the emigrant villagers said, "Feeding girls is feeding cowbirds," I would thrash on the floor and scream so hard I couldn't talk. I couldn't stop ...
>
> I minded that the emigrant villagers shook their heads at my sister and me. "One girl—and another girl," they said, and made our parents ashamed to take us out together.[6]

Hong Kingston also relates that "there is a Chinese word for the female I—which is 'slave.' Break the women with their own tongues!"[7] That women themselves were spiritually broken by such language and attitudes is attested to by Su Hua in *Ancient Melodies* (a book dedicated to Virginia Woolf and Vita Sackville-West).

Being the fourth child of my mother and the tenth daughter of the family, I was naturally neglected ... I often felt unhappy when I considered that I was only a girl. I always hesitated to talk or laugh because I was very sensitive about the fact that I was not wanted in my family.[8]

In light of these cosmic and social conditions, many commentators have tended to see the marriage resistance movement as an inevitable reaction to a system that brutalized women. For example, Arthur Smith, a nineteenth-century western writer on Chinese life, stated:

The reality of the evils of the Chinese system of marriage is evidenced by the extreme expedients to which unmarried girls sometimes resort, to avoid matrimony. Chinese newspapers not infrequently contain references to organized societies of young maidens, who solemnly vow never to wed.[9]

While the evils of the Chinese system of marriage would certainly be eschewed by any woman who thought she had alternatives, such evils were by no means the major explanation and a sufficient cause of marriage resistance. To view marriage resistance in this way is to be limited by the lens of hetero-relations. Smith and other commentators, while noting the prevailing conditions that oppressed women, fail to perceive that there was also another tradition that empowered Chinese women. The tradition of the "woman warrior" pervaded popular and cultural literature and folklore and encouraged female strength, resistance, and commitment to each other. It is this tradition that helps cast the "extreme expedient" of marriage resistance in the woman-identified light of a "chosen and delightful arrangement."

While not ignoring the tradition of female slavery in China, Maxine Hong Kingston brought to western attention the tradition of the woman warrior. "I learned to make my mind large, as the universe is large, so that there is room for paradoxes."[10] Hong Kingston relates how when Chinese girls listened to adult women "talking-story," they learned that they failed if they grew up to be "but wives or slaves. We could be heroines, swordswomen. Even if she had to rage across all China, a swordswoman got even with anybody who hurt her family. Perhaps women were once so dangerous that they had to have their feet bound."[11] The same mother who had uttered that "feeding girls is feeding cowbirds" communicated another tradition to her daughters:

At last I saw that I too had been in the presence of great power, my mother talking-story. After I grew up, I heard the chant of Fa Mu Lan, the girl who took her father's place in battle. Instantly, I remembered that as a child I had followed my mother about the house, the two of us singing about how Fa Mu Lan fought gloriously and returned alive from war to settle in the village. I had forgotten this chant that was once mine, given me by my mother, who may not have known its power to remind. She said I would grow up a wife and a slave, but she taught me the song of the warrior woman, Fa Mu Lan. I would have to grow up a warrior woman.[12]

The mythic tradition of the warrior woman is available in the popular literature that young Chinese-Americans read daily. Even in China-towns today, one can pick up Chinese comic books where the image of the warrior woman is present throughout the stories. Many of these stories contain images of magical women who perform great deeds of physical prowess. In this popular literature, one often sees images of husbands, for example, hiding behind strong women warriors who are their wives. Yet it is never implied, as in some western literature of this genre, that such a wife should trade in her husband for a man who is stronger than she. The same images of women are present in Chinese movies, where one finds a range of women from domesticated wimps to great hero women.[13]

The tradition of the woman warrior is historically real. During the peasant revolt of 1851–64, known as the Taiping Revolution, there were all-female combat divisions led by women. Women had their own separate army corps under the direction of Hong Xuanjiao. "Their very presence was said to have broken the morale of the imperial armies set against them."[14] When the Taiping forces established their capital in Nanking, there was a total of forty women's armies, each containing 2,500 soldiers.[15]

In the face of stringent opposition, many women organized themselves into battalions to fight for the Republican cause in the early 1900s. They had names such as the Women's National Army, the Women's Murder Squad, the Women's Military Squad, the Team for Military Drill, and the Amazon Corps of the Dare to Die Soldiers.[16]

The woman warrior tradition and history are celebrated in the great women poets of China. Ch'iu Chin also a revolutionary whose exploits received the greatest acclaim of all women warriors, fought not only against the Manchu dynasty but against all restraints on women. In her personal life, she often took the name Qinxiong, which means "compete with men." One photograph pictures her dressed in western male clothes with "quite a jaunty cloth cap."[17] Her poem "Women's Rights" is a feminist statement that combines her feminism with her belief that women should be militant and save the nation and themselves.

We want our emancipation!
For our liberty we'll drink a cup,
Men and women are born equal,
Why should we let men hold sway?

We will rise and save ourselves,
Ridding the nation of all her shame.
In the steps of Joan of Arc,
With our own hands will we regain our land.[18]

Jiu Jin placed herself at the end of the long line of women warriors in the tradition of Milan. She can also be situated in the company of the scholar-rebels and bandit outlaws of Chinese history and legend. "She learned fencing, riding and sword play and single-handedly she wished to rescue women and China from the 'darkness' and 'blackness' of their condition."[19] Her poetry was a source of inspiration to many women who came after her, and her execution established her as one of the great revolutionaries of Chinese history.

Ch'iu Chin was arrested by the Manchu government. She was beheaded in 1907 after her poems were used as evidence of her treason. Another of her poems highlights a freedom for her people that conjured up historically known women warriors and that was irrevocably linked to the freedom of women in China.

To the Tune
"The River Is Red"

How many wise men and heroes
Have survived the dust and dirt of the world?
How many beautiful women have been heroines?
There were the noble and famous women generals
Ch'in Liang-yu and Shen Yun-yin.*
Though tears stained their dresses
Their hearts were full of blood.
The wild strokes of their swords
Whistled like dragons and sobbed with pain.

*"Ch'in Liang-yu was a seventeenth-century heroine who, after the death of her husband, was appointed commander of his army. Shen Yun-yin (seventeenth century), after her father was killed by the rebel army of Chang Hsiang-chung, took command, defeated them and recaptured her father's body." From Notes to Poems in *The Orchid Boat*, trans. and ed. Kenneth Rexroth and Ling Chung (New York: The Seabury Press, 1972; new edition, published by New Directions in Newton, N.J., in 1982), p. 124.

The perfume of freedom burns my mind
With grief for my country.
When will we ever be cleansed?
Comrades, I say to you,
Spare no effort, struggle unceasingly,
That at last peace may come to our people.
And jewelled dresses and deformed feet
Will be abandoned.
And one day, all under heaven
Will see beautiful free women,
Blooming like fields of flowers,
And bearing brilliant and noble human beings.[20]

Ch'in Chiu's poems also indicate a strong tradition of friendship with women.

Two Poems to the Tune
"Narcissus by the River"

I

Lady T'ao Ch'ui-tse gave a farewell party
in the T'ao Jan Pavilion. My woman friend
Tzu-ying wrote couplets in Great Cave
calligraphy:

Like a young colt running past a crack in a wall,
The light and darkness of almost a year have gone by.
Wind sweeps the clouds from the sky.
We each go our separate ways.

I share her sadness and write a poem in answer.
I am going to Japan to study
And Tsu-ying returns to the South.

II

We have drunk wine and discussed literature.
Our hearts have beat together
With the same emotions.
Softly we sing together the old song
"The Sunlight in the Pass."
The sorrow of parting will follow our horses' feet.
The melancholy of farewell
Surrounds the city like a river.
Iron strokes, silver curves, your couplets
Are limitless in their meanings.
Take care of yourself. We can have no confidence

That one day we will see each other again.
We stand on the bridge, hand in hand.
The river and the evening clouds stretch away for a
thousand miles.[21]

Combine the tradition of the woman warrior in history and in the popular literature, the poetry of China's great women poets, and the tradition of female revolutionaries in many periods of Chinese history—and the marriage resistance movement acquires a historical and political context.

Kwangtung: The Locus of Marriage Resistance

The marriage resister can be seen as part of the same Chinese women's tradition that spawned the woman warrior. Her battle was against enforced marriage, and her resistance was just as fierce as her militant mythic and real counterparts. However, her resistance went beyond an antimarriage position to the integrity of a tradition of "loose women" committed in friendship to each other, often for a lifetime.

Most Cantonese grew up with some knowledge of this resistance. However, as Marjorie Topley, the anthropologist who did the original work on marriage resistance, notes, if references to this tradition had not been mentioned, albeit briefly, by western observers, the world outside China might never have learned of this female resistance movement that lasted for approximately one hundred years (in the particular form that this chapter describes). " 'The existence of this Amazonian League,' writes a missionary long resident in the neighbourhood, 'has long been known, but as to its rules and the number of its members, no definite information has come to hand.' "[22] This was not the kind of tradition that Confucianists would be eager to record, nor was it a tradition that latter-day Chinese reformists or revolutionaries, first nationalists and then communists, would have encouraged. In China the subject is ignored as connotative of

"feudal and backward" practices...The modern socialist woman is by definition a productive working member of the community, a manager of her household, and the bearer of the officially approved one child per family. There is no room for aberration ... It is the perceived wisdom that the practice not to wed, although its history is an ongoing one, has nothing to teach the contemporary Chinese woman.[23]

Women who resisted marriage or cohabitation had little interest in programs of marriage reform promulgated by the revolution and were thus once more, for revolutionary purposes, "goods on which one loses."

Most marriage resisters came from the Canton delta and worked in the sericulture industry, in areas such as Shun-te hsien, Nan-hai hsien, and a small part of P'an-yu, which is east of Shun-te. Women who worked in the silk trade had the opportunity to be economically self-sufficient, a condition enjoyed by few women in China. The organized marriage resistance movement started in Shun-te but eventually spread to other districts where women could work and economically provide for themselves and often for their natal families. Maria Jaschok, an anthropologist and historian, who has done recent work on the lives of unmarried women in pre-Communist China, writes: "No statistics can be found, but Sankar speculates that in Guangdong at least one out of ten was such an unmarried woman, an estimate confirmed by my own findings."[24]

The Kwangtung region of China, along with its economic attraction and sustenance for unattached women, had other features that bear mentioning. In contrast to the rest of China, many women here worked outside the home, not only in the silk industry but in the fields, on the streets, on the rivers and sea, and in various kinds of manual labor. Writer Ta Chen, in a statistical study of industrial labor in China in 1933, recorded that 66.6 percent of the total number of workers in the four main industrial regions of Kwangtung were women. In Shun-te, 81.2 percent of the labor force were women.[25] Women were most active in the weaving and spinning sides of the silk industry.

Agnes Smedley, writing about her travels in this region in the early 1930s, remarked that this labor force of women and girls often provided a large part of the family income, and thus such families might be less likely to force working daughters into marriage. Here then was an area in which girls could hardly be looked upon as no better than "cowbirds" or as "goods on which one loses."

As the economic strength of Cantonese women proved significant in creating a different fiber of woman—the marriage resister—so too did their physical strength and abilities. Women in the Kwangtung region had never accepted footbinding to the degree to which women in other parts of China had been forced. Thus, from early times women here were more physically equipped for hard work and had the mobility that was necessary for manual labor. Female infanticide in the silk area was almost nonexistent. Less significant perhaps, but rather intriguing, is the further fact that Cantonese women, as Maxine Hong Kingston relates, were regarded as the most beautiful in China. The latter may simply be a reflection of the degree of happiness that Cantonese women experienced compared with other Chinese women.

When the Kwangtung region is examined to determine differences in women's status, the factor that is always highlighted is dearth of males. It is often stated, or implied, that because of the migration of Chinese men to America and other countries, the women were "left to themselves." Depending on emphasis and interpretation, one can get the opinion that women sought each other by default.

Instead, one can say that politically the migration of men released women as a powerful force that was able to thwart opposition to the antimarriage movement and to their own intentions never to marry. The reduction of males in Canton can be seen as removing some barriers to female friendship in which women were free to more actively assert their Gyn/affection. In general, male emigration tended to strengthen the position of women overall.

Finally, writer James Dyer-Ball observes that Shun-te women were considered different and "more intelligent than others." Although Chinese girls were not formally educated, many girls from the Shun-te area were generally able to read. [26] Topley's sources indicated that girls from farming families received tutorial instruction in reading at what were called the "girls' houses." Ho talks of such women reading the classics.[27] Parents who noted the intelligence of daughters and their decision to marriage often accepted this as their "nonmarrying fate" and believed that such girls should remain unwed.

All of the reasons enumerated above were more or less influential in the emergence and development of an organized marriage resistance movement in the Cantonese district of China. In my opinion, a far more significant cause is the culture of woman-identification and Gyn/affection in which many Cantonese women were immersed from a very early age. For it is here that we find the internal conditions, common to these women as women, that promoted marriage resistance and female friendship. Having experienced the culture of female friendship at a young age, Cantonese girls created the social and political conditions for the survival of those friendships beyond youth.

For example, the early socialization of many young girls in the Shun-te villages occurred in so-called girls' houses which were homes organized by women where female children lived together. Girls resided in these houses until marriage or until many took vows of spinsterhood. It was customary for older girls in these houses to visit temples, religious places, and the theater in groups. Nineteenth-century writer Benjamin Henry observed that they "show their independence" by going "in large numbers" to the dramas associated with large religious festivals, sitting in a separate gallery reserved for their use.[28] Many of Topley's informants described the ties of friendship that existed among these girls, which encouraged sworn sisterhood.

> In some villages at the betrothal of one of their number, the members of a group would treat the occasion as if it marked her impending death and the "sisters" would wear mourning clothes to indicate her imminent removal from their midst . . . During this time they formed close friendships often involving lesbian relationships.[29]

The "sworn sisterhoods" that the girls' houses generated give evidence of the power of woman-identified culture developed at an early age, where it was normal for girls to expect a future with each other and where certain material conditions existed for that future to be realized. Basic to the marriage resistance movement in Kwangtung were these sworn sisterhoods.

Sworn Sisters and the "Chai t'ang"

There were various ways in which sworn sisters were pledged to each other. One accepted and institutionalized version of sworn sisterhood was that a pair of girls or women would take mutual vows never to marry and never to part company. The Chinese term for sworn sisters was *shuang chieh-pai,* "mutually tied by oath." Very often, these girls or women had spent a large part of their childhood together.

Sworn sisterhood, however, was not limited to twosomes. It often comprised a larger association of many women who were committed to each other in friendship and who formed an organized antimarriage grouping. Both Topley and Ho report that another term for such sisterhoods was *chin-lan hui,* or Golden Orchid Association. The Shun-te gazetteer, in an 1853 edition, notes that women's Golden Orchid Associations had long been prevalent in the district.[30]

The term Golden Orchid has a varied and significant usage. James Liu of Stanford University has suggested that it may be derived from a passage in the *I-Ching* that says, "When two persons have the same heart its sharpness can cut gold; words from the same heart have a fragrance like the orchid."[31] Further explanation of this expression is that gold never changes its color and is therefore symbolic of two friends "who never change their feelings for each other. . . the orchid too, has a lasting fragrance and symbolises the lasting 'fragrance' of friendship."[32] Winston Hsieh has speculated that the term signals the structure of the sworn sisterhoods that may "bud" or divide into subgroups as they become more expansive, "just as orchids bud into several flowers on one stem."[33]

Sworn sisters took their vows in a ceremony that marked the occasion. The religious nature of this ceremony portrays the spiritual dimension of sworn sisterhood indicated by such terms as *sheung kit paai,* "a pair tied in prayer," or *paai sheung chi,* "to venerate or respect knowledge of each other." In this way, the marriage resisters were like western nuns who also were organized into sisterhoods that had a religious aspect. The structure of their residences give further evidence of this spiritual dimension.

Sworn sisters often lived in what were called *vegetarian halls* or *spinsters' houses.* The former were originally residential establishments for lay members of the Buddhist faith and also for lay and clerical members of several semisecret religious sects that split off from a syncretic religion called *Hsien-t'ien Ta-tao,* "the Great Way of Former Heaven." These sects had long been associated with political militancy in China, had been suppressed, and had thus become semisecret.

The sects established themselves in Kwangtung in the middle of the nineteenth century and had particular appeal for women because they emphasized sexual equality and focused upon a mother goddess as the highest deity. Many of the marriage resisters and sworn sisters were associated with these sects which became entirely female in membership after severing themselves from the more male-dominated religious groups. Religious life, in whole or in part, was considered an appropriate way for loose women to live. As with western nuns, religion provided an encouragement and a reason for women to remain single.

The vegetarian halls, or *chai t'ang,* were associated originally with spiritual advancement and "self-cultivation," which is an important method for progressing spiritually in Buddhism and in *Hsien-t'ien Ta-tao.* Two major practices accompanied "self-cultivation": eating *chai,* a vegetarian diet, and sexual abstinence, which in the case of the marriage resisters was interpreted as heterosexual abstinence since, as we shall see, lesbian practices were fairly common among these women. The main demand for *chai t'ang,* or vegetarian residences, especially in later years when many emigrated to Singapore, came from unattached women who had taken vows of spinsterhood.

Since antimarriage groups were generally organized by village, the groups would often build what came to be called "spinsters' houses." Spinsters' houses (*ku-p'o wu*) were found all over the Shun-te area. In many instances, they were hardly distinguishable from vegetarian residences. However, vegetarian food was not a requirement for residents in the spinsters' house, and there was less focus on religious activities in general.

Both the *chai t'ang* and the spinsters' houses provided for unattached women in their old age, when they could no longer work. Inhabitants often had elaborate arrangements for saving money that was set aside for both retirement and death benefits. ". . . in some groups women put a fixed percentage of their monthly earnings into a fund for festival celebrations; they contributed to funds for emergency assistance to the families of the 'sisters.'"[34]

An important germ of inspiration for the resistance movement came from stories contained in the *shan-shu* or "good books," found in the libraries of many *chai t'ang*. Often they are also called "wooden fish books" because their stories were meant to be recited to the accompaniment of a "wooden fish," that is, a wooden instrument. Some scholars call them a "powerful source of propaganda" for women who resisted marriage. These books were authored largely by Buddhist nuns in the silk growing area of Shun-te to encourage unattached women and girls of this district to join a religious community.

"Good books," or "precious volumes" as they were also called, were put into writing during the Sung Dynasty. They were stories of exemplary women and were most often written in ballad or semiballad form without following poetic rules too closely. Some classical education was needed to understand everything contained in these works, but peasant women often learned them by heart and had someone explain their meaning.

The content of these stories is most interesting in examining their influence on marriage resistance. The subject matter of most of these books is women — women who lead pure and religious lives and therefore obtained spiritual and often material rewards. One of the most popular ballads has been translated as "Song of the Southern Sea." It is the story of Kuan Yin, the Goddess of Mercy, and a princess, who was believed in popular culture to have become a nun against her parents' wishes.

> Who faithfully follows my footsteps
> 　　May share in my infinite gain;
> And he who is brave to relinquish,
> 　　May know what it is to attain.
>
> With jasper and opal I deck me,
> 　　With the night-shining pearl I am crowned;

Look back on the way I have travelled,
    And judge if a better be found.

No husband to claim my devotion,
    No mother-in-law to control,
No children to follow my footsteps
    And fetter the wings of the soul;

As free as the winds on the mountain,
    Or the birds that soar up to the sun,
From morning till evening I wandered
    In the sombre hued robes of a nun . . .

There was a joy in the courts of my father,
    But I gladly exchange it for this,
A year and a day of delusion
    For an age of unspeakable bliss.[35]

The theme of many of these ballads is marriage as an impediment to higher spiritual advancement. For example, one story tells of a spiritual woman forced into marriage who refused to pray to her husband's ancestors. She was magically conveyed to a mountain nunnery, and eventually her husband became her disciple. The women in many *chai t'ang* at the end of a day's work would sit and discuss their favorite heroines from these stories. One account, related to Topley by a resident of a Singapore *chai t'ang,* was the narrator's own life story but bears remarkable resemblance to the stories contained in the "good books."

She was an unmarried immigrant worker from Tung Kuan and had decided early in childhood not to marry. One day she had a vision of Buddha, according to her story, and he told her she must practise "self-cultivation," eat *chai* permanently and remain a spinster. She told her family of this experience and asked permission to live at home and earn money. . . Her father refused however and soon her marriage was arranged. On her way to the home of her husband-to-be she tried to cut her throat but was prevented by the bearers of the sedan-chair in which she was travelling. She then jumped into a river and attempted to drown herself but "could not sink." Eventually she was taken back to her father and he took pity on her and consented to her remaining a spinster.[36]

Many of the resisters had "good books" that they had acquired at a young age. From these "precious volumes," they were encouraged in their convictions that refusing to marry was morally right, that resistance was a brave act, that men cannot be trusted, and that suicide can be a virtue when committed to preserve one's integrity.

Suicide was, in fact, made into a tool of public group resistance against forced marriage. Arthur Smith relates the incident of a mass suicide by a league of young girls who wanted to remain single.[37] The marriage of one of their group of six sworn sisters had been arranged by her parents. They then jointly made the decision to commit suicide by drowning together in the Dragon River. This became a famous story among the nonmarrying women and was widely quoted in more recent times by women who emigrated to Singapore.[38] Topley cites other similar records of suicides involving pairs of sworn sisters who lived in Hong Kong.[39]

The marriage resister saw her suicide within a tradition that viewed it as a public and honorable act. For example, historian Susan Mann states that "by the eighteenth century, the suicide of a wife resisting rape during a bandit raid had become a public event celebrated by both community and state."[40] In the same tradition, the marriage resister knew that her suicide would be extolled by future resisters who would judge her way of dying a final heroic act of not only private but public rebellion. That such suicides were often jointly engaged in by several sworn sisters was a confirmation of their public and political symbolism. This is not to romanticize female suicide but to invest it with a political dimension, a dimension not often ascribed to women as it is to men who commit such an act for a larger cause.

The "good books" also emphasized female leadership. The vegetarian and spinsters' houses became the institutionalized structures for this element of leadership where women could be independent and often rise to positions of authority within the group. Finally, such residences became substitute "families" offering a home to loose women among others of their own kind as well as giving them the economic facilities to ensure their continued existence.

The Pu lo-chia and the Tzu-shu nü

There were two types of resisters — the *pu lo-chia* and the *tzu-shu nü.* Both types often formed societies of six to ten members who designated themselves by titles such as "never-to-wed" or "all pure." They were generally made up of pairs of sworn sisters. *Pu lo-chia* is the Chinese term for women who were forced to marry but who did not consummate the marriage or cohabit with their husbands. It literally translates as "not going to the family," meaning the family of the husband, as all Chinese women became members of their husband's family.

Many women in Shun-te threatened suicide in the house of their new husbands if they were forced to stay there after the marriage ceremonies were completed. Some observers report that resistance women carried opium for this purpose and that they used charms and chants against the unwanted husbands. In addition, it is said that other nonmarrying women sought more drastic means of avoiding matrimony. "The sudden demise of betrothed husbands, or the abrupt ending of the newly married husband's career, suggest unlawful means for dissolving the bonds."[41]

Numbers of women who had been betrothed by arrangement went through the marriage ceremonies but refused to cohabit with their new spouses. In this case, the custom that developed was that the woman would return to her family of birth three days after her marriage. During the three days spent in her new husband's household, she would refuse any food or drink from her husband's family. According to vows she had taken in the sisterhood, such acts were looked upon as accepting permanent residency with him and would result in loss of membership in the antimarriage society.

It is said by women that the bride-to-be would sometimes be literally sewn into her clothes, the purpose being to preserve her virginity. She would also be warned to stay awake while in her husband's presence. If after three days were up, and when she returned home her clothes were still intact, she was considered to have passed the test and could remain a member.[42]

In-laws accepted this arrangement because often the new wife, after separating from her husband, would support him and his family. Sometimes, the *pu lo-chia* returned to her husband to bear children and, after this duty was finished, would not engage in further sexual relations with him. Many others who refused to return to husbands had to support concubines for them and also the children of such unions. Thus these *pu lo-chia* often incurred long-term economic obligations to their extended conjugal families. Sometimes all the members of the sisterhood contributed to this arrangement.

The second type of resister was the *tzu-shu nü*, literally translated as "never to marry." This type became known as "self-combers," women who comb or arrange their own hair. It was traditional at a Chinese woman's marriage that her long single plait of hair was bound up into a bun. The *tzu-shu nü* put up her own hair. This "self-combing" demonstrated to society that the nonmarrying woman's life was to be lived "as if married," that is, she could not be engaged to any man and her lifestyle was as sacred and honorable as that of a married woman.

That "never-to-marry" women took their unions with each other seriously is well exemplified in the ceremonies that marked the occasion of their coming together. A hairdressing ceremony initially signaled the woman's intention to leave home, and it was treated like a marriage ritual. As one *tzu-shu nü* in Singapore explained, "It is really like a marriage ceremony and the couple swear everlasting friendship and mutual help."[43]

In theory, it was only after this ritual that the status of the *tzu-shu nü* was accepted by society at large. Topley relates that, in practice, the ceremony often did not initiate the nonmarrying woman into her life as a *tzu-shu nü* but instead would take place several years after a woman took her vow not to marry. In this case, the ceremony would include many pairs of sworn sisters and would become a combined "golden orchid" and hairdressing rite.

Sworn sisterhoods existed all over China, even outside the resistance area. They were of many varieties. So pervasive were they that one continually reads references to them. One western woman, who became a sworn sister to two Chinese women, commented that the ceremonies which accompanied these pacts of sworn sisterhood (although they were not those of the *tzu-shu nü*), were hardly rituals of "facile friendship-making." First the two Chinese women explained with great solemnity why they wished her to be their sworn sister, an unusual wish expressed by a Chinese woman to a westerner.

"Shu Hua and I have been Blood Sisters for many years, as you know," Blossom explained. "Shu Hua spoke to me two nights ago in bed and asked me if I would consent to make you a Blood Sister with us, and my spirit was full of joy at this. First you shared our troubles, and then there was the long waiting in the Law Court, and finally we shared joy and peace together at Ch'ien Lung's Pool; so Shu Hua said that you are certainly our sister already in soul, and it is fitting you should become one by the correct rites."[44]

Then the ceremony ensued, complete with readings, prayers, blessings, and incense. "I could feel her soul calling to my soul, and I knew she was asking herself if any foreign woman, not to mention myself in particular, had sufficient sobriety in her character to endure the implications of the Oath of Friendship."[45] The ceremony ended with the prayer "that there might be nothing but truth between us."[46]

Lesbian Practices

The marriage resister had considerably greater freedom than women in other parts of China, including the freedom of lesbian friendship. Several sources have commented that numbers of marriage resisters appeared to be lesbians. Topley suggests that although it is difficult to know the extent to which the *tzu-shu* movement and sworn friendship involved lesbian affinities, many of her informants provided evidence of fairly frequent lesbian identification among the resisters who were forced to emigrate from China. "On the evidence of the immigrant women themselves such relationships seemed fairly common among women up to the age of about forty. Such relationships are widely believed by the Chinese to exist today in Singapore among domestic servants."[47]

When many of the Kwangtung resisters had to emigrate, they went to Singapore and took work as domestic servants. Sources also reported that Chinese housewives living there were reluctant to employ pairs of women as servants "because of the high emotional content that sworn-sister relationships appear to have...One housewife expressed the opinion that such women 'make use of your beds when you go out.'"[48] Topley adds that the general attitude toward such relationships was one of "amused tolerance" rather than hostility.

Hostility was not lacking, however. Agnes Smedley, traveling through the Cantonese silk area in the early 1930s, found quite an antagonistic reaction to the resisters. Smedley's male guide and interpreter spoke of the women workers with "hostility" and "contempt."

> His particular hatred seemed to be thousands of women spinners, and only with difficulty could I learn why. He told me that the women were notorious throughout China as Lesbians. They refused to marry...
> "They're too rich—that's the root of the trouble!... They earn as much as eleven dollars a month, and become proud and contemptuous... They squander their money!" he cried. "I have never gone to a picture theater without seeing groups of them sitting together, holding hands."[49]

So once again, women had "found love where they work" as well as finding work where they love.

Smedley's guide also informed her that these "despicable girls" evaded the law promulgated in 1927 prohibiting the formation of communist cells and trade unions in the filatures (silk factories) by forming Sister Societies. What is more, they had "dared strike" for shorter work hours and pay increments.

Smedley gives us a physical picture of these women in her written portrait, appropriately entitled "Silk Workers." "Long lines of them, clad in glossy black jackets and trousers, sat before boiling vats of cocoons, their parboiled fingers twinkling among the spinning filaments. Sometimes a remark passed along their lines set a whole mill laughing."[50] When Smedley saw this female labor force at work, she began to realize the positive effects of industrialism in the lives of these working women. The silk regions were the only areas in China where the birth of a baby girl brought joy instead of pain, because here girls were the main support of their families.

Smedley notes that "consciousness of their worth was reflected in their dignified bearing . . . They could not but compare the dignity of their positions with the low position of married women. Their independence seemed a personal affront to officialdom."[51] Thus, Smedley concludes, they were attacked as lesbians because they were loose women, that is, independent and unhusbanded women.

In this interpretation, any independent woman is *perceived* as a lesbian. Smedley might have added that many of these women *were* lesbians, that female independence does breed lesbianism, and that loose women have traditionally been vilified as promiscuous, free-spirited, and resistant to the rules of "officialdom," especially to hetero-order. As with their western sisters, such women were attacked for becoming the "masters of themselves," whether lesbian or not.

When Smedley's guide departed, she finally joined the workers by herself, and they gathered eagerly around her. "Two of them linked their arms in mine and began pulling me down the flagstone street. Others followed, chattering happily."[52] A broken conversation then ensued, punctuated by signs and gestures because of the language barrier. They were most interested in knowing whether Smedley was married and had children. When she answered in the negative, they became "interested and surprised." The evening together ended in singing and in the women accompanying Smedley back to her temple. Smedley concludes her portrait of the silk workers by saying: "As they streamed in long lines over the bridge arching the canal and past the temple entrance, I felt I had never seen more handsome women."[53]

In discussing lesbian relationships with pairs of sworn sisters, Topley found that some women admitted their own personal lesbian involvements, but only when they were told that lesbian relationships exist in Europe. More often, they told of knowing about such relationships among their friends.[54]

One woman gave Topley a unique religious rationale for lesbian practices that views the existence of lesbianism in quite a hetero-relational, but inimitable, way. She recounted that a woman may be predestined to marry one man again and again in various incarnations. In one of these incarnations, he may be born female. Since this "man" is her fate, she is attracted to the female incarnation of her "husband." Whether or not this could happen more than once, and thus not be such an unusual occurrence, was not clear.

Topley also relates that her sources called lesbian practices "grinding the bean curd."[55] This was a euphemism used by Topley's informants to indicate their belief that lesbians used a dildo made of fine silk threads and filled with bean curd. The image is also consistent with the ways in which lesbians have always been represented as "like men" or as "mannish women." Chang Hsin-t'ai, in his *Short Record of Travels in Canton,* reinforces this stereotypical view of the resisters.

> In the last ten years or so the custom has taken another turn; the sisters finally become "like trees which are joined by shared branches" [i.e., lovers]. When two of the women live together, one of them takes on the semblance of the husband. This custom evidently arose in the district of Shun-te, and later spread extensively into P'an Yu and Sha Chiao, with the result that it has expanded to such an extent that even in the provincial capital one can't avoid it.[56]

The author adds, in a final note of disapproval:

> To not marry because of homosexuality is truly against nature and very harmful to women's constitutions; but it's even more common for women to not marry until it's too late because of some change in their life plans, and then fall into homosexuality. This is really a major problem.[57]

The "major problem," however, became the continued existence of the marriage resisters in China.

Migration from China

The marriage resistance movement had existed for almost a century in China when most of its members were forced to migrate—in effect, a personal and political exile. Although the movement was forbidden by the nationalist government, all attempts to stamp it out had been unsuccessful.

When the communists seized power, the marriage resisters were branded as women leading "sad and lonely lives."[58] On the one hand, the People's Republic regarded the resisters as victims who had suffered "terrible hardships" after the filatures were closed and the women were put out of work. On the other hand, the communists frowned upon their resistance and considered it essentially negative and counterrevolutionary. "The spinsters' houses were gradually phased out. Many women were forcibly removed to the homes of kinsmen. Only those with nobody to take them in were allowed to remain."[59]

Jaschok claims that remnants of the resistance existed up to the Cultural Revolution: ". . . it was the imposition of a rigidly uniform social system that followed the victory of the Communist Party in 1949, and the attack on cultural relics of any kind during the Cultural Revolution (1966–1976) that eradicated the last institutionalized traces of this practice in Guangdong."[60] The collapse of the silk industry in the late 1930s had paved the way for the communist extinction of the resistance movement. This put thousands of unattached women in an economically disastrous position. Some *tzu-shu nü* and *pu lo-chia* retired early to their respective spinsters' houses and vegetarian halls. Those who were younger and had not saved enough money for such retirement sought work as domestic servants in Canton and other urban areas. Many others migrated to Malaya, Hong Kong, and Singapore. Some women left China earlier as the threat of Japanese occupation became a reality. "When the Japanese took Canton in 1938, many young unattached women escaped sexual exploitation by taking up residence in vegetarian halls."[61]

Of those who emigrated, many had to take work as domestic servants, the age-old fallback for economically deprived women. These women were called *amah* and did all the work of a household including washing and cooking. Topley tells us that "immigrant servants are generally preferred to locally born women by both Western and Chinese employers. Generally speaking it is probably their tendency to be unattached and to have a minimum of private life which makes them in greater demand."[62]

According to the 1947 census report in Singapore, 42,225 Chinese women (20 percent of the total female population aged fifteen and over) were "gainfully employed." Most of these women came from the antimarriage districts in China, were unattached, and took work in pairs. They lived in dwellings called *kongsi* and ran several kinds of loan clubs. A few *kongsi*, Topley says, were "partial anti-marriage sisterhoods" where women who came from the same area in China were reestablished in Singapore.

With the emigration of large numbers of nonmarrying women, many vegetarian halls were established. In 1955, there were approximately 250–350 *chai t'ang* in Singapore, 90 percent of which were inhabited by women. Topley's research indicates that much of their membership came from the *tzu-shu nü* and *pu lo-chia* women exiled from former Chinese resistance areas. In addition, Topley cites the existence of marriage resistance among locally born women in Singapore. "The local born section of the Chinese female working-class, however, is not entirely devoid of its confirmed spinsters."[63] Mostly all local spinsters came from poor families. Some left home in their teens because they had been put into positions of arranged marriages.

Although the women who were forced to emigrate organized no cohesive marriage resistance movement, as there had been in their former Cantonese homeland, they preserved much of the spirit and many of the traditions of sworn sisterhood. *Kongsi* literally means "a company," and the term was used of a number of Chinese associations. For the emigrant resisters, *kongsi* meant living quarters generally composed of women from the same region of China. These quarters housed four to fifty women who came from the identical or adjacent Chinese villages or districts. They provided decent living quarters for unattached women. Spatially, the *kongsi* ranged from a cubicle to a number of large rooms, even to elaborate club houses which maintained all sorts of connected benefit plans and regular social gatherings.

As in the Cantonese spinsters' houses, one woman held a position of authority by virtue of her seniority, her experience as a servant, or her initial role of organizing and renting the *kongsi*. "Members too, have an understanding that no woman belonging to a *kongsi* may take a job in a household from which a fellow member has been dismissed. Some of the *kongsi* in fact are something approaching a primitive form of trade guild in their facilities and objectives."[64]

One *kongsi* was established by two sworn sisters for thirty women. After the Japanese occupation, increasing rents forced them to give up their quarters. They then moved to a larger space. They calculated that thirty women would be just enough to pay rent, light, heat, and water.

Many *kongsi* ran "associations" or "clubs" which had a mutual aid or social purpose. Indeed, the *kongsi* were remarkable examples of voluntary associations that brought into being ingenious economic and social bases for independent working-class women. Often these associations created banks in which were kept thousands of dollars of the members' money and from which loans could be made to the members.

Sometimes money was put into the "bank" to be used for some future festival or celebration. One of the more famous of these celebrations was the Seven Sisters Festival. This was regarded by the local inhabitants as the special event of the nonmarrying women from the Canton district. Many *kongsi* had Seven Sisters Societies that prepared for the festival months ahead of time. The *amah* (domestic servants) took this opportunity to make special clothes for each sister and to create what would now be referred to as craftwork. Each *kongsi* also tried, in a friendly manner, to outdo others in planning and celebration.

The plethora of voluntary associations organized by the unattached *amah* is a testimony and tribute to their social and economic inventiveness. There were religious clubs, called *pai an hui,* or "associations for praying to or venerating the shrine." Often these were inspired by a desire for the harmony of the members or the success of their various enterprises, both of which were considered spiritual undertakings.

Long life associations (*jen shou hui*) were societies whose purpose was to raise money to meet the death, funeral, and ceremonial expenses of its deceased members. Sometimes they also provided financial help to the dependents or beneficiaries of deceased members. In a society where it was believed that the person after death needed attending, the long life associations provided groups of mourners consisting of sister members.

Some unattached women adopted female children, although it was not common for a pair of sworn sisters to adopt jointly. The reasons given for adoption were that the girl child would be able to care for her adopted mother in the latter's old age and that she could provide companionship for her. The hope of economic support also prompted adoption and was seen as a future insurance of filial piety. Many independent women adopted girls also as a way of encouraging another generation of women not to marry. Adopted daughters, however, were not always enthusiastic about their mothers' expectations of them.

A film that was especially popular among the unattached immigrant women living in Singapore depicted the story of a struggle between an older *tzu-shu nü* and her young adopted daughter. The latter wanted to renounce the practices of her adopted mother and felt she was being forced to take antimarriage vows. "The girl refuses to take tzu-shu vows, telling her foster mother that it is old-fashioned and superstitious to reject marriage; that nowadays marriage is much better for women than it was in the past, and that women should work to further their marital status."[65]

Because of such attitudes that developed in the younger generation, adopting daughters became less popular among the immigrant women as time passed. Such adopted daughters often wanted to marry and lost interest in their spinster mothers. Eventually, then, the marriage resistance movement waned, although there is some evidence of individual survivors living in Singapore and Hong Kong today.

The Political Worth and Weight of the Marriage Resistance Movement

Assessments of the resistance movement have been inextricably conditioned by hetero-relational standards. In general there have been two main evaluative patterns that hold sway in the sparse summaries of its political impact. First is the dynamic of psychologizing, and second is a simplistic and often cavalier dismissal of the movement as insignificant and apolitical. Often, these two evaluations are found in conjunction with each other.

Psychologizing pervades statements such as the following: "Most sources stress fear of marriage as the women's principal impetus."[66] Reducing female independence to this kind of cause has been a tactic consisently applied to many Gyn/affective women and movements who are not bound by the usual constraints of hetero-relations. It is a widely accepted assessment, in part because people do not think how absurd it would be to apply this psychologizing to other groups who resist dominant structures and systems. For example, nowhere do we read that individuals become socialists out of a "fear" of capitalism.

This pattern of psychologizing can also be found in explanations that equate marriage resistance with a "distaste for heterosexual relations." Such language is comparable to the reasons adduced for the celibacy of western nuns.

To be more precise, there may well have been a "distaste" for heterosexuality on the part of the marriage resisters, just as there was a "distaste" for slavery on the part of those who revolted against it. However, the language of "distaste" devitalizes the political weight and worth of any resistance movement and summarizes that resistance as an individual quirk or as a defect of the resisters' collective character. It trifles with the willful choice, the political philosophy, and the public actions of group movements, and it is consistently applied to women who choose to spend their lives with women and are indifferent to men.

In spite of the evident political quality of marriage resistance, other commentators dismiss the resisters as insignificant and type them as apolitical. My work on the marriage resisters could not have been done without Marjorie Topley's ground-breaking and original research. It is therefore unfortunate to find in Topley's doctoral dissertation on the movement the following assessment:

> By neither kinds of organisation [the *pu lo-chia* or *tzu-shu nü*], however, were new rights for women in marriage demanded. The anti-marriage movement of Kwangtung *cannot be regarded as any positive progressive movement;* the women *merely* refused to accept sexual relationships with men. [Italics mine][67]

Measured by Topley's own research data, her assessment can be proved untrue. Furthermore, progressivism is hetero-relationally equated with the demand for "new rights" for women in marriage. Why should those who opposed marriage in both its traditional and progressive guise be expected to promote the campaign for marriage reform? Finally, Topley's evaluation is an example of how the resisters are seen only in opposition to marriage and not in relation to their own structures of womanist existence. Presumably by the standards of hetero-relations, those who oppose hetero-reality cannot move beyond it because there is no "beyond." Reality, albeit "positive" and "progressive," is equated with hetero-reality.

In a remarkably glib fashion, Elisabeth Croll also dismisses the political worth and weight of the marriage resistance movement. Although Croll devotes a mere one page to the movement in her work *Feminism and Socialism in China,* she can definitively state — without supporting evidence and in-depth analysis: "The anti-marriage associations were an expression of opposition to the traditional forces of 'fate' but *they remained at the level of rejection* and furnished *a force of escapism rather than a significant force for change.*" [Italics mine][68] Once more, such statements are allowed to stand because of hetero-relational exegesis that equates a chosen, organized, and public separation from marriage and a creative construction of a woman-identified existence with apolitical dissociation from the world.

How does one contend with this charge of "escapism . . . rather than a significant force for change"? On the level of fact alone, Croll's simplistic dismissal is astounding. The resistance left a legacy that has had a vast political impact on women's lives in China today. Topley cites the 1973 research of Graham Johnson, a sociologist, who found what could be called a feminist ecology in the former resistance regions.

> In Shun-te many former members of the marriage resistance must now be members of the grandparent generation. One imagines that the high value they have always placed on freedom of movement for women — on their being unencumbered by children — and the low value they place on pro-

creation might today find their expression in the distinctive work patterns and extraordinary population statistics of the former resistance area.[69]

As further evidence of their feminist legacy, Johnson also cites more family planning success, lower birth rates, and more widespread practice of abortion in the Canton delta compared with nonresistance areas. Finally, the resistance ecology promoted an extremely high involvement of Cantonese women in collective work compared with the involvement of women outside the resistance areas.[70]

There are more Gyn/affective measures by which to measure the political worth and weight of the marriage resistance movement. We must analyze the legacy of the resistance not just in hetero-relational terms—family planning, birth control, and abortion statistics—but by more Gyn/affective revolutionary standards. And this necessitates analyzing women's resistance not just in male-defined revolutionary situations but in other contexts not perceived by men as revolutionary. The criteria for political weight and worth, as defined by men, often amount to the criteria for manhood—dramatic self- and group assertion, daring deeds, and open and rebellious confrontation with the state. What is granted the status of "political" is frequently measured by the old manly heroic ethic.

I offer certain concrete and specific guidelines as a yardstick for measuring Gyn/affective politics.

1. *In what ways did the resisters oppose male domination? In what ways did they resist hetero-reality?*

The resisters were adamant about not participating in the marriage system. Even the *pu lo-chia* who could not escape going through the actual marriage ceremonies would not cohabit with their husbands or would cohabit for a limited amount of time, anticipating a future unbound by the oppressive constrictions of married life. That they did not work for marriage reform, but instead worked for more woman-defined structures in which women could work, save money, retire, and have their own culture, is a remarkable proof of their movement operating outside the parameters of hetero-relations.

The movement not only inchoately resisted the Chinese system of male domination and hetero-reality but actively and publicly organized women against it. From Agnes Smedley's recounting of men's reaction to the resisters, it is obvious that many men found them chilling, for they represented the loose woman who was independent—intellectually, economically, emotionally, and sexually—from men. Further, these women went beyond resistance to male domination by developing not only the structures for women's survival against the system but for women's transformation of their own lives.

2. *If power cannot be measured by male standards, to what extent did these women change the concept and reality of power?*

Women together are generally regarded as not powerful because they are perceived as women alone, that is, without men. Thus criticisms such as Croll's—that the resisters were "escapists" who provided no "significant force for change"—are taken at face value because these women are evaluated from the perspective of what contributions they made to changing the structures in which women and men participate together. So once more, women together are women alone or, this time, women removed from reality. By Croll's measurement of the extent to which the resisters influenced marriage "morphology," feminist political power is defined as the reformation of hetero-relational structures and as the "right" to progressive marriage reforms.

Instead, one important measure of feminist political power must be defined by how women are able to change the quality of life for themselves and other women. Progressive marriage reform may be important for many women, but to measure by the marriage yardstick the political impact of a movement that had other goals in life than marriage—indeed, that resisted marriage publicly—is to ignore the expansive edifice of Gyn/affective power. Women's personal and political roles have always been measured by the ways in which they take responsibilities for others—that is, men and children. The extent to which women take responsibility for themselves and other women must be a significant factor in reassessing the concept and reality of power in women's groups.

3. *To what extent did the resisters change the quality of life for themselves and other women? Or who benefited from their life and labor?*

Exact numbers are not available, but marriage resistance was a movement that encompassed thousands of women who were able to live a freer and more independent life because the movement was a social and political force to be reckoned with. It provided women with a sense of difference, importance, and autonomy, which was unknown to most women in China and from which emerged a woman-identified culture. Compared with the situation of Chinese women in general, the resisters were architects of their own lives, earners in the labor force, and activists who created a social world for the women with whom they interacted. Their life was a public testimony that women could emerge from oppressive conditions and become acting participants on their own behalf. They created a community for women who had no family and made explicit their vital connections with one another. The social, cultural, and economic structures they built were in place for the women who came after them. And finally, many of these women supported relatives and extended families who, without their support, would have been in dire straits.

4. *What were their patterns of interaction, and did these become visible to the society outside the resistance movement?*

What remains striking—of political weight and worth—is the public commitments women made to each other. The Gyn/affection of marriage resisters was not merely a personal pact. Their commitments were public and empowered their social and economic lives. Their patterns of interaction generated many distinct forms which were well-known in the society at large. For example, the reality and rituals of sworn sisterhood were consistently recorded by the gazetteers. Chinese newspapers frequently carried accounts of such ceremonies. Many of their other customs were noted publicly; for example, their going to the theater in groups where they established their own sense of space and place, behaving in an independent fashion, and their economic self-sufficiency, which produced the age-old negative reaction that women who earn their own living and are unattached "have too much money to spend."[71] Their social and economic forms of organization established Gyn/affective patterns of interrelatedness and mutual recognition that constituted a way of female life and living unknown to most Chinese women.

5. *Were women's groups, such as the marriage resisters, sex-segregated (against their will) or sex-separated (by choice)? (Also, one must note that, in some cases, groups of sex-segregated women became sex-separated women.) Did this choice confer power?*

I have demonstrated, throughout this chapter, the *chosen* dimensions of marriage resistance—the fact that women elected resistance to marriage in the face of a society that utterly condemned their unattached existence as nonexistence. The personal and political courage of this choice cannot be underestimated. Many women would have chosen suicide rather than submit to marriage. Separation from marriage, however, was augmented by the creation of a social, economic, and cultural existence primarily with women. Theirs was a life of no "mere" segregation.

The bias against separation runs deep in feminist writings, I think, for several reasons. Separation is not distinguished from segregation. Also, it is simplistically equated with a separatism which is uncritically defined as an escapist and apolitical dissociation from the world. And it is always regarded from the perspective of mere "separation from" rather than from the perspective of a personal and political integrity gained.

In writing about the harem, Leila Ahmed perceives this bias against female separation in feminist literature as a western construct.

> But our thoughts in this area are on the whole still clogged with unexamined assumptions: that women secluded and barred from the society of men but wonderfully free to be with other women, are, necessarily, women *deprived;* that societies that practice rigid segregation of the sexes are necessarily, and by definition, in all ways more oppressive to women than sexually integrated societies.[72]

Ahmed contends that within segregated groupings of women, such as the harem, women were free to do many things that western women could do only at peril to their lives. Also because the harem was forbidden to men (*harem* itself stemming from a word meaning "forbidden" and "holy"), women could "share living time and living space, exchange experience and information, and critically analyze — often through jokes, stories, or plays — the world of men."[73] In her analysis of the harem, Ahmed does not naively assert that this segregation was a panacea for women. Indeed, it was a "space to which women are compelled into and confined within."[74] Yet she concludes that such "a female homosocial world" can promote "both an awareness of male oppression, and female independence of mind."[75]

A female separation from the system of hetero-reality, which carries with it the drive for a more woman-defined existence that makes its mark on the world, is rooted in and is a manifestation of worldliness, not an exit from the world. (See Chapter IV for an expanded discussion of dissociation from the world and Chapter V for a fuller treatment of worldliness.) Separation has received critical press because there has been little attempt at sorting out the complexities of the issue. The question is seldom asked to what extent such spheres confer power on women; rather, the automatic assumption is that women are deprived of power because of their "women together" existence.

Further, if worldly impact is the genuine concern of the critics of womanist separation, then serious attention must be paid to the ways in which other groups have always attained rather than lost power by establishing separate spheres. For example, I have argued elsewhere, in an article advocating separate Women's Studies programs, against the charges that such programs ghettoize feminist knowledge.

> It is highly unlikely that traditional disciplinary content and methodology will change in a more woman-centered direction until Women's Studies is autonomous and self-defined enough to make a true impact on such disciplines. Religion departments would not be doing sociology of religion, for example, if there had not emerged a self-defined and autonomous discipline of sociology which determined its own content and methods.[76]

The separation that women's groups have chosen must be granted the same political weight and worth of other separate spheres when they can be truly shown to change the quality of women's lives, to confer power on women, and to assist women in making their mark on the world.

Resisters and Nuns

The history of the marriage resisters is also the history of *hetaerocracy*—the Rule of companions, in which female friendship is restored to prime order. Like their western counterparts, the resisters created their own social economic, and cultural locus for the institutionalization of female friendship. Because the resisters were unallied with any male dominant system, however, their hetaerocracy lasted only a century in its organized and systematic fashion.

There are many comparisons between the two groups. Both made conscious decisions not to marry and made those decisions public. The vow of chastity on the part of nuns and the pacts of sworn sisterhood on the part of the resisters were affirmed in religious and public ceremonies celebrating their promises.

Many resisters also emphasized heterosexual chastity in their lives. Their tradition of eating *chai* was a further evidence of moral purification, originally linked with spiritual growth and "self-cultivation" in Buddhism. From a Gyn/affective perspective, the emphasis on chastity in both groups must be seen as a mode of empowerment that protected them from male promiscuity and, in China, from sale and degradation as prostitutes, slaves, or domestic drudges; more important, it also can be seen as a means of integrity that enabled their rule of hetaerocracy. In both groups, heterosexual celibacy functioned as empowering and not as repressive.

The religious existence of both groups gave a spiritual and sustaining dimension to their unorthodox life choices with women. Their spirituality endowed their friendships with meaning and permanence, and in many cases such friendships lasted until death. The union of souls which was foremost in the ideal of convent spiritual friendship had its counterpart in the resisters' attention to spiritual advancement with each other. The reading of good books, or "precious volumes," parallels the tradition of meditation and spiritual reading in convents, often solitary but also shared.

The physical space that both groups of women created with each other cannot be underestimated. Setting up households together gave women the spatial location necessary for the sharing of a rich inner and worldly existence. It enabled them to provide a home and "family" for women who came after them and who were also attracted to such a companionship of equals. It helped them to conceive other structures in which they carried on their work and activities, such as the educational and social welfare institutions that nuns created and the cultural and loan associations developed by the resisters.

In the social, cultural, political, and economic spheres, both groups also created structures of empowerment for women that left their mark on the world around them. Chapter II chronicled the educational, political, and cultural aspects of convent living, especially during the medieval period. We have examined in this chapter the accomplishments of the resisters in devising unique social and economic arrangements that enabled women to lead lives never before known in Chinese society. Such structures were not omnipotent or without problems. But power is never absolute or without problems. Many critics who charge women's groups with being apolitical seem to demand that they exercise a type of absolute power in the world, a demand seldom imposed on other oppressed groups.

As unattached women whose friendship with each other motivated great achievements, nuns were hardly "superfluous women." Nor were the resisters "goods on which one loses." Both defied the hetero-relational stereotype of the loose woman as lewd woman—she who is free for men—and reclaimed the original meaning of loose woman—she who is free for women. In the tradition of the ancient *hetaira*, nuns and resisters restored female friendship to its original state, investing it with a primary purpose and passion. They were "happily unmarried."

This did not mean that both groups of women escaped vilification by hetero-relational standards or that scholarship does not continue to judge them by these same standards. Whenever women are together, doing unconventional deeds, they are categorized as not real women. The categories are repetitively prolific: manly, deprived, sexless, frigid, lonely, broken, lewd, whorish, escapist, apolitical, insignificant. Or their womanist origins become redefined as male-originated. Thus scholars attribute nuns going into convents and Chinese women resisting marriage to the scarcity of men or the prevalence of "nonprogressive" marriage structures.

Truth, or historical representation of reality, does not have to tally with the facts or the testimonies of the historical actors themselves. The historian or other interpreter, by gazing backward into the historical landscape, has been so accustomed to using the canons of hetero-relational scholarship that often good feminist scholars take them for granted in their own work. What actually happened gets lost in the conformity to so-called objective (hetero-relational) standards. For example, scholars will overlook the independent causality of women's choice to live, work, and be with each other in favor of scarcity or fear of men. Or, at best, Gyn/affective groups are seen as exceptional women, without past and without future. Gyn/affective history is treated not as "historical" but as "sheer occurrence," presumably springing from nowhere and having nowhere to go.

The task of Gyn/affective scholarship is to save Gyn/affective women and deeds from the futility that comes from oblivion — oblivion not only from lack of recognition but from the wrong kind of recognition. Indeed, that has been the task and purpose of this entire book and, in particular, of these two chapters on loose women.

The critique of hetero-reality and the representation of women who have resisted it does not mean that the obstacles to female friendship cease to exist. The history and culture of female friendship are replete with obstacles to Gyn/affection. And those obstacles must be named for what they are. In the genealogy of this book, however, they are not the final word about female friendship. They are only the next word!

IV
Obstacles to Female Friendship

To put it starkly and simply, the Second coming of the Witchcraze will employ different methods. This time, women are trained and legitimated to do it to each other.

> Mary Daly,
> *Pure Lust*

Friendship does not abolish the distance between people, but it makes it vibrant.

> Walter Benjamin,
> *Understanding Brecht*

If I am not for myself, then who is for me?
If I am for myself alone, then who am I?

> Rabbi Hillel,
> *Sayings of the Jewish Fathers* [sic]

T here are many impediments to female friendship. A work on women's friendships should not romanticize the subject by omitting these obstacles from serious consideration. Such obstacles are present among different kinds of women—those who are feminists and those who would not define themselves as feminists. In fact, among both groups of women, the obstacles have surprisingly similar patterns.

The most blatant obstacle to female friendship is the prevailing patriarchal adage that "women are each other's worst enemies." This theme has many variations, and a chorus of male voices through the centuries has echoed Jonathan Swift's words: "I never knew a tolerable woman to be fond of her own sex." It would be easy to dismiss this chorus by virtue of its sex or to emphasize the unintended clue given in Swift's remark that the women whom men find "tolerable" are not fond of their own sex. So women disidentify with other women in order to make themselves "tolerable" to men.

However, women utter similar words. A study chronicling women's attitudes toward female friendship revealed the following. From a secretary: "To attach too much importance to friendship with women is adolescent"; from a computer programmer: "It will be viewed as 'latent' lesbianism."[1] It would be easy to ignore these voices by saying that women internalize men's attitudes about them and about their relationships with other women. The problem is that, although this may account in one way for the cause of women's antifeminist behavior, it does not assuage the awful reality of woman-hating-woman conduct when it happens in our own and other women's lives. It is the reality of this behavior with which this chapter is concerned.

By blaring the hetero-relational message that "women are each other's worst enemies," men have ensured that many women will be each others' worst enemies. The obstacles to female friendship get good press. The message functions as a constant noise pollution in women's lives and is heard in many different places. Constant noise about women not loving women is supplemented by the historical *silence* about women always loving women. Women-hating-women take their sustenance from the silence that surrounds women-loving-women. It is this double message that strangles the growth of Gyn/affection. Women need to be aware of the contexts in which this double message arises as well as the mechanics of how it functions to stonewall the evolution of female friendship.

In the course of writing this book, I have asked students, friends, and various other women to list what they felt to be the primary barriers to Gyn/affection. The lists were lengthy, although women tended to characterize the obstacles in similar ways. What I came to realize, however, is that although the concrete obstacles could vary among different groups of women, the contexts from which they sprung are remarkably common to all women. And so if it is true that putting a subject in context illuminates it, then talking about the contexts in which the obstacles to Gyn/affection arise is an important step toward eradicating the obstacles themselves.

Friendship gives women a point of crystallization for living in the world.* It gives form, shape, and a concrete location to women who have no state or geographical homeland and, in fact, no territorial ghetto or diaspora from which to act. Friendship provides women with a common world that becomes a reference point for location in a larger world. The sharing of common views, attractions, and energies gives women a connection to the world so that they do not lose their bearing. Thus a sharing of personal life is at the same time a grounding for social and political existence. By the same token, anything that militates against women's-being-in-the-world—against a female worldliness—undermines a strong female friendship that has political consequences, namely, Gyn/affection.

Unfortunately, the contexts in which many women live their lives enhance a worldlessness rather than the worldliness of which I speak.

---

*In the following chapter, I discuss the notions of "world," "worldliness," and "worldly integrity" much more fully as part of my vision of female friendship. For purposes of this chapter, where I stress the necessity for women to be in the world and where I use three forms of worldlessness as contexts in which many obstacles to female friendship arise, it is necessary to be clear about my use of the word *world*. I define *world* in the following ways:

1. The earthly state of human existence; this present life.
2. The pursuits and interests of this present life; temporal or mundane affairs.
3. The affairs and conditions of life; the state of human affairs; the state of things.
4. Most pertinent: The sphere within which one's interests are bound up or one's activities find scope; one's sphere of action or thought; the "realm" within which one moves or lives.

I am fully aware that *world* is often used as synonymous with the cosmos and that much feminist literature has defined it in this way, wishing to establish certain connections between women and Nature. However, I use the term *world* to mean the public realm. Or, as Hannah Arendt phrased it, "The world lies between people." (Hannah Arendt, "On Humanity," in *Men in Dark Times* [New York: Harcourt, 1968], p. 4.) I am restricting the meaning of *world* to these parameters, for the time being, because my point in this chapter is to extract the ways in which women are dissociated from, assimilated to, or victims in the world.

Neither female worldliness nor female friendship can grow or deepen within the contexts of dissociation from the world, assimilation to the world, or victimism in the world. Since these contexts prevail in the lives of many women, the obstacles to Gyn/affection also arise within them. Worldlessness produces friendlessness.

Dissociation from the World

Because women have been the eternal victims of male tyranny, because survival has been the key focus of female existence and feminist political thought, because women have almost everywhere lacked involvement in and control over the political world in which we have lived, and because the world is man-made, many women have developed a dissociation from the world. Hannah Arendt, more than most philosophers, has discussed the concept of worldlessness. Arendt's notion of worldlessness, although originally developed and analyzed in the context of the history of the Jews and of Judaism, has much relevance for women and feminism today.[2]

Women in general have assumed a worldlessness almost by default, that is, by virtue of the passive and derivative positions into which they have been forced throughout history and in almost every culture. Other women, such as some feminist separatists, have made dissociation from the world a political ideal and reality. The difficulty in both cases is that when dissociation becomes a prominent mode of existence—as in the former example where women derive much of their meaning and reality from husbands, lovers, fathers, or male bosses, seldom experiencing the world directly, or as in the case of some separatists, who make dissociation the basis for affinity with other women—female existence becomes segregated from the rest of the world. Philosophically this can make women narrow in vision; politically it can make them very vulnerable. Even radical and voluntary dissociation from the world, originally undertaken as a necessary and daring feminist political stance, can produce a worm's-eye view of the world that exposes women to attack. A major consequence of dissociation is that women can become ignorant of conditions in the "real" world, conditions that may militate against their very survival.

In a world that views women as superfluous, that is, as not needed, marginal, unimportant, and to be dispensed with, women add to this superfluousness by dissociating themselves from the world. The more women dissociate, the more catastrophic the effect can be—the further women are removed from a definite share of what should be a common world, that is, a world held in common by all who inhabit it.

Let it be understood that I am not identifying dissociation with the necessity for women to live "on the boundary" of hetero-relational society. Women will always be "outsiders" to this culture, as Virginia Woolf and others knew. However, there is a worldless dissociation from patriarchy and a worldly dissociation. The dissociation that I criticize is not that of women coming together separately to then affect the "real" world. Rather it is a dissociation that proclaims a withdrawal from that world. It is a dissociation that is usually accompanied by a "downward mobility" of mind and of money. It often creates an apathy toward political, intellectual, and financial existence as well as an apathy toward one's physical appearance which becomes a symbol of one's disregard for the man-made world. It behaves as if money and status are things that women already have (or could have if they wanted), can easily discard, and can easily replace. It calls upon "patriarchy as excuse" to rationalize the inactions of not getting a job, not going to school, not taking economic and professional strides that would locate a woman in the "real" world.

Dissociation excludes women from access to the world. It thus excludes women from power, money, and interaction with others, the most basic conditions of worldliness. Dissociation gives women the illusion that they can retreat into an undisturbed time and space where a semblance of freedom can be preserved. However, as Arendt has pointed out, such a stance leads to "the freedom and untouchability of outcasts."[3] The politically dissociated feminist plays the revolutionary in a community of other like-minded women but does not really impinge on the dominant male ethos. She remains an outcast from the world, not a rebel "on the boundary" of it.

On the other hand, the dissociation from the world that is not chosen for consciously defined feminist reasons—an interpretation of the world that women largely derive from men—is reinforced by women's lack of knowledge about women as a common people. In contrast to other oppressed groups, women do not possess the past of a cohesive and self-conscious community with its own political traditions, philosophical vitality, and history—or should I say that this past is one that most women know little about? The rootlessness of women in their own group identity as women contributes more than anything to the worldless, unrealistic, and nonpolitical perception that many women have of the world. This rootlessness is responsible also for the lack of female friendship, the friendship that is truly Gyn/affective as a political virtue.

Gyn/affection cannot be sustained where women have "the great privilege of being unburdened by care for the world"[4] because Gyn/affection is a political virtue with a political effect. Female living, especially feminist existence, cannot take place outside the *polis*.

Any strong and critical reality of female friendship, any mode of friendship that aims to restore power to the word and reality, cannot be created within a dissociated enclave of women who have little knowledge of or interest in the wider world. Women's friendships cannot be reconstituted in a vacuum of dissociation from the wider world. Any women's community that dissociates itself from a wider world cannot take the place of a wider world.

Dissociation from the world produces dissociation from women. It restricts Gyn/affection to a separate community created by withdrawing from the world. Thus it deprives Gyn/affection of its political power and makes of it a personal matter only. Women may acquire a strength that is sustained by radically chosen dissociation. However, as Hannah Arendt reminds us, strength is not political power.

> ... strength and power are not the same ... power arises only where people act together, but not where people grow stronger as individuals. No strength is ever great enough to replace power; wherever strength is confronted by power, strength will always succumb.[5]

Radically chosen dissociation from the world is a temptation as women are constantly confronted with a world that men have fabricated. It is even more tempting to ignore the babel that sustains the man-made Babylon. Women do this, however, at our peril.

Women who dissociate from the world either by political choice or by involuntary derivative status must put something in place of that world. Many have resorted to therapism.

Therapism: The Tyranny of Feelings

Therapism is what elsewhere I have called "therapy as a way of life."[6] The phenomenon of therapism, as it is manifested among women and in the women's community, includes not only going into therapy and often staying there for years but making of one's relationships with women a therapeutic context. Therapism is an overvaluation of feeling. In a real sense, it is a tyranny of feelings where women have come to believe that what really counts in their life is their "psychology." And since they don't know what their psychology means, they submit to another who purports to know—a psychiatrist, counselor, or analyst. In this sense, we might say that therapism promotes a psychological hypochondria with women as the major seekers of emotional health.

There are, of course, instances in which women justifiably seek help in a therapeutic setting. I am not criticizing this genuine need. However, there seems to be little recognition given to the fact that therapy is becoming a way of life among women and that it is necessary to ask where the individual need for advice and counsel leaves off and the tyranny of feelings begins. It is remarkable that women who bemoan their lack of money for books, cultural events, and the like somehow obtain the money needed for weekly or biweekly therapy sessions. Feminist therapy is a booming business. Many feminist restaurants, bookstores, health centers, and credit unions have gone out of business completely or remain on the brink of financial survival. Yet feminist therapy thrives. At the very least, women should examine why this is the case.

One reason is the premium placed on the disclosure of self. The disclosure of self has become the territory of therapy. It is a particular kind of disclosure, however, that employs a mechanistic model of building, adjusting, and tinkering with the self as though it is some external object in need of repair. It is a brand of disclosure that confuses genuine self-revelation with the perpetual manifestation of intimate feelings. Refusal to tell all is regarded as repressiveness, as a denial of one's inner self. And as a result, the women's movement, like society at large, has fast become a therapeutic society where self-exposure ranks as one of the highest virtues. Women must show and tell all. Little about body or mind can be mysterious. Thus women engage in massive psychological strip-teases that fragment and exploit the inner life. It is increasingly more difficult to lose one's job, health, or lover without having to go into therapy about it.

Certainly people must be able to free themselves of torturous feelings, pent-up emotions, and troublesome trials. There may be times when women will seek out therapists for help. Just as there is a genuine need to share such feelings, there is also a need to protect and withhold. And the therapeutic context may not be the best place to share such feelings. Genuine self-revelation should not be confused with perpetual therapeutic manifestations.

Therapeutic manifestations have consequences far beyond the actual therapeutic setting. Michel Foucault has put it this way:

> ... we have ... become a singularly confessing society. The confession ... plays a part in justice, medicine, education, family relationships, and love relations, in the most ordinary affairs of everyday life, and in the most

solemn rites; one confesses one's crimes, one's sins, one's thoughts and desires, one's illnesses and troubles; one goes about telling with the greatest precision, whatever is difficult to tell.[7]

These words make clear that psychology has created a new type of person—the human confessing animal. "The obligation to confess . . . is so deeply ingrained in us, that we no longer perceive it as the effect of a power that constrains us; on the contrary, it seems that truth, lodged in our most secret nature, 'demands' only to surface."[8] Self-disclosure becomes equated with liberation. In this sense, therapy becomes a way of life that affects the way we speak, the way we think, and the way we relate to other people. As a way of life, expression of feelings becomes a kind of ritual proclaiming that expression alone, independent of the consequences produces change in the person. Expression alone exonerates, purifies, and redeems.

In this context, Sara Scott and Tracey Payne, writing in the British radical feminist magazine *Trouble and Strife,* call therapy a "mental laxative." Emphasizing therapy's preoccupation with the past, they maintain that therapy "leaves us reaching constantly backwards into our own past experience rather than outwards to the experience of other women to find explanations for our lives. Once women find and *express* these past 'blocks', supposedly women will be 'whole' and happy".[9]

The irony of all this is that in an age that is obsessed with the revelation of self, true and deep subjectivity is hard to find. Hannah Arendt pointed out two reasons for this. First, psychological introspection annihilates the actually existing situation by dissolving it into mood. At the same time, it lends an aura of objectivity to everything that is subjective.[10] Thus an inner life is reduced to an exercise in therapeutics. Therapism reifies subjectivity, that is, it thingifies it, by externalizing and wrenching the inner life out of its depths. Too easily, the inner life becomes the outer life.

Second, in introspective self-disclosures, the boundaries between what is intimate and what is public become blurred. Intimacies are made public, and those who refuse to engage in the publicizing of intimacy are viewed as uptight and repressed, in need of a psychological purging. The importance of feeling one's self feeling is the norm. Life acquires reality mainly in the course of confessing it and subjecting it to a constant psychological probe. Not the emotions themselves but the telling of emotions becomes definitive for reality.

What does all this have to do with female friendship? For many women, feminist therapy has become a substitute for female friendship. Others have noted what a Russian emigré has said about friend-ship in America: "Americans go to a psychologist because of the need for friends."[11] There is a sense in which women in continuous therapy purchase friendship by the hour from those in the therapeutic role. Often these women do have friends with whom they discuss their intimate lives. However, they claim that there is something "different" about talking with a therapist.

For example, one woman related to me the story of a friend who had undergone the break-up of a ten-year relationship with her lover. The ending was extremely nasty and, for one month, my friend listened to every detail of the break-up, offering advice, comfort, and her own presence of friendship. One day, her friend told her that she was going to see a therapist. My friend questioned her about the need to do this. Her friend replied that she was going into therapy "to get some advice." "But what could be different about the advice that a therapist will give you from that which I have offered?" my friend asked. Her friend pondered awhile and then answered: "But I pay her!" My friend concluded, "Well, pay me then!"

As Tracey Payne says of her own experience in therapy: "Looking back on it I see very little that I could not have got from close friends or a CR group, but at the time therapy also offered 'freedom'. In particular freedom from my past. I felt that if I kept 'shovelling shit' fast enough I could catch up and be free of it . . . I also believed that 'sorting myself out' was a good thing in itself."[12]

In a confessing society, friendship often becomes reduced to "sorting myself out" and/or to co-counseling—literally when two women set up this formal arrangement with each other, or figuratively when women make of their relationships with other women a context for constant self-disclosure. Feelings become facts. Feelings also become matters of probing and preoccupying interest. As Pat Hynes has phrased it, women become "overly specialized emotionally."[13] Political matters are explored largely in the context of how one "relates" to them. Ultimately, friendships of this nature become a form of gossip—gossip about one's self.

In therapism, what is missing is passionate exchange. The sharing of feelings predominates over the revelation of passionate truth. Mary Daly has made a crucial distinction between this kind of feeling and passion. She calls the former *plastic* or *pseudo-passions*.

In contrast to real passions, plastic passions are free-floating feelings resulting in more and more disconnectedness/fragmentation. Since they are characterized by the lack of specific and nameable causes, or "objects," they must be "dealt with" endlessly in an acontextual way, or within a pseudocontext.[14]

As an example of a plastic passion contrasted to real passion, Daly compares fulfillment to joy. Fulfillment she sees as "the therapeutized perversion of the passion of joy."[15] Fulfillment is almost like being stuffed or filled by an external source. Joy is a movement that comes from within a person. A fulfilled woman is "completed" or "finished" elsewhere. A joyful woman engages in consistent self-directed movement for more of her deepest Self and that of her friends.

Therapy as a way of life filters out the passion and lets the feeling through. It is almost as though the depth of a woman is sifted out and the diffused feeling retained. Therapism promotes low levels of intensity. In this sense, feeling is what one might call the banality of passion. The "therapeutizing" of friendship is based on a particular loss of Self, the loss of the passionate Self, and the loss of the original Self who was one's original friend. Having lost this originality, women continue to relate to each other nonoriginally. The examination and exploration of feelings become a substitute for a more passionate intimacy and sharing. There is a loss of depth and a loss of the intensity of female friendship. Hetero-relational patterns flourish in the wake of the loss of original Gyn/affection.

In close friendships, there is a hunger for truth, beginning with the truth of each other. Therapism replaces truth with an overdose of navel-gazing self-disclosure and blurs the difference between the two so that profound truth is equated with perpetual self-manifestations. It takes self-revelation, an important part of any friendship, out of the context of the passionate revelation of a woman's life as truly lived and pretends that such revelation can exist only within the context of the actual therapist-client relationship or within the informal therapeutic context of friends who act as sisterly co-counselors.

The breeding ground for therapism is the dissociative context in which many women live. When a woman becomes dissociated from the real world, even though that world is man-made and corrupt, events and people may more easily acquire a reality that is out of place. For example, a woman's self—not her deepest Self but the self that feels itself feeling—takes on a proportion that is wrongly sized. When this happens, the expression of feelings may become equal to or greater than, for example, the expression of political action or ideas. To take Virginia Woolf's famous words and use them in a different

context, women then become "magnifying mirrors"[16] reflecting themselves back to themselves at a self-absorbed size.

The dissociative context of women in general, or that chosen by
some feminist separatists, creates a dissociated "community" that can
become a totalistic environment which subjects those who inhabit it to
homogeneous norms and values. As analyzed by Robert J. Lifton,
totalistic environments usually succeed in claiming "total ownership of
each individual self within it. Private ownership of the mind and its
products—of imagination or of memory—becomes highly immoral."[17]
Dissociation, whether in the case of women in general or feminist
separatists, creates a kind of totalistic environment that subtly functions
as an apparatus for constraining truth and fostering "correct" behavior by
making total exposure the rule. Women who do not engage in perpetual manifestations of their feelings, whether at the coffee klatches of
shared housewifedom or within the women's community, are judged
wanting. Within such an environment, a woman is deprived of both
external worldly information and internal reflection, both of which are
necessary to maintain a sense of place in the real world and to preserve
a Self separate from it. Within a dissociated context, life may acquire
"reality" more easily by exposing one's privacy in the almost mystical
manifestations of shared feelings. Confession becomes a constant form
of communication with other women. Therapism has replaced
friendship.

While therapism exists in other than dissociative contexts of
women, women in such situations have become singular victims of it
because most women, by virtue of sex role segregation from the major
political realities, are already affected by dissociation from the world. If
one adds to this other layers of dissociation, for example for politically
chosen feminist reasons, a more amenable context for exploitation of
the inner life is created.

The women's movement has not only helped create a new class of
professional counselors known as feminist therapists but has also
made the context of many women's relationships with each other into
a world without walls. This phenomenon of "show-and-tell" relationships is, I maintain, another form of Self and horizontal violence. It
does violence to women's strong and original Selves, and it does
violence to women's friendships by keeping women in a prone position vis-à-vis each other, the position of one who constantly chooses to
feel herself feeling, thus diverting attention away from the active use of
inner resources by dissipating energy in constant manifestations of
self. Instead of becoming deep friends, women become "technicians of
human relations."

Relationism: The Tyranny of Relations

What I am dubbing "relationism" often accompanies therapism. Relationism is the reduction of friendship to relationships that get constantly "examined" and "dealt with" in much the same way that therapism examines and deals with all sorts of feelings.

Relationism also has its new class of professional experts. They are called "attraction theorists" and as they "oversee" the "field of friendship," they can, among other things, technically explain the difference between "companionate love" and "passionate love." Like the "attraction theorists," women "in relationships" often make of them a technical enterprise by "dealing and dealing" with them until they can be "dealt with" no longer. Personal style, erotic interchange, gestures, facial expressions are all material to be used to draw out a meaning or significance beyond the gestures themselves. This kind of relationism objectifies women and their relationships in much the same way that women become objectified in a hetero-relational context. It defines women always "in reference to" someone else.

Relationism materializes the etymology of the word *relate* by making women into "relatable" creatures, that is, a class that "refers to" something or someone else—that which is ever being brought into relation with something external to the Self. The consistent focus on dealing with relationships in which many women are immersed reinforces dissociation from a wider world of meaning and significance. Such relationism prevents the development of deep Gyn/affection.

Relationism exists in several contexts. Within a hetero-relational context, where women derive their meaning from the men in their lives, relationism takes the form of women being constantly focused on men. The men in women's lives often become the topic of discussion when women friends come together. This kind of relating fosters frivolous friendships that are chiefly characterized by women talking about men and swapping stories about "good men," "real men," "gentle men," or the various other varieties of male consorts. Many lesbians, however, especially within the context of separatist dissociation from the world, fall into similar patterns of focusing on the women in their lives. Reticence to speak about one's personal relationships is viewed as a leftover of a secretive patriarchal mentality and as a politically repressive barrier that inhibits social intercourse among women. Thus, dissociation of both varieties gives women a new profession, which is actually an old profession—the profession of "professional relating."

As "professional relaters," lesbians often channel the bulk of their energy into relationships in which they frequently move from one erotic relationship to another. Lesbians have been critical of the hetero-relational imperative that prompts women to see themselves always in relation to men. However, "living for women" in the reductive sense, where women's lives are "bound up" with their relationships, can become the analogue of "living for men." Lesbian relationism is not much different from hetero-relationism if women in such circumstances must always "be in a relationship." In the grip of such relational "fever," it seems that lesbians have, in one sense, replaced men with women as relational objects. The hetero-relationist adage "Thou as a woman must bond with a man" is modified to "Thou as a woman must bond with a woman." Lack of an erotic relationship is often seen as lack of a significant self.

The relationship-centeredness of many women, heterosexual or lesbian, makes others the center of a woman's life. It displaces a necessary Self-centeredness and often negates a work-centeredness since, when a relationship fails, all else fails. Women become depressed, paralyzed, and unable to continue other commitments, especially their work lives. Relationism, or the relationship-centeredness of women, is thus an obstacle to female friendship because it draws a woman's energy away from her Self, her original friend, always to others. No genuine Gyn/affection can be created which does not come from a strong Self. Relationism promotes a surrender of Self and of a positive and necessary Self-centeredness.

Perversions of "The Personal Is Political"

The proliferation of relationism and therapism promotes the proliferation of women's private lives. In the beginnings of this current wave of feminism, there was much emphasis on "the personal is political." This was and still is a crucial feminist insight. It signaled that what had been relegated to the personal domain of a woman's existence—areas such as the family and sexuality—were areas of political consequence. The saying "the personal is political" encapsulated the truth that such traditionally regarded personal areas of life, largely inhabited by women, could no longer be segregated out of the political arena. Indeed, areas such as the family and sexuality now came to be viewed as bastions of patriarchal power and as prime centers of sexual politics.

There have been many perversions of this original insight. "The personal is political" has undergone reduction and misinterpretation. For example, many women took "the personal is political" to mean "the personal is public knowledge." In this view, anything that is intimate, private, or personal becomes matter for the public domain. One of the latest versions of this is the movement called "lesbian sadomasochism" in which, as Kathleen Barry has noted, the ultimate perversion of "the personal is political" occurs.

> Whatever your "feelings" or "desires" are, because you are a woman, a lesbian, a feminist, does not legitimize asserting them as a *political* right . . .
>   It is this kind of thinking that extends the concept of oppression until it is utterly meaningless . . . If we are to connect our personal experience of oppression to political strategy, this strategy must be based in certain identified values of what promotes and enhances human life over what objectifies it.[18]

So-called lesbian sadomasochism has similarities to therapism in that it also arises in a context where expression of feelings is the norm, this time even the political norm. Denial of such feelings is seen as political repression. Thus liberation becomes equated not only with the freedom to follow one's feelings but with the campaign to create a political movement out of publicizing those feelings.

There have been others who have criticized what they regard as perversions of "the personal is political." Not all of these critiques have been as astute as Barry's. Jean Bethke Elshtain's work is one example of a "displaced critique"—a critique that is misfocused—in her use of what she has termed a "politics of displacement." Elshtain argues: "Nothing personal is exempt, then, from definition, direction and manipulation—neither sexual intimacy, love, nor patenting . . . if politics is power and power is everywhere, politics is in fact nowhere."[19]

The problem, in my opinion, is not the politicizing of personal life. It is the *publicizing* of personal life. Nothing personal can be private. Nothing personal can be hidden from public scrutiny. The distortion resides in the fact that everything that is personal becomes publicly exposed under the rhetoric that "the personal is political." Thus, calling everything "political" generates a ruse for making everything personal, subject to the public and collective judgment of the women's community.

Within the context of certain self-identified separatist groups whose politics is based on dissociation from the world, the "personal is public" phenomenon has taken root. What often happens, what often is rationalized as a necessity for shared collective existence, is the breaking down of all sorts of private limits. As one critic has put it, "first go the clothes; then the easy feelings, then the tough feelings, then the real secrets, and finally the entire inner self. Supposedly after this soul-baring orgy, we will then experience a new freedom, or equality, or openness, or something."[20] Relationships in particular are a fertile area of discussion. One of my former students expressed her exasperation with the "personal is public" mentality in the following way: " . . . it is seemingly a categoric imperative for everyone and anyone to have an opinion about what everyone is doing. I HATE IT."[21]

No genuine Gyn/affection can come of this. Even when women are not aware of misinterpreting "the personal is political," because they sincerely believe in the sharing of private living, one must ask what is really being shared under such circumstances. Is it really a profound inner life? Is it the fruits of a thoughtful and creative existence?

Gyn/affection needs private space and time. This privacy is quite different from dissociation upon which therapism and relationism thrive, fostering the illusion of an undisturbed time and space separate from the world to which only "the relations" have access. Rather, privacy fosters involvement in the world because it adds a quality of reflection to life and to the selection of friends—what Alice Walker has called the "rigors of discernment." Discernment helps us to regain perspective about our Selves and others. Without this habit of reflection, we lose the feel of our own Be-ing, the sense of integrity that makes us who we are.

Assimilation to the World

The opposite of dissociation is assimilation to the world. Assimilationist women desire to succeed in the world of men by effacing the fact of their femaleness. The assimilationist strives to lose her female identity, to go beyond it, to be regarded as a person in a world that grants the status of persons only to men. She does this by assimilating to the male dominant world on its terms.

I am not advocating that women constantly proclaim "I am woman" on the job or in whatever worlds they move. However, an assimilationist woman disidentifies consistently with women. For example, she may ignore or, worse, accept oppressive attitudes and actions such as sexual harassment or the denigration of other women made in her presence. She may even initiate discussion of antifeminist topics to prove she is "one of the boys." In other words, when she is oppressed as a woman, she does not respond as a woman.

In a society that is not only hostile to women but is pervaded by what Andrea Dworkin has named woman-hating, it is possible to assimilate only by assimilation to antifeminism also. Explicitly or implicitly, assimilationists sever ties with other women, whether they are in the company of men or women or both. The irony of this is that both men and women will always perceive them first and foremost as women. It is unfortunate that assimilationists do not recognize, or ignore, this perception, wishing it will go away, when it never will.

A common way in which women assimilate is by exaggerating declarations that they are not feminists or by taking pains to proclaim that they have moved beyond feminism. The former women may affirm that they believe in equal pay for equal work, but they dissociate themselves quickly from other women who believe in the same things or from women who go further. In the latter case, many women use the term "postfeminist" as a badge of maturity. Thus assimilation, in both instances, becomes a form of dissociation from women.

Another irony of such dissociation from women, and especially from feminism, is that often assimilationist women engage in quite extraordinary activities that are feminist in the sense that these endeavors require unconventional capabilities, courage, determination, and persistence. Also, they are often pioneers in their respective fields. One thinks of women scientists, truck drivers, welders, and presidents of colleges who not only are excellent at what they do but who frequently are more astute and humane than men in the same areas. However, many of these women, when asked, would deny any kind of woman-identification. Penney Kane wrote in *Homemaker's Magazine:*

> Women seem to be espousing feminist principles, on the one hand, and dissociating themselves from the movement, on the other . . . Letters in response to our articles are touching, personal, and supportive. Many readers are eager to report discrimination, or to recount how they handled being treated in a patronized manner, or succeeded despite obstacles. Yet, when I introduce myself as a feminist, many women react as though the term were scatological.[22]

At best, assimilationists identify with feminism as "a lifestyle or an attitude or feeling of vague sympathy with women or an assertion of modernity."[23]

Assimilation spells the end of any strong reality of female friendship before it begins. For the assimilationist, men and/or male-defined structures are what counts. To become part of the male dominant society, women have to believe or pretend that they are both persons and women in the ways that men have defined both for them. What is demanded of assimilationist women by the male dominant culture is that they behave in ways that distinguish them from ordinary women—for example, they are encouraged to be bright, articulate, upwardly mobile professionals—but at the same time they must exhibit acceptable manners and modes of man-made femininity such as charming behavior or feminine clothing. The complicated psychology learned well by the assimilationist woman is how to be and not be a woman, or how to be the woman that men still recognize as one of their own while avoiding the woman who recognizes her Self and women who are Self-defined.

The assimilated woman is the new androgyne. She often combines so-called masculine and feminine roles, or she mixes a "masculine" career with a "feminine" marriage and/or motherhood. She is often referred to as the "new woman." This new woman is a blend of the so-called cosmic polarities of masculinity and femininity, yin and yang. It is as if she overcomes such cosmic polarities within her own persona and lifestyle. Two culturally fabricated halves, masculinity and femininity, have been glued together once more to produce the complete person, the woman who supposedly "has it all." The assimilationist woman creates her own person in a hetero-relational image, this time incarnating such an image of complementarity within herself. Thus she sees no necessity for Gyn/affection within a life that seeks male definition for completeness in all sorts of ways.

Sexual Liberation

The road to assimilation is the road to conformism, this time conformism to new stereotypes that assume form under the guise of "liberation" and "new woman" rhetoric, but conformism nonetheless. This brand of assimilationism often displays the verbiage and outward lifestyle of liberation, particularly sexual liberation.

Sexual liberation may take the form of a liberated marriage in which both partners have careers and do the housework and childcare, although men seldom bear an equitable share of the latter two.[24] Or it may take the form of an "independence" in which a woman has multiple sexual partners of her own choosing and timing but becomes committed to none. The liberation of women, lesbian or heterosexual, as defined by the mores of the sexual revolution is often from "sinful" or, in more modern parlance, repressive sex to the expression of self through "fucking." As Shulamith Firestone wrote a long time ago, "her sexuality eventually becomes synonymous with her individuality."[25] Sexuality becomes not only a "polymorphous perversity" but a "polymorphous rebellion" against anything that is perceived as repressive.

Swinging, gay sex, bisex, S&M—the list is endless—all become superficial substitutions for sexual intimacy.

What the traditional woman regarded as sexual slavery, the "new woman" regards as sexual liberation. It is a sexual liberation that assimilates its values from the male left or from the gay male movement. One of its most recent manifestations is, again, so-called lesbian sadomasochism, in which self-defined feminists and lesbians display a new aspect of assimilation—assimilation to the ethic and lifestyle of "genital sex is what counts." This gets "refined" to "the kind of genital sex is what counts."

Firestone was prescient in *The Dialectic of Sex* where, in writing about sexual liberation, she anticipated the arguments of latter-day lesbian sadomasochists long before there was such a movement. "To be plain old needy-for-affection makes one a 'drip,' to need a kiss is embarrassing, unless it is an erotic kiss; only 'sex' is O.K., in fact it proves one's mettle."[26] So-called lesbian sadomasochists would go further and say that only certain kinds of sex "prove one's mettle," and—to pun on the obsolete meaning of this word—one's sexual "mettle" is proven by "mettle" (read "metal" as in collars, chains, spikes, and other such "exotic" paraphernalia). They assert this under the guise of "freeing" women from their traditional role of "affectionate sexuality" which, they claim, lacks vigor and is indeed "wimpy." So-called lesbian sadomasochism confines sexuality to highly charged sex acts, substituting forceful and often violent sex performances for ardor and intense passion.

Although lesbian sadomasochism may arise in a context where women are dissociated politically from the wider world, at the same time it assimilates women very forcefully into a leftist and gay male world of sexuality. S&M is part of a "politics of assimilation" in that its values and style are derived from the male-directed left and gay male worlds. In her article "Sadomasochism: The New Backlash to Feminism," Kathleen Barry has pointed out that the promoters of lesbian sadomasochism are leftist and left-identified women who have become allies with heterosexual leftist women. Together they have been at the core of the so-called feminist pro-pornography movement. From their leftist perspectives, such S&M proponents as Gayle Rubin downgrade radical feminist issues such as sexual harassment, rape, and pornography as insignificant in comparison to "real" issues such as women's economic oppression.

The sadomasochistic mentality and movement assimilate women into a sexual liberation that is none other than the unrestrained expression of male-defined sexual behavior, where sexual liberation is tantamount to doing whatever one "feels" like doing. We confront again the tyranny of feelings, where feelings are portrayed almost as deterministic sexual drives that must be expressed at all costs. This is a very reactionary mentality which in one sense replicates the cultural conception of male sexuality. Men have always been portrayed as "needing" to express their "natural" sexual urges. So-called lesbian sadomasochism entitles women to vent similarly conceived "natural" sexual urges, giving women full "equality" of unobstructed sexual expression.

On another front, the promoters of lesbian sadomasochism assimilate philosophies and activities of the gay men's movement. Gay men as "style setters" in the women's fashion industry have popularized clothing and make-up for women that promote the masochistic look. In addition to retaining the 1950s black leather fashion, many gay men have added whips, chains, spiked bracelets, studded collars, and swastikas to their wardrobes, creating a veritable armamentarium of sadomasochistic style. So-called lesbian sadomasochists have been quick to assimilate and copy this style. John Stoltenberg has pointed out that "we are witnessing the convergence of what was once deemed a 'gay sensibility' with what was once deemed a 'heterosexual sensibility.' That convergence is conspiously a male sensibility, and it now reveals itself fully as thriving on female degradation."[27]

In gay male sadomasochism, one of the partners "temporarily mimics powerlessness." Stoltenberg illustrates how,

> true to their privileged status as genital males in society, the partners are at liberty to trade roles in private without jeopardizing their status in the culture in any way. Between two homosexual males then, there exists the possibility that "consent" in sadomasochism may be meaningful: Its meaning is in their prior agreement to reify each other's manhood.[28]

Women are not "phallic peers." Their "consent" to so-called lesbian sadomasochism can derive its "meaning" only from their status as victimized peers, one of whom merely role-plays the part of the powerful.

> The lesbian sadist pretends in private to have more power than she has in the culture . . .
> A male homosexual may feign powerlessness relative to another, perhaps more violent, homosexual man; a lesbian may feign power relative to another, more masochistic, woman. Neither masquerade alters the objec-

tive reality that in society at large, men hold power over and against women through force, and both masquerades are erotic manifestations of that reality.[29]

Gay men transmit the message that sadomasochism is sexual liberation which "transcends gender." As with many other male-defined versions of transcendence, it is transcendence by graft. It merely grafts onto a relationship between women, a mode of "fucking" that has been developed for and remains oriented to men.

The *Oxford English Dictionary* gives as a primary definition of *assimilation* "the action of making or becoming like; the state of being like; similarity, resemblance, likeness." Other subsidiary definitions give further enlightenment: "the becoming conformed to; conformity with . . . conversion into a similar substance." Assimilating the male objectification of women, women conform to treating each other as objects.

Strong and loving Gyn/affection breaks the subject-object sexual system. So-called lesbian pornography—that is, pornography developed by men in which women are depicted in supposedly lesbian postures—reduces women to object-object interaction. Likewise, lesbian sadomasochism is one more way of putting women back into place as sexual objects. This time women objectify each other.

Under the banner of sexual liberation, the banishment of repressive sexuality is claimed. Enter repressive tolerance!

The Tyranny of Tolerance

Proponents of S&M have accused their adversaries of promulgating a dogmatism about what is right and wrong for feminists. More often the accusation is that those who oppose sadomasochism foster rigid values of political correctness. There is a curious reversal here. Where indeed does the dogmatism reside?

A dogmatism of tolerance has infected the women's movement. As a dogma, tolerance asserts that there should be no value judgments made about anything. Using the rhetoric of not imposing values on others, women buy into a dangerous philosophy in which they strip themselves of the capacity for moral judgment. What they do not realize is that values will always assert themselves. When women do not take responsibility for generating and representing their agreed-upon values, they become pushovers for the tyranny of others' values. It is the tyranny of tolerance that fosters a loss of feminist will—the will to shape history in a value-defined way.

Like "the tyranny of structurelessness," the tyranny of tolerance has promoted an ethic of value freedom that has been allowed to stand as an unexamined principle among certain groups of women. From an unexamined principle, it is a short distance to an unexamined life.

The sources of this ethic of value freedom are several: women's natural reaction to the tyranny of patriarchal values that are absolutist and unbending; resistance to the kind of control this has given men over women's lives; the uncritical acceptance of leftist values of valuelessness; and the equating of morality with moralism. Moralism, a traditional preserve of women, is rightly eschewed by feminists. As Andrea Dworkin has defined it, "Moralism is the set of rules learned by rote that keeps women locked in, so that intelligence can never meet the world head on."[30] Moralism constricts values and prevents women from engaging in meaningful ethical activity and from making genuinely moral decisions. In contrast, what Dworkin calls "moral intelligence" constructs values. "Moral intelligence is active; it can only be developed and refined by being used in the realm of real and direct experience. Moral activity is the use of that intelligence, the exercise of moral discernment."[31]

The assimilation of value freedom as a guiding principle has locked many women into a new dogmatism just as rigid in its own ways as the old—the dogma that moral or ethical judgment itself is oppressive, counterrevolutionary, and antithetical to politics. Committed to value freedom, many feminist groups found it most difficult to establish priorities, articulate goals, and define the basis for any political action which opposed and criticized other women's priorities and goals. Women found it easy to assert judgments that were in opposition to clearly accepted male dominant values. Paralysis set in when judgments and actions came into conflict with those of other women, especially women from within the ranks of those supposedly committed to the same cause.

In the name of some amorphously defined feminist community, value judgments and the will to enact them in opposition to other women are seen as divisive. However, what kind of consensus can be built on the unwillingness to make judgments? Social and political life stem from values, choices, and activities that are defined with clarity and exercised with commitment. For example, many women vaguely "feel" that so-called lesbian sadomasochism is wrong but hold back from translating that "feeling" into an articulate position and opposing action. No one, they say, has the right to judge the behavior of others or enforce one's own values. Philosopher Hilde Hein has said:

We have become reluctant to be labeled as moral crusaders in an age when human potential has degenerated to "doing your own thing." We are conditioned to making bland observations and cynical jokes in response to obscenities of a national scale and perversity of universal magnitude. We are numbed to the point of being at home with cruelty and despair. Sado-masochism is but one more absurdity to be greeted with a blank stare. But to do that is to yield to yet another assault upon our own decency . . . We cannot capitulate to the liberal dogma which treats as normal and neutral the volitional debasement and humiliation of one human being by another.[32]

The tyranny of tolerance dissuades women from tough-minded thinking, from responsibility for disagreement with others, and from the will to act. Worse, it allows oppressive values to surface without being rebutted.

In an age of ethical relativism, women forget that although a truth may be relative, it is relative to some particular framework of values. Even value freedom is a value statement. There is no such thing as pure relativism. Anything is seen from the eye of the viewer, from one of many angles or frames of reference. The fact that truth may be relative should not lead to the judgment that all values are on the same scale. From what purely relativistic vantage point could that judgment be made, for it is indeed a judgment and it is no more purely relativistic than any other judgment.

The tyranny of tolerance deprives not only individuals but also a political movement of its capacity for discernment. It saps a moral passion and purpose from feminist politics. It de-ethicizes issues of power so that decisions too often get made from, for example, a cost-benefit or purely consequentialist analysis. When politics is disjoined from ethics, politics frequently is reduced to policy. The hostility toward values and the facade of tolerance divest the women's movement of its radicalism. An active boldness is domesticated into a passive tolerance.

Tolerance is essentially a passive position.[33] Marcuse has labeled this "repressive tolerance" because, by neutralizing values, it serves mainly to protect the fabric by which society is held together. What is defined as value freedom may appear to be sensitive to and respectful of others, but in reality it makes people passive and uncritical. "Tolerance is turned from an active into a passive state, from practice to nonpractice."[34]

The tyranny of tolerance affects Gyn/affection in a significantly negative way. It vaporizes the "rigors of discernment." The passivity and uncritical mindset that it develops in women prompt them to apply the same lack of standards to selecting friends. Women who lack the "rigors of discernment" form nondiscriminating friendships.

Discernment, from the perspective of the tyranny of tolerance, is viewed often as a form of elitism. As writer and photographer Joreen notes in her classic essay "The Tyranny of Structurelessness," "Elitist is probably the most abused word in the women's liberation movement. It is used as frequently, and for the same reasons, as 'pinko' was used in the fifties."[35] Women forsake their powers of discernment because they are intimidated by the fear of being labeled "elitist." The tyranny of tolerance equates discernment with elitism and in doing so promotes a state of mind and a social context in which distinctions are leveled and sameness prevails.

In her remarkable essay "*One* Child of One's Own," Alice Walker gives this advice to women of color:

> What was required of women of color was to learn to distinguish between who was the real feminist and who was not, and to exert energy in feminist collaborations only when there is little risk of wasting it. The rigors of this discernment will inevitably keep throwing women of color back upon themselves, where there is, indeed, so much work, of a feminist nature, to be done.[36]

Many of these words can be paraphrased and applied to the formation of women's friendships. One might then wish to say:

> What is required of women friends is that they learn to distinguish between those who are real friends and those who are not and to exert energy in developing friendships only when there is little risk of wasting it. The rigors of this discernment will inevitably keep throwing women back upon their Selves where they will find their original friend.

It is significant that Walker refers to the *rigors* of discernment. It is a word that conjures up associations of strict, harsh, severe, exact, and scrupulous—associations with which women do not readily identify. Yet if we can think of discernment as a habit of mind and heart, specifically a habit of reflection that is rigorous in the best sense of the word and that is not an easy or passive habit, as tolerance is, we will have achieved greater insight into our friendships. Cicero's words are instructive in this context: "you ought to love after you have made a judgement; you should not form the judgement after you have loved."[37] This is not to say that the habit of discernment will always guarantee the right friends. It will, however, promote a "common sense" about the possibilities and even tne failures of female friendship.

The absence of the "rigors of discernment" has fostered the attitude that feminism makes all women friends. This is not only non-discerning; it violates all comon sense. It sentimentalizes female friendship, giving women the illusion that feminism can provide something it was never meant to do. If all women can be friends, then no women are really friends.

Many women have made the mistake of expecting to be friends with women based on certain things they have in common: flashes of ideas, analytic genius, erotic energy, lively interests, political commitments, professional goals. All of these qualities may provide the possibilities for friendship, but they may not generate the reality. Discernment is a habit and, like any habit, it takes time and has to be exercised in such a way that the whole of what constitutes a friendship can be grasped.

The habit of discernment teaches us to be loyal to our Selves, to have faith in our own insights, and to claim these as a power of scrutiny in our interactions with others. Discernment is not foolproof, nor can it guarantee that friendship lasts forever. What it provides is insight— even insight into our mistakes.

The Assimilation of Silence

A common way in which women are assimilated into the male domi-nant world is by the simple silence that surrounds the reality of Gyn/affection. At the beginning of this chapter, I remarked that the con-stant noise about women not loving women exists in tandem with the historical silence about women always loving women. The silence that prevails erases the fact that women have been each other's best friends, supportive kin, devoted lovers, and constant companions. Silence here has worn a funereal garb that sports several fashions.

Perhaps the biggest silence is the muting of many women's direct experience of female friendship. This amounts to a silencing of female friendship before it has a chance to begin. For other women, the disabling of the direct experience of friendship is wrought by throwing sand in women's eyes about the nature of female friendship—that is, it is portrayed as adolescent, immature, and/or latently homosexual. Feminist writer and activist Julie Melrose has suggested that this is tantamount to "making experiential reality (i.e., 'being with other women in a positive way feels good') secondary to male intellectual reality (i.e., women can't/shouldn't be friends)."[38] Thus women's direct and positive encounter with Gyn/affection is mediated by men's version of it. Direct female participation is assimilated by male non-participatory pronouncement.

It is important to understand that total silence is not always the issue. Rather, silence takes more subtle and often partial forms. The ways in which women's relationships with each other are categorized constitute a dramatic technique of silencing that plays its part off center stage. Categorization changes the definition and shape of women's reality, especially when it is professionally done. For example, when Freudian psychology relegated women's friendships to the realms of "sickness," "arrested development," and "immaturity," it silenced the direct experience of female friendship for many women—literally by snuffing out its existence, or possibility of existence, and categorically by misnaming the reality. As experienced and interpreted by women in a post-Freudian age, female friendship becomes aberrant.

Categorization promotes reductionism. Once a woman sees Gyn/affection categorized reductionistically, she sees herself reduced. Categorization promotes dissociation and assimilation at the same time. It prompts women to dissociate themselves from the demeaned category while being assimilated into more acceptable hetero-relational categories.

One of the ways in which female friendship is silenced by categorization is to proclaim it "exceptional." For example, in Joseph Lash's extensive and enlightening biography of Helen Keller and Annie Sullivan, the profound friendship between the two women is described as "exceptional," that is, as rare. Throughout the book the author and various persons who appear in this remarkable story comment on the utter uniqueness of the friendship between the two women. "The tie between you and our dear Annie is as close as any tie can possibly be. I dare say plenty of people have told you that there is nothing like it in history or literature."[39] One might reasonably say that there was nothing like this friendship "in history or literature." However, what was exceptional about these two women was not the intensity of their friendship. Many women have had the profound affection that they experienced with each other. What was unique was the way in which Annie Sullivan became a conduit for Helen Keller's knowledge of and feeling for the world. Not many women's friendships have been written about, and this one probably reached the public eye because of Helen Keller's extraordinary journey from darkness to light and Annie Sullivan's astounding role in "the creation of a soul."[40]

Female friendships are, of course, exceptional if by *exceptional* one means better than average and deviating from the norm, the norm of hetero-relations. However, when Gyn/affection is portrayed as exceptional in the sense that I am criticizing, it is usually meant to convey that women's friendships are rare, that is, not prevalent, or are out of the ordinary course and reach of most women's lives. So many women who learn about the deep and enspiriting relationship between Helen Keller and Annie Sullivan are led to believe that most women cannot rise to the occasion of such a friendship. Thus even the most marvelous messages of Gyn/affection are muted by this kind of exceptional portrayal. The category "exceptional" functions to lead women away from learning just how prevalent such friendships between women have been throughout history and in almost every culture.

In the same way, anything that women do that is out of the ordinary realm of hetero-relations or that deviates from those norms has been categorized as exceptional. Women construction workers, scientists, weightlifters, karate experts, and lesbians are categorized as exceptional because they step out of the prescribed hetero-relational roles. There are many more women weightlifters and lesbians (jarring juxtaposition of categories intended) than both men and some women realize! However, because these women are not visible to the eyes of hetero-relations, they are classified as exceptional. The convoluted logic of hetero-relations has even made the category "exceptional" a compliment for women.

Another mode of silencing is to put anything out of the ordinary that women do into a hetero-relational category, thereby depriving it of its women-identified and women originated power. Thus men create so-called lesbian pornography using heterosexual poses and postures. Or women who lift weights are exhorted to look and act like Linda Evans, the Krystle of the TV soap "Dynasty"—strong but contained by man-made femininity. Many weightlifting books and brochures show women how to build up their strength—relatively speaking—while not developing "unsightly" muscles. Women are not encouraged to sport their muscles but to develop a firm, trim figure that makes them more attractive to men.

Increasingly, any out-of-the-ordinary things that women do become hetero-relationized. Women and women's acts are then assimilated into the appropriate hetero-relational category. Feminism itself has been subject to such assimilation. One prominent feminist was dubbed "the feminist who likes men." Since most feminists are depicted as not liking men, the message is that any real woman, indeed any real feminist, likes men. Women-defined feminism is silenced for women who read such descriptions.

There is also the silence that Virginia Woolf wrote about so clearly in *A Room of One's Own.* "Chloe liked Olivia . . . Do not blush. Women do like other women."[41] Many women are aware in themselves of an attraction to other women. Women often acknowledge this on some level, even if that level is moving dramatically away from the attraction.

Other women are embarrassed by any explicit display of the attraction. The embarrassment, the "blush," stems from a fear that their best-kept secret will be divulged, and they along with it. With many women, this "blush," in a post-Freudian age, is a fear that female friendship will be interpreted as lesbianism. Many women go to great lengths to avoid any possibility of this interpretation.

I think, however, that Mary Daly has named what happens at a deeper level in many women's hearts and minds when she refers to the taboo against "Women-Touching women." Daly quotes Freud who gave some insight into the nature of the "taboo":

> The prohibition does not merely apply to immediate physical contact but has an extent as wide as the metaphorical use of the phrase '*to come in contact with*.' Anything that directs the patient's thoughts to the forbidden object, anything that brings him [*sic*] into *intellectual contact* with it, is just as much prohibited as direct physical contact." [Italics mine][42]

Daly adds to this: "Anything that directs a woman's thoughts to the forbidden object, her Self, anything that brings her into intellectual contact with her Spiritual Touching Powers, is just as much prohibited as direct physical contact with another Female Self. This extension is inherent in the Total Taboo against Women-Touching women."[43] While the taboo against "Women-Touching women" is indeed sexual, it is not only that. More fully, it is a "Total Taboo" against women touching the extended range of our original Selves and other women.

It is also the case that women are not necessarily embarrassed by attraction to other women but by the sheer fact of the presence of other women around them. For example, one woman pointed out that men are timid about approaching women in twos or in larger groups. An obstacle to female friendship, she notes, hearkens back to events such as junior high school dances where girls would separate "purposefully from one's female friends because the boys were too chicken to ask you to dance if you were with other girls: more likely if you were alone and therefore 'accessible.' "[44] Many women, in many different ways, avoid female friendship so as to make themselves "accessible" to men.

These "junior high" scenarios tell us much about the impediments to female friendship. Women together in quantity, never mind in quality, serve to keep men away. If women gathered together in numbers are viewed as nonaccessible to men, how much more unapproachable are women who are joined together by choice and passionate bonds. If some women relinquish the sheer numerical presence of women for hetero-relational trysts with men, more women will relinquish the qualitative energy of Gyn/affecion when they fear the "Total Taboo" of "Women-Touching women."

Women shun the company of women, often because they believe women are boring. Within the ways that hetero-relations have absorbed women's adventurous spirits, of course women have been tamed by patriarchy. And, unfortunately, women are boring whose liveliness has been contained by the "bore-ocracy" of hetero-relations. As student of communications Denice Yanni has pointed out, this opinion that women are boring is reinforced by hetero-relational media that portray women as "only *one dimensional*" characters.[45] This one-dimensionality of women, as depicted in the daytime and nighttime soaps, especially in the characters of women like Sue Ellen and Pam of "Dallas," is that of women who ultimately exist for men. (If Sue Ellen goes back to J.R. one more time!) "Cagney and Lacey" is probably one of the few prime-time television programs that deviate from this portrayal of one-dimensional women, yet even it is careful to contain Cagney and Lacey's adventures by Lacey's Harvey and Cagney's recurring bouts with boyfriends. The message is that while these two women are spectacular and adventurous cops, they are indeed normal hetero-relational women who are the same as other women, that is, hetero-relational.

Silence about the adventure of Gyn/affection prohibits the naming of the taming of many women. Silence about the adventure of Gyn/affection drowns out the truth that women are bored only with what men have forced women to become. Women are bored only by themselves and other women who have no original and independent Selves and who have nothing of their own with which to arouse women.

That female friends arouse other women is a truth that women must tell, for it has been stifled by its very opposite. Man is said to be the one who arouses a woman in all ways. Thus when an original woman does stir another woman, she is labeled "not a woman." She is said to be "mannish." It is important to understand, however, that "mannish" in this context means what man has reserved for himself. Since men have appropriated the arousal of women to themselves, a woman who profoundly arouses other women is defined as acting "like a man" when the exact opposite is true. It is she who acts most like a woman because her original Self is awakened and capable of calling forth the same originality from other women. If men withhold money, creativity, and independence from women, why shouldn't they withhold women's affection from women? If man decides that only he should give women money, creative crumbs, and the threads of quasi-independent living, it should not be surprising that he will also reserve women's affecion for himself. Hetero-relations tames the originality and the capacity in women to arouse the originality of their Selves and other women.

Taming begins early in a young girl's life. Mothers as "token torturers" often function as taming vehicles. Whether it is the actual mutilation of a young girl's body by clitoridectomy, the restraining of active and mobile physical movement, the replacement of strong female body language by feeble feminine posture training, or the discouraging of athletic development, or whether it is the binding of a young girl's adventurous spirit, curious mind, or independent quest for Self-knowledge, women who experience the mother or other female kin as "tamers" often take the path of dissociation from women, not wanting to be tamed further or to move in the company of the "tamed."

The taming of women also happens on a widespread social and political level. "Thirty-six million women can be tranquilized in a year and the nation does not notice it, does not miss their energy, creativity, wit, intellect, passion, commitment—so much are these women worth, so important is their contribution . . . so essential is their vigor."[46] The irony in these words could be multiplied over and over in the face of rape, pornography, battering, reproductive technologies (new and old), and the ways they tame women's Self-defined and autonomous existence. However, if the hetero-relational ideal is that of a restrained and tame woman, then why would anyone notice, comment, or object? More to the point, why in the midst of a tamed population of women would *women* notice, object to, or miss the lost possibilities of a vital and vibrant female friendship? The taming of women ensures that many women will promise not only "indifference to the fate of other women"[47] but also indifference to the friendship of other women.

Women are assimilated by the hetero-relational ideology that men are a woman's greatest adventure. Women learn not to expect a lively future with women. Men become the future—the eschatological saviors that women need only await. "Her youth is consumed in waiting, more or less disguised. She is awaiting Man."[48] The adolescent boy makes his way actively and adventurously toward adulthood. The young girl is trained to wait tamely for the future to happen to her. (Perhaps this is one more reason why men have always been so focused on women's "coming," as in "did you come?") Many women's entire lives are consumed in waiting not only for the promised man but for the hetero-relational promised land. "Soap operas invest exquisite pleasure in the central condition in a woman's life: waiting—whether for her phone to ring, for the baby to take its nap, or for the family to be reunited shortly after the day's final soap opera has left *its* family still struggling against dissolution."[49] Soap operas never end. "Tune in tomorrow," but tomorrow creates more waiting. Will Horace find out that his wife is having an affair with his ex-girlfriend? (Indeed, such a plot might, for a moment, make even soap operas interesting!) The myriad ways in which women wait amount to a kind of "waiting sickness."

The ways in which women have been trained to wait are impediments to the formation of female friendships. Often women wait for other women to initiate Gyn/affection, without taking the initiative themselves. They fear making the first move. Here women assimilate the hetero-relational model in which women have waited for a phone call, a proposal, the expression of a preference, the offer of a contract, a job, a future. Waiting can be fatal, however, for it breeds a passivity and discourages risk-taking. Ultimately, it convinces women that they are not responsible for their own futures.

Women must overcome this major obstacle to Gyn/affection by initiating all sorts of activities with each other —affection, thinking, and the doing of deeds. The gift of female friendship is that it initiates Self-movement. The woman who befriends her Self and other women realizes that she cannot "shed the burden of time" waiting for a future in which someone, this time a woman, will hand her back her lost Self.

Hetero-relations rest on the fiction that women must wait with "great expectations" for the promised man and his promised land. Gyn/affection must be based on the active initiation of female friendship. It is a kind of friendship that must be actively sought rather than passively expected. Many women thought that by becoming feminists, female friendship would automatically follow. So women waited, expecting that friendship with other women would be the natural result of shared consciousness raising, common political goals, and collective organizing. But this was just another form of waiting.

Like all genuine movement, female friendship must be actively aroused. Women must awaken each other to the possibilities of friendship, especially within the context of a hetero-relational world where women have learned that only men arouse and excite women. Men have made of women "movable" property but have not permitted genuine movement. Female friendship can teach women that what they mistook for movement, within the framework of hetero-relations, was mere "touching." As Mary Daly has noted, all women in patriarchy are a "touchable caste."[50] Gyn/affection promises profound movement and deep stirring or, to reiterate the famous phrase of Virginia Woolf, "Women alone stir my imagination."

Craving adventure, women are often repelled by other women's inability to take risks. Inherent in the hetero-relational argument that women are boring is that all women are the same, the same in timidity of living. "It is the acceptance of risk that wins him his power."[51] Although Elizabeth Janeway did not apply these words to women's perception of other women as timid, they are important in this context. However, in hetero-relational "adventures," women often have not distinguished between male risk and recklessness and the ways in which men turn risk into reckless behavior, a behavior that frequently masks necrophilic obsession.

Real risk, existential risk, is taken by those women who challenge hetero-relations and who have the courage to claim their original Selves and their female friends. The refusal or the inability to take the risk of Gyn/affection is at the heart of the loss of female friendship. Not taking the risk of female friendship limits the possibilities of female life and living in every way imaginable. It shuts off womanist imagination. In assuming the risk of creating Gyn/affection, women change the terms of our existence in this world. Gyn/affection demolishes hetero-relations, primarily by withholding belief from men and male-defined existence for women.

The hetero-relational dogma that "men are women's great adventure" can persist only where women do not take the risk of challenging it. In rebutting it, women show that what women often settle for with men is not genuine adventure but mere stimulation.

With rising levels of hetero-relational taming, women's capacity to experience Self and woman-defined adventure declines. Increasingly, in this anesthetized society, more and more external male-defined stimuli are needed to provide women with a sense of being alive. However, stimulation is a form of escape. Having no recourse to the original woman-defined Self, women fill the emptiness. Hetero-relations becomes a quick transport away from one's original Self and that of other women. Diversion becomes a goal for women suffering from the deficiency disease of hetero-relations. Unfortunately, for such women the disease is mistaken for the cure. Women continue to seek ever new hetero-relational stimulants. Such stimulation is, at best, short-lived and, at worst, destructive to Self and others. It anesthetizes women's capacity to live creatively, shuts off imagination, and ultimately promotes women's assimilation to a world they never created.

Many men have talked about their fear of being tamed by women. So strong is this hetero-relational adage that it has become a dogma of hetero-relational psychology—the fear of "castration by the mother (woman)." This disguises the real wreckage of hetero-relations—that women have been castrated* by men and, further, that women are tamed by women who have been tamed by men. The silence behind all this noise about the male castration complex is that women are tamed by the hetero-relational woman. Of course, mothers (women) do not initiate the taming of daughters (other women). Men and hetero-relations began the taming of the mother as mentor (see the section "Mothers and Daughters" in the following pages of this chapter).

Women crave adventure, but in a hetero-relational world they settle for stimulation. Stimulants blunt a woman's clarity of mind, strength of will, scope of vision, and mastery of the world. The biggest stimulant of all is constant doses of hetero-relations.

Victimization in the World

Victimism provides a third context in which the obstacles to female friendship take root. I use *victimism* to describe a milieu in which women's primary female or feminist identity seems to be grounded in women's shared state of having been victimized by men. In relationships with each other, such women emphasize their heritage of shared pain, although the ways in which various women have been victimized differs by age, class, race, and other factors.

Kathleen Barry has described how victimism functions in creating a role and a status out of the reality of being a victim.

> The status of "victim" creates a mind set eliciting pity and sorrow. Victimism . . . creates a framework for others to know her not as a person but as a victim, someone to whom violence is done . . . The assigned label of "victim," which initially was meant to call awareness to the experience of sexual violence, becomes a term that expresses that person's identity.[52]

Victimism transforms the historical and cross-cultural reality of women's victimization by men into a psychosocial identity whereby women take on the status of victim as a primary self-definition and role. Once this occurs, women are portrayed as helpless in the face of male tyranny. In both a political and a personal sense, victimism becomes the first and final word about women. Victimism promotes the belief that a woman's self and women as a group are forever in bondage to their history of pain and oppression.

*As Mary Daly long ago pointed out, "to castrate" essentially means to deprive of power, potency, creativity, and ability to communicate.

In this context, I am concerned that victimism does not become the basis of a woman's self-definition and disempowerment. Certain self-defined feminist groups have grossly misused this kind of critique, and it is important to dissociate my concerns from theirs. For example, FACT (Feminist Anti-Censorship Taskforce) et al. have attacked anti-pornography civil rights legislation—crafted by writer Andrea Dworkin and lawyer Catharine MacKinnon and supported by a multitude of black and poor neighborhood groups, women of color groups, Jewish women's groups, lesbians, prostitutes and ex-prostitutes, and hundreds of women who have risked public exposure and harassment testifying on behalf of this legislation—by claiming that it promotes the woman as victim stereotype.

> ... the ordinance perpetuates a stereotype of women as helpless victims, incapable of consent, and in need of protection ... Further, its stereotypes of women as powerless victims undermines women's ability to act affirmatively to protect themselves.

It is not the antipornography ordinance that perpetuates the woman as victim stereotype. It is the pornography itself and FACT's twisted support of pornography by appealing to a nonexistent ordinance stereotype of the woman as victim. It is they who keep women as victims—bound and bowed.

There are different ways in which victimism is displayed by women, some suble and some not so subtle. More subtly, women often relate to each other as victims when they come together out of a shared pain, stressing that what they have in common is only, or mostly, that shared pain. Constant and one-dimensional focus on the sharing of pain can drive women away from strong female friendships by obscuring the historical reality that women have been and can be for women in other than sisterly suffering ways. The emphasis on victimism also bolsters the conviction that female friendship can arise only for negative reasons: that is, because men are so bad or in reaction to the atrocities promoted by a misogynist culture. Here female friendship seems spawned by the results of the oppression of women. Thus in a better world, presumably one in which men "behave," female friendship might not be necessary.

Women who bond as victims often spend a good deal of time immersed in the narrating of experiences of victimization. This is necessary and profitable as a catalyst for the sharing of strength that can often emerge from the many states of atrocity to which women have been subjected in a woman-hating world. And it is an important step in moving women away from thinking that their horrendous experiences have been peculiar to their individual selves or, worse, have been their fault. However, constant "dealing" with the experience of suffering, whether in therapy or in women's relationships with each other, prevents women from moving beyond the endless circle of not only repeating the experience but repeating the experience of the experience, often to others who share the same or similar experiences.

This leads to a peculiar type of "relationism" where women spend an inordinate amount of energy "relating" such atrocities to other women and cultivating associations with women that are built on their shared status as victims. Victimism militates against Gyn/affection because the kind of relating that women engage in is that of continual narrating of pain. Women who bond in victimization are, in real ways, encouraging women to remain victims in order to sustain the bonds.

More overtly, women relate to each other as victims when they make a cult of failure. Many women can be wonderful in adversity but not in success. Here I am not speaking of the so-called fear of success syndrome discussed originally by Matina Horner. Rather I am talking about a distrust or even outright resentment that is often expressed in women's groups when one of their own succeeds in some particular and noticeable way. The reaction is often that, in escaping the circle of the oppressed, she becomes a pariah.

Alice Walker addresses this issue in an essay, originally written for the *Black Scholar* in response to Robert Staples's article attacking "angry black feminists" Ntozake Shange and Michele Wallace.

> Try not to think how successful they are. Try to blot out how much money Shange has made. Don't be pissed off at how beautifully she writes, or with what courage and vulnerability. Resist the temptation to blame her for all those audiences from Marin and Scarsdale. Remember if you can that she didn't know they were coming. Think big.[53]

These words could be addressed to many women who succumb to the politics of victimism by regarding failure in the man's world, or downward mobility, as the only "pure" feminist politics. Such women mistake worldliness for assimilation to the world.

Sustained and one-dimensional emphasis on victimism reduces the history and bonding of women to an eternal state of atrocity over which women have never exerted any countercontrol. In this view, the history and bonding of women is shaped by external male-dominated forces that mold women's existence. This is a form of behaviorist political theory which stresses the deterministic omnipotence of environment, this time the environment being patriarchy.

While it is necessary for women to recognize the prevalence and longevity of antifeminism across historical ages and cultural lines, the imperative for such recognition should not lead women to the conclusion that the force of antifeminism is almost natural and without end—so overwhelming that any will to feminist action and female friendship is lost.

Victimism ultimately negates Self-definition and Self-responsibility in the world. When women do not define themselves beyond the role of sufferer, then women will settle for the world as men have made it. There will be little inclination to create a different world. Victimism means being overwhelmed by the world. It makes women world-sufferers rather than world-makers. It establishes women in the world negatively. Women's commonality is reduced to our shared oppression. There is the unstated and, hopefully, unintended, premise that feminists might lose our feminist identity if antifeminism disappeared from the world. Although a feminism that highlights women's oppression as victims is oriented to the very real worldly issues and realities that affect women—for example, abortion, reproductive abuses, rape, and the like—it is swallowed up by victimism when its impetus and its purpose are contained by these atrocities.

Women have indeed been broken by men. Yet men would make it the case that it is they who have been damaged by women. For example, they blame mothers who gave them too much or too little attention or wives who dominate or are too dependent on them. Men have always claimed the wounded role. The overcoming of brokenness by women as well as the rejection of men as broken creatures in need of women's restorative power is necessary to the process of female friendship.

Women, as a people, cannot be held together and cannot move in the world linked primarily by a common enemy or by a negative identity of victim. Only within the framework of female friendship can a woman live as a woman, working for a reconstituted world, without exhausting herself in the struggle against woman-hating and without despairing at the enormity of the task.

Mothers and Daughters

Adrienne Rich has written: "Before sisterhood, there was the knowledge—transitory, fragmented, perhaps, but original and crucial—of mother-and-daughterhood."[54] Nancy Richard has added: "A woman's first relationship is with her mother. We learn to relate to other women both from this relationship and in reaction to this original bond."[55] While the mother-daughter relationship is in no way deterministic for the forming of female friendships, it has had a persuasive influence in the development of Gyn/affection.

Much has been written about mother-daughter relationships, and I do not intend to cover that ground again. However, it is important to examine the mother-daughter relationship insofar as it has proved to be a major obstacle to women forming close friendships with each other and insofar as it has unfortunately provided the soil for the growth of female victimism. My intention here is not once more to blame mothers, as is the usual tack, but to analyze the ways in which the mother-daughter bond, or lack of it, has been based on victimism—the victimization of the mother by a hetero-relational life and the victimization of the daughter by mothers who pass on to daughters a tradition of dissociation from women.

We know about the freight of the mother-daughter relationship defined within the parameters of hetero-relations: the daughter witnesses the mother who can't or won't help her; the mother who may ignore not only literal rape of the daughter by the father or father-figures but "rape" by a woman-hating culture; the mother who encourages the daughter to submit, be silent, be formed; and the mother who rises up in rebellion but who pays for her resistance.* Even when the mother defies hetero-relations, the daughter beholds the mother's victimization for doing so. The historical prototype of this is daughters who were forced to watch mothers literally burned as witches during the Inquisition. The historical examples multiply when we take the toll of daughters who have been forced to watch deviant mothers "burned" by battering, madness, institutionalization, therapy, drugs, and the ever-present female domestication of body and mind.

There is, of course, more strength conveyed to daughters by mothers who have been "burned" for hetero-relational deviance than by mothers who have not defied hetero-relations. However, on a practical level, there is small comfort because maternal deviance may often deprive the daughter of the presence of the mother. On an existential level, however, it gives the daughter some presence of the mother as mentor.

*I am not saying that this is the only legacy that mothers leave to daughters. There are many other empowering traditions that all sorts of mothers have left to all sorts of daughters. This point, I hope, is obvious in other examples throughout this book. I am trying to portray, in this chapter, the mother-daughter interconnection in the context of how it has functioned as one obstacle to female friendship. Certainly, it has not always, or even primarily, functioned in this way. But it has done so often enough to warrant analysis.

Mentors impart education and knowledge of the world. The word *mentor* comes from a Latin root meaning "to remember, think, counsel." However, education that daughters receive from mothers, within the confines of hetero-relations, does not provide the knowledge of remembrance—remembrance of the original woman, she who creates her Self. It is not an original or woman-defined knowledge. It does not impart to daughters the advice and counsel of Gyn/ affective worldliness and power.

Within the roles of hetero-relations, the mother has not been allowed to be a mentor to the daughter. At best, she is a misguided mentor; that is, what counsel she can give is well-meaning but misdirected.

> In a world of hetero-relations, where women are primarily for men, the majority of mothers teach their daughters to be for men. That is, to live "safely" in the world of hetero-relations . . .
>
> In teaching their daughters to be for men, mothers fail to tell them at what cost. Nor can they themselves know . . . Mothers "protect" their daughters from violence in the world men have "created."[56]

Nancy Richard, who wrote these words, describes the mother as a woman who can exercise protectiveness without having the power of protection. So women turn to men for what they think is "real" protection, knowledge, and power.

To know, to really know the ways in which women are contained by hetero-relations would be the definitive Gyn/affective education that mothers could convey to daughters. But women too often become "the daughters of educated men."

Hannah Arendt associates knowledge with the quest for truth. [57] Gyn/affective knowledge would teach women the truth about hetero-relations and what women need to know to live truthfully. It would be a trusted knowledge that would come from an experienced and trusted advisor, a true mentor. It might be the kind of knowledge that Sido imparted to Colette.

> What Colette so loved in Sido was a special kind of female strength. She loved what her mother knew about the world—which way the wind was blowing, where it was raining. Sido was close to nature and alert to portents. She made barometers out of oats and could tell whether it would be a cold winter or not based on the number of skins an onion had. These were ancient female arts, the talents of shamans and witches, and they were practiced in a culture that neither demeaned nor tamed them.

> Sido does not seem to have lived in the patriarchy. Or Colette did not see her in that way. Both mother and daughter had a shared distance from and benign contempt for male authority.[58]

This is a profound description of the mother as mentor. It is, however, at second hand. We have Colette's own words about the absence of hetero-relational constraints on the mother-daughter relationship: "No half-grown males anywhere, no sign of a man . . . The deep peace of a harem, under the nests of May, and the wisteria shot with sun-light . . . and the hands of my mother at the back of my neck, deftly braiding my hair."[59]

The best education that mothers can give to daughters is the example of their own lives. Would that all daughters could say of their mothers: "I am the daughter of a woman . . . who herself never ceased to flower, untiringly, during three quarters of a century."[60] This is true mentoring.

> The idea of mentor as an experienced and trusted counselor has all but vanished. The counselor has become the therapist, who tries to replace the authentic relationship where the mother/daughter relationship has "failed" and the mentor is not available. She or he becomes the mediary between the mother and daughter. Women spend as much time, if not more, with their counselors working through—dealing with the confusion between loving and hating their mothers and between feeling swallowed up and at the same time cast out by their mothers than they ever had in authentic relationship with their mothers.[61]

An unmentored daughter is an unnurtured daughter, unnurtured in the strength she needs to Survive as an original woman in this world. Daughters, as compared to sons in a hetero-relational family, are more undernurtured in all ways by mothers and pressured prematurely to become nurturers of others—mostly of men. What also happens in this context, as Denice Yanni has pointed out, is "a silencing of woman's own needs for nurturing by making her the primary nurturer."[62] Since nurturing is "the most acceptable mode of behavior for women, her most accepted style of relating, women are more likely to extend themselves—and be rejected—as nurturers."[63]

This nurturing syndrome affects women in many different ways, some quite subtle. I have often noted that in Women's Studies classes women students have great difficulty discussing critically each other's opinions and judgments. Some are hesitant, unsure, and generally unfamiliar in this new and alien territory of critical judgment. Others consciously refrain from critical repartee because they equate it with a male adversarial mode of interaction that is perceived as an attack. With many students, the temptation is to assume a traditional nurturing behavior with each other and to cover over critical classroom exchange and analysis by gestures of support and caring. Often the issues, as well as any meaningful and tough-minded analysis of them, thus get dropped. Students do not move beyond nurturance and support while desperately wanting to go beyond, both in an intellectual and analytic context. However, they do not want to risk what it takes to face head-on the critical and sometimes disagreeable interactions with other women.

The lack of mother-mentoring can follow a woman throughout her life. Caught in the "safety net" of hetero-relations, women pass on to daughters—daughters who become mothers, teachers, counselors, and friends of women—a grab bag of survival tactics. Such tactics do not provide the kind of "Surviving" that Gyn/affection provides, "not merely in the sense of 'living on,' but in the sense of living beyond"[64] —in this case, beyond hetero-relations. These are the survival tactics of women who are still the victims of hetero-relations. They give women the capacity to suffer and to endure and/or to manipulate their way safely and skillfully through the world that men have given them. However, they breed neglect for women and for a strong Gyn/affective extistence. And they often create guilt about the wrong things.

The Politics of Guilt and Guilt-Tripping

Guilt and guilt-tripping often accompany an ideology and lifestyle of victimism. Guilt produces an identification with oppressed individuals and groups that is often based on pity and sorrow for their plights. Guilt is also similar to a knee-jerk reaction that is almost Pavlovian; that is, it reacts without thinking and often uncritically to what is perceived as oppression. At times, this has produced a demand from some women for uncritical acceptance of the actions of certain individuals and groups because they are members of an oppressed class. Kathleen Barry gives this example:

> When I was researching female sexual slavery in Europe and in the U.S., I came across several instances of lesbian pimps—that is, lesbian women who sexually enslave and pimp other women. They were at least as vicious, enslaving, and exploitative of their own women as any male pimps were. There seemed to be only one difference: they were treated more harshly or severely by the criminal justice system, which tries very hard to ignore or

not interfere with male pimps. Now, it is true that lesbian pimps are not typical of either lesbianism or pimping. But that does not mean that *any* form of pimping should be ignored or that lesbian pimps should be given special consideration by feminists because as lesbians they are treated more harshly by the criminal justice system. I think the same logic applies to the charge that the rape crisis movement is racist because black men are dealt with more harshly by the system. The fact of patriarchal racism neither excuses black men from raping women nor removes the responsibility from feminists to ensure that more white men are apprehended and brought to trial for rape.[65]

I have quoted these words at length because they provide a good analysis not only of an uncritical acceptance of oppression but of a seriously wrong conclusion that is an outgrowth of a politics of guilt. Here women draw conclusions about heterosexism and racism that are severely limited by a lack of judgment and of the "rigors of discernment." Here guilt dulls critical perception and the ability to sift out real racism, for example, from what is sentimentalized as racism.

Guilt also produces guilt-tripping. This is evident in women's groups where some women berate other women for racism, classism, and/or heterosexism. It fosters a policy and a style of antiracist, anticlassist, and/or antiheterosexist consciousness and behavior that is based on terrorizing other women in both an intellectual and a social way. Guilt-tripping usually is expressed in the negative; for example; a woman may say that another woman has "no analysis of race" rather than expressing an educative and affirmative position on race herself.

The guilt-tripped, as well as those who are guilty, often seek safety in invisibility; that is, they often confess their guilt in a public forum. As Nietzsche phrased it, "Talking about oneself can also be a means to conceal oneself."[66] Hiding among the "oppressors," the guilty and guilt-tripped often beat their own breasts and confess their own history of oppressive behavior. Supposedly, if one names one's self as an oppressor, one cannot be accused of oppressing. This may hide what is really a need for safety, security, and "cheap grace."

What often becomes of primary importance in women's circles is that women *acknowledge* their guilt. Acknowledgment of guilt often becomes a license to judge others.

The enthusiastic and aggressive confessor becomes like Camus' character whose perpetual confession is his means of judging others: "[I] ... practice the profession of penitent to be able to end up as a judge ... the more I accuse myself, the more I have a right to judge you."[67]

This identification with victimism also creates a pattern of women placating others by deprecating themselves. It is like a ritual where the guilt is not really driven out, as at least it was in religious rituals of atonement, but instead where it becomes redistributed among the guilty and the guilt-tripped. This has the further effect of prompting women to act oppressed or play the victim in other life circumstances. Women who act strong, who are not depressed or hangdog, are suspect. Many women find it much easier to bond with each other in misery, out of a shared weakness of spirit, and as victims.

A posture of continuous self-abasement and confessionalism vis-à-vis lesbians, poor women, women of color, disabled women, and/or aging women is neither courageous nor change-producing. Instead, it enlarges the circle of victimism, with women this time enforcing the identity and behavior of victim. Women of discernment should be as skeptical of such obsequiousness as we would be if such behavior came from men. The politics of guilt and of guilt-tripping do no women any good.

The energies invested in bearing and acknowledging guilt, as well as in guilt-tripping others, do not enable constructive action against oppression. They produce, instead, confessional stagnation creating a preoccupation with guilt itself. When women redistribute guilt among themselves, and especially use guilt-tripping to do this, it makes women forget the "main enemy."[68]

The sharing of guilt may create an illusionary sense of oneness for a time, but it fosters no stronger unity that outlives the sharing of pain.

> The humanity of the insulted and injured has never yet survived the hour of liberation by so much as a minute. This does not mean that it is insignificant, for in fact it makes insult and injury endurable; but it does mean that in political terms it is absolutely irrelevant.[69]

Put in different words, suffering, endurance, victimization, and the sisterhood of the oppressed create nothing beyond themselves.

The politics of guilt and of guilt-tripping other women is being used more and more to confer a kind of insider status on certain women who can claim multiple-victim history—that is, oppression by sex, class, race, and/or the other myriad forms of oppression produced by a patriarchal culture—or who acknowledge their history of being a multiple oppressor. Those who will not, or cannot, claim one or more of a multiplicity of oppressions are driven to outsider status. In a very real sense, women thus create another form of Virginia Woolf's "Society of Outsiders" among ourselves. Instead of using multiplicity of oppression in a positive way, it becomes a negative wedge that divides women from each other.

Pat Hynes was the first to point out that what is also emerging in this context is an "arithmetic of oppression ... whose correctness is measured by its containing the proper factors of addition."[70] This method of addition can never adequately account for the infinite variety of specific oppressions because some addend will always be missing. Instead, Hynes sees that the "imperative for radical feminism... is to find the language and theory which describes in precise detail every manner of suspicion and separation that has dulled the passion for a community of women."[71]

It is crucial to recognize the uniquely victimized and multiple oppressive conditions of many women's lives by race, class, and/or lesbian existence. When one is oppressed by distinct and varied conditions, one must respond not only as a woman but as a black women, a Jewish woman, an aging woman, and/or a lesbian woman. Nor can women who have not been oppressed in such ways stand apart from these conditions of other women's lives. Women cannot blithely act as if we are all women in the same way. Different oppressions must be singularly assessed and acted on, per se, not because they automatically confer "special status" but because they carry insight into both the diverse conditions of women's oppression and the possibilities for diverse friendships among women. Lucy Dawidowich puts it this way, using the Holocaust as an example:

> To refer to the murder of the 6 million Jews as *distinctive*, as *unique*, is not an attempt to magnify the catastrophe that befell them nor to beg tears and pity for them. It is not intended to minimize the deaths of the millions of non-Jews ... [it] stands apart ... not because of any distinctive fate that the individual victims endured, but because of the *differentiative intent* of the murderers and the *unique effect* of the murders ... The annihilation of the 6 million Jews brought an end with irrevocable finality to the thousand-year old culture and civilization of Ashkenazi Jewry, destroying the continuity of Jewish history.[72]

Feminists cannot afford to subsume any oppressive condition under the ecumenical category of female suffering. We cannot blur the distinctiveness of victimization by race or class or anything else, thereby rejecting political and moral responsibility for the consequences of these distinctly different oppressive conditions of many women's lives. Yet, by the same token, we cannot allow these distinctive differences to erase or extinguish our commonality as women who are oppressed as women and who bond as women.

In the final analysis, acknowledging differences and the responsibility for multiple forms of oppression must proceed from what Bonnie Atkins has called a "politics of identity."[73] Alice Walker gives a good example of the "politics of identity.":

> ... in America white women who are truly feminist—for whom racism is inherently an impossibility—are largely outnumbered by *average* American white women for whom racism, inasmuch as it assures white privilege, is an accepted way of life. Naturally, many of these women, to be trendy, will leap to the feminist banner because it is now the place to be seen.[74]

It is in this context that Walker advocates the "rigors of discernment" that I spoke of earlier in this chapter. This discernment, she reminds women of color, will enable them "to exert energy in feminist collaborations only when there is little risk of wasting it."[75] Walker adds further:

> To the extent that black women dissociate themselves from the women's movement, they abandon their responsibilities to women throughout the world. This is a serious abdication from and misuse of radical black herstorical tradition: Harriet Tubman, Sojourner Truth, Ida B. Wells, and Fannie Lou Hamer would not have liked it. Nor do I.[76]

Andrea Dworkin has given us some of the best antiracist analysis that proceeds from a feminist "politics of identity." In analyzing how black women are used in pornography, she says:

> As long as her skin shows, her cunt shows. This is the specific sexual value of the black woman in pornography in the United States, a race-bound society fanatically committed to the sexual devaluing of black skin perceived as a sex organ and a sexual nature. No woman of any other race bears this specific burden in this country. In no other woman is skin sex, cunt in and of itself—her essence, her offense.[77]

There is no subsuming of race here under the universal category of feminism. Rather there is a keen analysis of the connections that women as women must make if analysis and action against multiple forms of oppression are to have feminist integrity. The works of Alice Walker and Andrea Dworkin are excellent examples of antiracist analysis and action that proceed from a "politics of identity."

Feminists cannot be guilty or guilt-tripped for creating the range of oppressive conditions under which many women live. We must instead act out of responsibility, not out of guilt. We must fight against women assuming guilt, a guilt that is as corrosive to the female spirit as is the guilt of a young female victim of incest who becomes convinced that she is responsible for her father's crime against her. Women too often take on the guilt that properly belongs to the Fathers.

When women are consumed by guilt and act out of it, or when guilt-tripping occurs, the possibilities of female friendship are meager. The politics of guilt and of guilt-tripping reinforce the notion that women can come together only by acknowledging a shared pain, thus again re-cycling the pain among ourselves. If a woman assumes the primary identity of being oppressed, or of being in some way an oppressor, women indulge in suffering.

An "arithmetic of oppression" instills in women a distrust of women who are not, for example, of the same race, ethnic group, or not of the same abled status. Women then learn to trust only women of their own kind. There is, of course, a real necessity for placing primary trust in women who share a similar history. Women cannot simplify female friendship or make Gyn/affective harmony a matter of "cheap grace." Female friendship, especially friendship that is formed across lines of diversity and difference, is a complex, delicate, and strenuous process. We cannot afford to romanticize female friendship or imagine that we can leap over the boundaries of differences to instant Gyn/affection. However, we can afford to leave the guilt and guilt-tripping behind, putting the possibilities of friendship ahead of us.

Women's Alienation from Personal and Political Power

Victimization creates a complex relation between women and power. On the one hand, many women tend to regard power ambivalently, as something to be avoided, something that corrupts, and something that is always used over and against others. On the other hand, many women who have been subjected to the perversities of patriarchal power have risen up in resistance against it and seized power for their Selves and other women. Women have had a dual relation to power. However, it is the first notion—that power is to be avoided—which has proven to be an obstacle to Gyn/affection. Many women, having been the victims of patriarchal power, have assumed uncritically that power in itself corrupts. This is often accompanied by an alienation from their own sense of personal power—what Paul Tillich has called the "power of being"—and from other women who assert their individual power of being within women's groups.

Power can be defined in many ways. In more recent times, it has often become synonymous with political power. However, if we are to think of power outside its corrupting nuances, we must begin with the power of being and speak about the ontological foundation of all other forms of power, especially of political power.

> The self-affirmation of a being in spite of non-being is the expression of its power of being. Here we are at the roots of the concept of power. Power is the possibility of self-affirmation in spite of internal and external negation. It is the possibility of overcoming non-being. Human power is the possibility of man [*sic*] to overcome non-being infinitely.[78]

In my opinion, it is in women's alienation from their own power of being that other female problems with power begin.

There are different ways in which this alienation is manifested. Often in women's groups there is an automatic and uncritical acceptance of and demand for collectivism as the best way to structure a group. Along with this comes an insistence on "nonhierarchical" structures. While the desire to organize collectively is an understandable reaction to women's experience with oppressive, institutional, and patriarchal hierarchies, it can take disturbing directions that derail the development and deepening of female friendship.*

For example, this insistence on collective structures often levels real differences that women have in competence, commitment, and capacities. When differences in talent or leadership are asserted, women who feel less powerful are threatened. Sherry McCoy and Maureen Hicks in an article entitled "A Psychological Retrospective on Power in the Contemporary Lesbian-Feminist Community" give an excellent example of this:

> An ethic which has been accepted in many feminist groups says, "If woman A exerts power in way that causes woman B to feel less powerful, A shall have committed an error." This leaves very little room for the exercise of power or leadership, because one must be constantly on guard lest efforts at giving direction and offering suggestions be seen as the usurpation of a less vocal woman's power.[79]

The real issue here is why doesn't woman B and others like her take their own power rather than accusing other women of depriving them of it.

---

*I am not saying that there have been no successful collectives. I am aware that some collectives have managed to avoid the problems of which I speak, but these are exceptions, not the rule. There is no normative pattern, therefore, of positive collectivism that makes me believe that collectives are all that they are supposed to be or that they are the alternative to structures in which authority and responsibility are delineated.

Many women do not take power because their history of victimization has resulted in a severely diminished power of being. Lacking this personal power, such women will devalue women who express a power of being. Women who manifest individuality or directiveness may be outrightly berated for setting themselves apart from the group. Under the rhetoric of "collective," "noncompetitive," and "equal," women who achieve, who are ambitious, and who are successful in what they do are relegated to the status of pariah. Not wanting to be "exiled" from the group, some strong women may placate weaker women by deprecating or diminishing their own Selves and deeds. Or they may choose to leave the group and may become disillusioned with women. Women's alienation from personal and political power endows the collective group or the community with false power.

> To many women, the [women's] community became an entity with a life of its own. As such it held the power to pass judgment and, as a new-found home for the homeless, it took on a mighty significance . . . Traditionally, women have been denied access to "legitimate" (male) power and authority . . . When women reach adulthood, they often have little sense of how to go about obtaining direct personal power, let alone what to do with it even if they had it . . . Because women have not experienced firsthand the aggregation and utilization of power, we have been left to devise our own concepts of what power is, what it should be, and how it functions. Conceptualizing the community as a bastion of omnipotence reflects the immaturity of our experience with respect to power.[80]

Nonhierarchical structures often encourage a kind of parasitic person who may derive her own "power" from feeding off another's. Such women often use the rhetoric of equality as a means of guilt-tripping other women who demonstrate "the possibility of self-affirmation in spite of internal and external negation," to repeat Tillich's words. Any exhibition of personal power by another is seen as an implicit criticism of one's own inadequacies.

The hostile reaction toward any woman's display of strength or achievement is often accompanied by an uncritical rejection of any form of group requirements or order. All imperatives are regarded as elitist, repressive, and/or power-mongering. Of course, as Joreen long ago demonstrated in "The Tyranny of Structurelessness," there is no such thing as an unstructured group. So-called nonhierarchical structures often encourage the emergence of more unstructured hierarchies— covert power-mongering and strictures—that end up far more rigid than most overtly structured groups, since people in the "nonhierarchical" group have no accepted ways of rebutting the unstructured hierarchies that inevitably form.

Nonhierarchical dogma can damage Gyn/affective power because it can give a misplaced focus to "equalizing political power" when various women in the group have no center of individual power from which to build. Thus the situation frequently becomes one in which women either drain off the common power of the group or of strong individuals in the group or vent their inadequate feelings about power on other women who manifest it.

> ... equalizing power may not be an appropriate goal in every group. An automatic insistence on "nonhierarchical" structures may be an overreaction to our experience with oppressive institutionalized power imbalances. Real differences in competence, responsibility, and commitment demand acknowledgment, and this may take the form of delegating greater authority to those members of a group who are prepared to accept it.[81]

The uncritical imperative to form groups based on collectivist principles may function as reactionary, that is, as a reaction to our status as victims of patriarchal power. "Our power structures need to be judged by whether or not they enhance individuals' ability to achieve their own potential, not on whether at a given moment some women are given greater authority."[82]

Another bane of the nonhierarchical group is the habit of indirect power it encourages women to cultivate. Women in general have often not used their direct personal power. Instead, many have resorted to indirect power by funneling their own ideas and desires through men or even by manipulating men to do their bidding. This indirect use of power is often mimicked in collectivist settings. Where direct power of being is not called forth by the values of the group, the encouraged ethic is indirectness. Women will then often seek influence through indirection. Not projecting a direct sense of Self or of one's values is regarded as "politically correct." "Blending" with the group is preferable to "standing out." The qualities that distinguish a woman are not called forth, and her distinctive power is rendered invisible. However, the group can still be manipulated by individual women who are willing to seize power through indirect means.

The uncritical acceptance of a nonhierarchical model may spawn a whole different set of injustices. As many critics have noted, collectivism prompts women to pursue internal goals—what we might call domestic affairs—at the expense of necessary and needed external tasks, tasks that reach outward to a wider group. Dynamics of group processing, ways of interrelating within the group, and problems of communication among group members are dealt with and sometimes are dragged out interminably. Such internal affairs can be "talked to death" or, more appropriately, given a false "life."

False life is not real power. Within the enclave of such a group, women may be under the illusion that they are challenging the structures of patriarchal power. Yet no real power emerges from a group that silences its best and brightest voices for a false sense of group equality. And certainly no strong friendships can be formed among women who have no power of being. If, as Aristotle said, "the friend is another self," that Self must know its own power of being. She must be her own friend.

Woman as the Ultimate Victimizer of Women

There have been real betrayals of women by other women—by women who supposedly shared a similar feminist spirit and vision and by women whom one once called friends. Women have also held unrealistic expectations of women friends such that when these were not fulfilled women felt disillusioned and abandoned. It is important to distinguish between the real betrayals and the unrealistic expectations, although the two often produce the same results—disaffection from other women.

Sisterhood that was created in the struggle against all forms of male tyranny did not mean that women automatically became friends or that they shared a common world beyond the struggle. Many women who fought hard in the common cause of feminism felt that this would give them more than it did. And when it did not, they got "burnt out." Kate Stimpson has remarked that "burnout" is really another form of anger. We might then ask, Anger at what? I would answer: Anger at women who disappointed or betrayed. Anger over the investment placed in other women. Anger over giving more than one got back. Anger at the inability to transcend irreconcilable differences and divisions. Anger at the lack of recognition, respect, and thoughtfulness that women failed to give to each other. Anger over the loss of a happiness that women hoped to find with women.

Many women who became feminists during the 1960s and 1970s were "trashed" by women whom they had come to see as friends. "Trashing" sometimes took the form of a public denunciation in which women were castigated for some "politically incorrect" position. More often, the rupture happened in private. Since women were not prepared to confront betrayal and disloyalty from women, especially women they had come to trust, often the response was to conclude that "women were no better than men." Thus many women became disaffected from other women and turned back from woman-identification. In the last decade, numbers of women became alienated from other women and from feminism. Mary Daly refers to this as a "crisis of feminist faith," where women came to believe that the " 'illusion' is feminism itself."[83]

There are many ways to analyze this phenomenon. It is instructive that women who turn back from women and woman-identification seem to be saying that to be wounded by a woman is to be a kind of "ultimate victim." Having known victimization by men, and having expected it to come from these quarters, women did not forsee it coming from other women. Yet it did, and more frequently than many of us would like to acknowledge. Turning away from women, however, in the wake of horizontal violence and betrayal, is like proclaiming that no one can deal more mortal blows to women than other women. Of course, there is one level on which this is true. Because we expect much more from women, women do wound more deeply. This is only a partial truth, however. Partial truths can be enveloping, but the trouble with partial truths is that they are simply not whole truths. The whole truth is that, in a woman-hating world, women will internalize and externalize antiwoman values and behavior. The best that women can make of this is to know precisely that this behavior will occur, face this knowledge head-on (but perhaps more importantly "heart-on"), and act in a more Gyn/affective way because of and in spite of this knowledge of the mind and heart.

The strength of our commitment to women is finally tested in hard times—even when women throw female friendship back in our faces. As women of reality, we must know all of the forces that are ranged against us, including the awful force of women-betraying-women. We must grasp this knowledge, feel it, and then move on—to other women. This requires persistence and stamina—the power to stay with women.

When women turn away from women, they choose a different kind of victimization. They say, in effect, that they are already too wounded to be wounded again, this time by women. This attitude, however, makes women the ultimate wounders of women. It also proclaims that to be hurt by a woman is to be an ultimate victim beyond which nothing can victimize. Of course, women are not consciously aware that they are subjecting themselves to a more subtle kind of female victimism. However, this is what happens in reality.

Disaffection from women produces a nihilistic attitude toward feminism and female friendship. During the mid-twentieth century, especially the post-Holocaust and post–atomic bomb era, male poets and philosophers had an extended fascination with the meaning of nothing. Andrea Dworkin has said of this nihilism, ". . . they make romance out of this alienation so as to avoid taking responsibility for what they do and what they are."[84] A similar alienation has infected women, not to the point of romanticizing disaffection from women but to the extent of eschewing responsibility for one's unrealistic expectations of women and of not acknowledging a certain sentimentalizing of female bonding which expected too much and then backed away when it wasn't delivered.

This sentimentalizing can take the form of placing uncritical trust in women in general or in women who define themselves as feminist. Categorical trust, like categorical truth, cannot sustain itself; it cannot sustain those who exercise it, and it certainly cannot sustain female friendship. Categorical trust makes friendship, as Emerson said, "too good to be believed." To place uncritical trust in anyone, even honorable women, is foolish.

It is not wrong that women expect much from other women. We should expect that women will not behave as men have. In expecting much, however, we cannot expect women to be more of everything— more moral, more trustworthy, more giving, more intelligent. And, especially, we cannot expect women to be more of everything in a way that makes women less forgiving of women who fail them.

Nihilistic disaffection is the easy way out. The safest victims of our disappointment and rage are those of our own sex. It is simple to negate the values of feminism and of female friendship that were formerly held. It is much more difficult to confront the disillusionment and make up one's mind and heart to once more choose for women.

Disaffection from women must be supplanted with a more realistic Gyn/affection. We must resist the idea "that we are doomed to eternal victimization by 'the other': first patriarchy—now other women."[85]

Conclusion

The obstacles to female friendship finally serve to remind us that friendship is ongoing. Befriending women means continuing to befriend others even after deep friendships may be lost, or working through the obstacles in the hope that a friendship will be able to continue.

Friendship is a process of "repeated acts." In this sense, friendship is a habit that reoccurs in the face of betrayals, ruptures, and disaffection from women. It is a creative habit that, to take Mary Daly's words and use them in another context, "does not happen through wishful thinking but through arduous practice, through repeated acts."[86] Repeated acts of friendship must fly in the face of the "paradise lost" of former friends.

There is an enormous amount of practical wisdom about friendship that can come from its failures as well as its successes. In the grip of failure, there is always the temptation to ask, "Is/was it worth it?" Was it worth the time, energy, intensity of feeling, and the giving of Self? If Gyn/affection is indeed a political virtue with political effects, these questions must be answered from a different vantage point, possibly with other questions.

When a friendship awakens a woman to the possibilities of a deeper life and then denies the fulfillment of those possibilities within the friendship, was/is it worth it? Would it have been better to have been left unaffected by a particular friendship, even if that particular alliance did not last? We might all take heart from Alice Walker's words, spoken in the context of the civil rights movement but very applicable to the crisis of female friendship:

> Part of what existence means to me is knowing the difference between what I am now and what I was then. It is being capable of looking after myself intellectually as well as financially. It is being able to tell when I am being wronged and by whom ... It means being part of the world community, and being *alert* to which part it is that I have joined, and knowing how to change to another part if that part does not suit me. To know is to exist.[87]

If female friendship does any of this, in spite of the rents and fissures in its fabric, it is well worth it.

The obstacles to female friendship, for many women, have given them a reason to back away from other women because they feel that too little is gained from Gyn/affection. They ignore the gifts of female friendship that have been given. Female friendship has given us the experience of each other, and it has given us the gift of Self. It has given us a purpose, and it has shown us that we can be for women. It has demolished the facade of hetero-relations that draws us away from our Selves and each other. It has given us a history in which we learn that women have always loved other women. It has given us an understanding that a life of mere survival is insufficient for the spirit. It has given us the ability to express our love for women in different ways. It has given us lives that are touched by women, breaking "the universal patriarchal Taboo against Women-Touching women." It has given us that which is "most seriously forbidden to us." That it did not give us this forever, or with the friends with whom we originated, is not the issue. For what it has given us is the vision and possibility of it ever-recurring.

V

A Vision of
Female Friendship:
Two Sights-seeing

The space to be for now
Is not here, nor there,
But between the shape of the world
And the soul spark.
Here means the edges of sharp, spare,
Full and narrow
Like notebooks, jots, columns, tittles,
And the sky between high rises.
There means at the edge of light.
Nail your tongue and feet and fingers
Firm in the space
Not here, not there
Which is the same as saying
In neither and both at this one time.

> Catherine Barry,
> "The Space,"
> *Views from the Intersection*

Mama exhorted her children at every opportunity to "jump at de sun." We might not land on the sun, but at least we would get off the ground.

> Zora Neale Hurston
> *Dust Tracks on a Road*

I've dreamt in my life dreams that have stayed with me ever after, and changed my ideas; they've gone through and through me, like wine through water, and altered the colour of my mind.

> Emily Brontë,
> *Wuthering Heights*

The possibilities of female friendship are founded on vision. Vision is all the more important to discuss against the backdrop of the obstacles to female friendship and against a fabric of friendship frequently torn by disagreements, disruptions, and dissensions.

There are many ways to speak about vision. Every meaning, however, is possessed of a certain tension. This tension can be "felt" in the word's dual dictionary definition and in any attempt to live out a vision. At one and the same time, vision means "the exercise of the ordinary faculty of sight" and "something which is apparently seen by other than ordinary sight."[1] Another way of phrasing this tension is to ask how, indeed, it is possible to see with the ordinary faculty of sight, that is, to maintain a necessary realism about the conditions of existence, and to see beyond these conditions, that is, to "overleap reality." *Or, how do women live in the world as men have defined it while creating the world as women imagine it could be?*

Men have established the patterns of language and of meaning in which acceptance of the present state of affairs is known as "realistic" and efforts to create a more feminist or woman-defined world are pejoratively called "utopian." Thus, women who emphasize the necessity of vision are vulnerable to charges of distracting other women's attention away from the real problems of women's oppression and to accusations of romantic simplification or sentimentalizing. Anyone who proposes to speak about vision, especially that of seeing beyond the ordinary faculty of sight, is temporarily daunted by the "vision," or should I say the "specter," of being labeled "soft-brained."

A vital aspect of the beginning of this wave of feminism was its visionary power. For better or for worse, feminists have grown more "mature" in their aspirations, to the extent that maturity is often equated with a rejection of vision and with a hard-nosed realism that forecloses a sense of the feminist future, even before its possibilities appear. Feminist "maturity" seems to mean putting away the ideals of an earlier feminist "adolescence," including the very language of a woman-centered future.

In the "maturity" of feminist writing, scholarship, and action, we are witnessing a phenomenon that has occurred in other areas. Thinkers are turning away from the responsibility to generate ideals. For example, nineteenth-century sociology generated images of what society might be. Since then, sociology has become a discipline primarily

concerned with measuring and analyzing what is. Keith Melville has
faulted sociologists with creating "a science of the future, concerned
not with what should be, but with the formulation of predictive
statements about what probably will be."[2] Quantifiable calculations
and computerized predictions — hard-core futurism — have replaced
critical idealism and visionary thinking. We witness the same turna-
bout in the realm of philosophy. Philosophy, especially the themes and
questions raised by metaphysics, has become primarily analytic, reducing questions of being to the analysis of language, a language that
further reduces meaning to mathematical symbols and equations.

Idealism has always been suspect, but today it's more so when the
truly real issues of health, education, and welfare are further removed
from women who need them — and this is the majority of women. As
one economist has stated: "We don't have male poverty in the United
States anymore. We only have female poverty."[3] Or, as a front-page
story on poverty in the *Boston Globe* noted:

> "All other things being equal, . . . if the proportion of the poor who are in
> female-headed families were to increase at the same rate as it did from 1967
> to 1977, they would comprise 100 percent of the poverty population by
> about the year 2000."
>
>   . . . In the public mind, the 1970s is generally thought of as a decade of
> progress for America's women . . . These gains have been real and historic.
> But, in reality, there has been progress for only a few.
>
>   . . . In other words, women as a group are worse off than they were a
> decade ago.
>
>   . . . The 1980 National Advisory Council on Economic Opportunity
> report, released in October, concluded that "to the extent that there have
> been winners in the War on Poverty during the 70s, they have been
> male — and mainly white . . . The much more rapid decline in poverty for
> men has meant that the inequality in life-chances between men and
> women has grown considerably over the past few years."[4]

The further hard-pressed material conditions of many women's lives
are such that:

— Two-thirds of the world's illiterates are women.[5]
— Women earn 59.4 percent of what men earn.[6]
— Women are vastly more underemployed than men. While women
   represent over 50 percent of the world adult population and one-
   third of the official labor force, women perform for nearly two-
   thirds of all working hours and receive only one-tenth of the world
   income. Women also own less than 1 percent of world property.[7]

— Every seven minutes, a woman in the United States is raped.[8]
— Every eighteen seconds, a woman is battered.[9]

In this context, the sheer mention of a vision of female friendship sounds "unreal" to many.

Women, however, cannot afford to disregard or dismiss the visionary task, especially the task of seeing with more than ordinary sight. Nor can we let despair about the overwhelming character of the state of female atrocity mire us in the man-made world. A truly critical edge is one that is informed by a vision that expands the horizon of "real world." The world is more than men have made of it. Yet women must also be able to live in the man-made world affectively and effectively.

An undivided vision is based on *two sights-seeing — near- and far-sightedness.* This is the *essential tension* of feminism. It is present in every aspect of women's lives. Women must learn how to live with and in that tension. This means not being crushed by the contrast between what the world is and the way it ought to be.

Dual vision includes, on the one hand, a keen recognition of the conditions of female existence in the man-made world. This means an acute near-sightedness that sees keenly with the ordinary faculty of sight. Realism of the world as men have fabricated it is necessary to maintain more than ordinary sight — or a feminist far-sightedness — that does not become far-flung or escapist. On the other hand, realism about the conditions of female oppression and the man-made manipulations of female existence in this world may carry us beyond heterorelational structures, but at the same time there must be far-sighted thinking and action that suggest where we are going.

Women must reject the false vision and sentimentality of heterorelations precisely because this is a distorted vision of our Selves. This does not mean that women should reject vision, however. It does mean that women will shape our vision so that we will not only enable our own freedom from men but will also create the conditions of female friendship.

This book is based on the conviction that it is not possible for women to be free, nor to be realistic about the state of female existence in a man-made world, nor to struggle against those forces that are waged against us all, nor to win, if we do not have a vision of female friendship — if women do not come to realize how profound are the possibilities of being for each other as well as how deeply men have hidden these possibilities from us.

Dual vision poses a tension but not a contradiction. Realism about the conditions of man-made existence must be illuminated by a vision of feminist imagination that acts. And the feminist visionary task must root itself in the real world, or else, as Pat Hynes has remarked, like an electrical charge that has no ground, its unguided energy will become dispersed in all directions.[10] Virginia Woolf phrased it this way: "Energy has been liberated but into what forms is it to flow?"[11]

Dual Vision: Its Forms

Materialism and Idealism

To live in and with dual vision is a delicate act for women because this tension takes many forms. There is the idealist-materialist tension. Too much "materialism" (that is, the world view that sense experience and material existence alone are the "really real") about the man-made world can mire us in it. This can have several consequences. Women can become so angry that the anger goes nowhere and, ultimately, turns back against one's Self and other women. Or women can become paralyzed by the conditions of patriarchy, eventually using these as an excuse for not engaging with the real world because they see nothing beyond these conditions.

There is also the kind of materialism which, lacking any idealism, dismisses the need for imagination and far-sightedness. This stance often asserts that the bread and butter issues of women's lives are the only things that are really real and that it is almost an insult to talk about the necessity for women to see "with more than ordinary sight." It refuses to recognize that, for many women, there must be something more that prompts women to seize the means of daily bread. Without a deeper "reality," material bread and butter realities pale.

Too little "materialism" about the man-made world encourages an enfeebled, empty, and escapist vision which can overlook the blatancy of woman-hating, thereby conditioning women not to react, oftentimes even to the most extreme and urgent states of female atrocities. Here the condition of women's oppression becomes something against which belief rebels. Discussion of women's oppression becomes almost embarrassing, as though dwelling on it is immature, sophomoric, and the product of a morbid political consciousness. In this way, many women have obliterated the depths of these atrocities from their consciousness.

Too little "materialism" also fosters an indwelling, spiritualized, or abstract consciousness that distracts from the "real" conditions of women's lives. "Seeing with more than ordinary sight" becomes "a veil that spreads over the hard reality of existence. It tempts us to a self-sufficient life in the world of images and thoughts."[12] The feminist future always seems brighter than hetero-relational reality. This has prompted some women to define the world only in reference to the future or in reference to the world of Nature. Many view the world of institutions and artifacts as unreal—the total product of male fabrication. But the world is more than the world of Nature. Institutional structures, while artifactual and imitative, and often corrupt, are part of the real world.

Two sights-seeing asserts the fundamental movement between materialism and idealism, no matter which is declared to be the starting point. If women start from the viewpoint of consciousness, asserting the primacy of values or ideas, women must move at some point to "materialize" this consciousness. If, on the other hand, the starting point is the material conditions of women's lives, women must move at some point in the direction of "idealizing" when matter becomes consious of itself—of its whys and wherefores, of its meaning, and of its depth. Even many Marxists, namely some of the Frankfurt school, had a vision of hope that one could call transcendent in the sense that it moved their theory beyond the material realm of objective possibility to horizons beyond that realm.

I have sometimes been asked to describe what my basic philosophical stance is. The answer is that I am a critical idealist and a critical materialist. Reductive materialists have a way of making me emerge from the matter at hand soaked in idealism. And dogmatic idealists send me fleeing back to the material conditions of women's existence. The process of women's friendships moves constantly between the material and ideal. There are the ideal conditions in which Gyn/affection flourishes, and there are the material conditions in which Gyn/affection exists. The aim is to bring these two together. A critical idealism does not project ideals into a future but finds the origins of these in women's past and present. Every ideal of friendship must create a foundation for itself in women's existent reality.[13]

Idealism, however, is not simply the restoration of the past or the elevation of old matter into new creation. One cannot, for example, use the marriage resisters or nuns as models to be lived by, but rather as instructive examples for the forms that female friendship can take. Idealism has a power, the power of expectation and possibility, to transform the material conditions of women's lives. Yet the movement between the two will always reassert the challenge of the material—to concretize the ideal—to actualize "something that is seen with more than ordinary sight" into the ordinary.

Goodness and truth, for example, may be ideals that one looks for in a friendship. It is impossible to find abstract goodness and truth, but it is equally impossible to find material goodness and truth manifested in a person unless there is some ideal by which goodness and truth can be recognized. We need ideals of goodness and truth, but not separated from the real matter of women's lives.

To use another example, it is important to any literature on female friendship that the ideal of passion be talked about. Unless, however, the material history of women's passion for each other is illustated, passion has little reality. Idealism cannot abandon its search for "goodness," "truth," "passion," or "friendship." It must have a theoretical independence, but it has no material independence that is cut off from the actual existence of female friendship and from the matter of women's lives as we live our friendships day by day.

Optimism and Pessimism

Having viewed many of the obstacles to female friendship, we see that a vision of Gyn/affection certainly raises the optimism-pessimism tension. There is no fundamental movement between optimism and pessimism as there is between materialism and idealism. Rather, hope expresses the correct tension between the two. Tension is not always a neat dialectical movement between two opposites in which a third reality proceeds from a preceding two (thesis-antithesis-synthesis); nor is it an "androgynous" unifying of what are perceived as counterpoles. Rather, hope goes beyond optimism and pessimism about female friendship, correcting the lopsided vision of both. Hope is a movement that forms between optimism and pessimism and then moves beyond the two. It gives women the staying power not to be crushed by the contrast between what the man-made world is and the way it ought to be. "It is precisely hope . . . that neither falls into despair nor sinks into a quietistic confidence."[14]

Hope about the possibilities of female friendship is not naive. It is tempered by the many obstacles that have divided women in the "maturity" of our associations with each other. Hope must be grounded in several things: in the spirit and reality of friendship that lives on in one's Self and in other women; in the fact that women have always been for women in all times and places; and in the continuity and consistency of women's friendships that cross all lines.

Hope is not necessary when things go smoothly, when there is a euphoria about the possibilities of women together, as there was in the first stages of this particular wave of feminism. Many women came through the feminism of the 1960s and 1970s jaded, "turned off," and disillusioned by other women. Often, women who "should have been different" turned out to be "just as bad as, if not worse than, men." Moreover, on a political level, violence against women often issued in horizontal violence. Even something like the defeat of the ERA (for the moment) dulled the spirit of togetherness. All of this can result in a profound pessimism about female friendship. Worse, it can lead to a grim cynicism that is emphatically and consistently critical about the inadequacies of women to develop and sustain Gyn/affection.

Both hope and friendship are easy when things proceed well. Hope is hard to hold, but is no less called for, when things are not as good as we expected them to be, when sisterhood does not seem as powerful as it once was or as once we felt it to be. However, the failures of friendship can never destroy the presence of its past in our lives, and certainly not its possibilities.

A hopeful vision of female friendship is not based on some ontological essence of female energy or vitality that women naturally possess by virtue of a more refined capability for love, caring, and respect for others. Rather it is anchored in the historical, cultural, and material bonds that women have created for our Selves in spite of the "State of Atrocity." The obstacles to female friendship and the divisiveness that often attends diversity serve as correctives to a shallow sentimentalism about women's affinities with women. Such difficulties remind us that to ground Gyn/affection in a natural capability of women to bond with each other is a false optimism that will betray itself. Misplaced optimism and shallow sentimentalism are two sides of the same coin.

A feminist vision realistically assesses the obstacles to female friendship. It is also keenly aware of the "State of Atrocity" in which many women exist. Seeing with "the ordinary faculty of sight," or being in the world as men have created it, is to know that the faculty of vision will not make such facts of female existence disappear. Yet the same vision, when it sees "something which is apparently seen otherwise than by ordinary sight," knows that such realism is not the whole perspective. Vision, as near- and far-sightedness, is neither false optimism nor disillusioned pessimism. Female friendship alone cannot vanquish the oppression of women, nor can it guarantee that friendship lasts forever. It can create and sustain hope in the midst of a world that suppresses Gyn/affection.

This kind of vision gives women "the hope that the earthly horror does not possess the last word."[15] Whatever that "earthly horror" is — whether it is the "State of Atrocity" in which many women live their lives or the experience of a friendship that has failed — hope tells us that our present existence is not ultimate and that there are alternatives. Hope also ensures that, in the face of the obstacles to female friendship, women will not capitulate to a nihilistic and conservative attitude which sums up past failed friendships as wasted time and energy.

Hope strengthens our negation of man-made "order." Images of a feminist future and continuous action to make this future realized in the present are generated by the capacity to hope. Hope promises that the past and present are not absolute. Yet hope must be grounded in a past and present that directs women's actions to a realization of the future.

Some feminist literature and culture have been based on a shallow and sentimental optimism that is hard to distinguish from wishful fantasy. It is "utopian," in the worst sense of that word. To be sure, hope can be expressed in dreams, fantasy, and utopian novels, but it is only hope insofar as it portends a "genuine futurity."[16] There is a sharp difference between visionary thinking that possesses a "genuine futurity" and the often colorful but nonetheless abstract flightiness of some feminist fantasy.

Historically, vision and hope have been the territory of religion. Judaism and Christianity, for example, have always preached much about "promise." However, for the most part, patriarchal religions stifled women's hopes, depriving women of the ability to create a Self-directed and woman-oriented future. Or they displaced female hope to various male saviors, gurus, and eschatologies. The promise of women's Selves never came into being. A patriarchal church, along with all sorts of patriarchal promises (heavens), became the definers and custodians of women's future. And even the future, which patriarchal religions promised, insipid as it was, could only be longed for.

Patriarchal religion is not synonymous with religion, as fascist politics is not synonymous with politics. Therefore, my vision of female friendship is spiritual or religious, in spite of the the reductions and distortions of both words in some feminist circles. Unfortunately, spirituality has taken on the characteristics of a cult and has been reduced to a product rather than a process. Many women seem somehow to acquire spirituality, as a product, along the feminist way, in the manner of what theologians would call "cheap grace." As children wear the inner tubes of car tires to swim in a lake, many women seem to "wear" spirituality to help them paddle in and out of the world around them. In contrast, spirituality as process has certain points of departure leading to other points of arrival, with the whole journey grounded in the real world of feminist action and women's existence in this world.

Women are not the main offenders in reducing religious reality to something it is not. Patriarchal religions and spiritual movements have done far worse in this area. In spite of these debasements of the spirit and spiritual reality, my vision of female friendship is spiritual and religious. For me, Gyn/affection raises questions of "ultimate concern" or meaning for women. It is therefore, in part, a religious quest which goes beyond patriarchal religion's identification with God, gods, or religious organizations. A vision of female friendship is religious in the most basic sense — being derived from its accepted Latin root, *religare,* meaning "to tie" or "to link." As one author has commented: "[religion's] role in human life is not to *add* something but to *unify* and to *direct* what is already there. The religious drive is . . . the contextual drive, as it were, manifested in all the others, the comprehensive drive through which they are related."[17]

It is in this sense that I am calling a vision of female friendship religious or spiritual. I maintain that Gyn/affection has the power to help tie women's lives together, to make connections that have not been made, and to provide a unifying and directing influence in all other areas of female existence in this world. Female friendship creates a network of meaning that transcends women's past, our ordinary lives, and our present.

The reality of Gyn/affection begins a journey into an "Otherworld" that, as Mary Daly has described it, is "both discovery and creation of a world other than patriarchy."[18] It is the perception of female friendship as "Otherworld Journey," as "more than," which also imbues it with religious meaning. The transcendent possibilities of female friendship may be viewed as illusion or as "really real" depending on whether one transforms question into answer, absence into presence. One of the differences between those who see feminism as a spiritual force — as well as a political and intellectual one — and those who don't is "not a disagreement of fact but an incommensurate way of experiencing."[19]

My vision of Gyn/affection sees female friendship as having revelatory power and as a realization of transcendence which creates for women ever-new possibilities of this-worldly existence. The "Otherworldly" power of female friendship revitalizes the power of women together in the real material world of female life and living. At the same time that female friendship poses the question and promise of far-off Be-ing, it grounds women in the real proximity of Gyn/affective Be-ing—one that we our Selves create in concert with each other.

The visionary journey of any oppressed group "envisions" a kind of salvation, "an evolution to higher consciousness on the part of society, even when society cannot. Even when society is in the process of killing them for their vision."[20] Vision enables hope to inhabit the spirit. Hope works for female friendship in spite of the past failures of friendship. It strives to make female friendship ever-present. That we shall reach the full vision of friendship, we have no certainty, only hope.

Theory and Practice: Thought and Action

Another tension that inheres in female friendship is that between theory and practice. Within the history of modern philosophy, as well as the current wave of feminism, theory and action have been falsely separated.

In recent times a distrust of theory has arisen. Feminists have also been susceptible to this distrust, reacting negatively to the sterile rationalism and abstraction of patriarchal thought. However, theory comes from the Greek *theorein,* which literally translates "to see." It is, therefore, an integral part of vision.

> Our tradition of political thought began when Plato discovered that it is somehow inherent in the philosophical experience to turn away from the common world of human affairs; it ended when nothing was left of this experience but the opposition of thinking and acting, which *depriving thought of reality and action of sense, makes both meaningless.* [Italics mine][21]

Here, Hannah Arendt asserts the fundamental movement between theory and practice, not so much in the sense of gluing them together but of restoring an integrity to that which never should have been separated.

Creating a chasm between theory and action deprives thought of consequence and action of deliberative depth. Thinking is an activity, and action is a "thought-event." When the unity of the two is restored, people will think twice before saying that "theory has no bearing on practice" or that "theory is easy and practice is difficult." To speak of theory and practice in this way reinforces a naive dualism. Theory is the reservoir of practice. It is the animating source of its purposiveness. It should be present in practice, as should practice in theory. The unity of the two is necessary to the integrity of each. Many have focused on the necessity to move from theory to action. Far fewer have emphasized that it is equally important to move back to theory once having acted or in the midst of acting. The integrity of theory and practice will always generate tension, but tension and separation should not be equated.

The integrity of thought and action, theory and practice, is the integrity of philosophy and politics. That integrity produces a *thinking participation* in the world. It enables women to enter the world as those who think. Thinking has often been an escape for intellectuals from the world, and in reaction to this many women have discarded theory, advocating its dismissal as a political act. However, right and rigorous thinking locates women in the world. There is no place for the absence of thinking in a Gyn/affective world. Mindlessness, clichés, superficial action, and sameness of conduct all result from this relinquishing of thought.

The need to think is inspired by the quest for meaning.[22] Thus, thinking should never be dissociated from the world of participation. One clue to this, as Arendt reminds us, is that the term *vita activa* (active life) was invented by those who "were devoted to the contemplative life and who looked upon all kinds of being alive from that perspective."[23] Andrea Dworkin has put it in a somewhat different way:

> The creative mind is intelligence in action in the world... The world is anywhere where thought has consequences... Thinking is action; so are writing, composing, painting; creative intelligence can be used in the material world to make products of itself. But there is more to creative intelligence than what it produces. Creative intelligence is searching intelligence: it... demands to know the world.[24]

There is a fundamental integrity between the theory and practice of female friendship that must always be emphasized. Female friendship must create a kind of "thought-landscape" where thinking is a vital part of the real world and where action is profoundly thoughtful. Friendship must equip women for the activity of thinking and for the thoughtfulness of activity. I am not saying that the practice of friendship will always keep pace with the theoretical ideals of friendship. However, when it doesn't, what usually has happened is that the tension between theory and practice has been lost. The practice and activities of friendship may turn sour, because thinking about friendship has ceased to be active. Perhaps the friendship becomes taken for granted and is not enriched by the liveliness of thought. Or the thinking may become stale because the practice of friendship has been lost or diminished by a kind of philosophical withdrawal from the day-to-day living of friendship.

Many women in their disdain for abstract and meaningless male rationalism assume that there is a fundamental falsity to any kind of theory. Because there have been so many conceptual filters set up between women and our experience, conceptualization, thinking, and theory are eschewed altogether. The result is an antagonism to thinking in any form. Dale Spender has written that "patriarchy has found it profitable to turn us away from the intellectual."[25] Mary Daly has pointed out that "since *intellectuality,* in the fullest sense, implies knowing one's own mind, the depreciation of a woman's intellectuality affects all aspects of her life, shrinking her physical and emotional energy, narrowing her sights."[26] When women do "turn away" and "shrink" from intellectuality, they are distorting feminist vision whose original impulse was not to attack the intellect but to dethrone masculinist and phallocratic rationalism as the sole means of knowing. "We need to redefine theory and theorist; we need to see theory not as something which is to be resisted, but something we can use in our own interest. And we need to see that men have no monopoly on theory; theorising is an activity engaged in by *all* human beings."[27]

Out of women's reactionary attitude toward thinking and theory has developed an anti-intellectualism that values practice without theory. However, any female or feminist action that lacks the complexity of thought often becomes rhetorical. Rhetorical action, like rhetorical words, is devoid of depth. Often it may be a clever and colorful rhetoric whose power derives from its ability to assail our sensibilities rather than to arouse our thought. It is a kind of rhetoric that rushes at us with something like "Words are the absolute in horseshit."[28] Words like this often succeed because they employ "the thought-terminating cliché." Robert Jay Lifton has given insight into what he calls "loading the language," a technique especially employed in totalistic environments.

The most far-reaching and complex of human problems are compressed into brief, highly reductive, definitive-sounding phrases, easily memorized and easily expressed. These become the start and finish of any ideological analysis. In thought reform, for instance, the phrase "bourgeois mentality" is used to encompass and critically dismiss ordinarily troublesome concerns like the quest for individual expression, the exploration of alternative ideas, and the search for perspective and balance in political judgments. And in addition to their function as interpretive shortcuts, these clichés become what Richard Weaver has called "ultimate terms": either "god terms," representative of ultimate good; or "devil terms," representative of ultimate evil ... "progress," ... "liberation," "proletarian standpoints" ... fall into the former category; "capitalist," "imperialist" ... fall into the latter. Totalist language, then, is repetitiously centered on all-encompassing jargon ... relentlessly judging, and to anyone but its most devoted advocate, deadly dull: in Lionel Trilling's phrase, "the language of nonthought."[29]

Rhetoric is not only expressed in words, however. Without theory, practice becomes a kind of rhetorical action that lacks complexity. Many women have equated theory itself with rhetoric. This has been true of much patriarchal theory and also within certain academic feminist circles. However, just the opposite is true — that is, rhetoric flourishes where there is an absence of thought. Rhetoric becomes a substitute for thought. And any kind of feminist practice that is not permeated by feminist theory is mere rhetoric, reducing action to a series of artificial flourishes and ostentatious gestures.

Instead of expanding women's reality, rhetorical practice constricts it. For example, women often take on the rhetoric/practice of friendship, as I noted earlier, by talking about it and "dealing" endlessly with their personal relationships with women. I termed this "relationalism," where the deeper conversation between two persons that constitutes part of a good friendship is missing. This kind of relating reminds one of what Nadezhda Mandelstam, in *Hope Abandoned,* described as the rhetorical style of those who mouthed the "correct line" of Russian communism: "we were struck by the fact that nobody *conversed* anymore ... On the other hand, there was no end of talkers, all vying with one another."[30]

These words have wider implications beyond the realm of female friendship, of course. In much literature and living, feminist and otherwise, we have rhetorical practice instead of thoughtful action:

— assertiveness instead of strength
— policy instead of power
— egocentrism instead of individuality
— posturing instead of action
— "gayness" instead of happiness
— gestures instead of movement
— sensation instead of passion

Much of what passes for feminist theory also lacks thought. Instead it is often a preoccupation with esoterica, or with what the male academy has defined as "real" theory. Academic feminists have been exaggeratedly focused on semiotics, deconstruction, and psychoanalytic thought. What gets accepted as feminist theory in the academy is rarely woman-originated and defined. Instead, theorists whose work can be evaluated within the male paradigms of Marxism, psychoanalysis, and/or deconstructionism—to name three examples—or who relate to these theoretical traditions in major ways, are the center of theoretical analysis and of seminars and courses on feminist theory. As a more specific example, French feminist theory courses in American universities are dominated by the theories of psychoanalytic feminists or by semiotics. The radical feminist theory of someone like Christine Delphy is rarely emphasized. This, of course, is not all that unusual since the same thing happens in American feminist theory courses. Many of these courses begin and end radical feminist theory with Shulamith Firestone and are utterly reductive in their typology of what radical feminist theory is about.

So there is theory and there is theory! The kind of theory I have been advocating throughout this section is a *thoughtful theory*—one that *restores the thoughtfulness to thinking*. Or, better still, thinking is the theory; thoughtfulness is the practice.

The Conditions of Female Friendship

Thoughtfulness

Thinking is a necessary condition of female friendship. The thinking I advocate is better described by the word *thoughtfulness*. In my use of it, *thoughtfulness* is characterized on the one hand by ability to reason and on the other by considerateness and caring. It is this kind of thoughtfulness that is necessary for Gyn/affection.

The commonly accepted definition of *thoughtfulness* is concern for others, attentiveness to others' needs, and considerateness for others. However, the word in its primary sense means literally "full of thought." Other meanings are "absorbed in thought," "meditative," or "characterized by careful reasoned thinking." Thus the word thoughtfulness contains a dual meaning and poses another tension. I contend that these two meanings must come together and be expressed in Gyn/affection.

Thoughtlessness has contributed much to the divisions and dissensions among women. Joan Schwartz has written a biting yet trenchant poetic commentary on thoughtlessness in the women's community. In a poem entitled "In Search of a Warm Feminist: An Unpoetic Poem to a

Poetic Problem," she writes of an encounter with a "famous feminist" who was invited to speak to a college community.

> She confronts us in our isolation
> She speaks to our losses — and our gains
> She utters our words in a voice that is our own
>   But that we cannot duplicate (though we would, we would).
>
> She tickles us with her metaphors
> She teases us with her irony
> She taunts us with our failures
>   our bourgeois life
>   (How banal, but we are not immune)
>   our other diseases
>   (against which we have not been inoculated by
>   a dose of SDS vaccine
>   the needle of leftist bacilli
>   attenuated and weakened but
>   necessary for antibodies against our bodies)
>   our selves
> her working-class background
>   (we of course are all
>   Middle-Class from before
>   Betty/Simone/dawn
>   Even our Russian peasant ancestors
>   Don't count
>   Even our first jobs at 11 which Were
>   counted out at 40¢ per hour
>   which paid the family electric bill.
>   We are still in outer darkness).
> her working-class anger
>   (Never mind the anger of the waitress goaded
>   into a stream of abuse
>   At us — the undeserving rich,
>   the feminists who are responsible for our sins
>   And hers too)
> Our provincialism
>   (We reward her with a week
>   of our pay for an hour
>   of her reading
>
>   but offer her cold surroundings
>   and shabby equipment
> Out of our warehouse of plenty
>   and yet expect
>   to be recognized as human)

    We laugh in ripples at our shared pain
    We laugh in tidal waves at her mockery of us
       Our foolish offerings
    We pay
       not in toilet tokens
       though we might
       as we shit buckets of guilt
       but in
       self-lacerating laughter for our sins
          of living in the academic community
    No community at all

    She rips us off by hating us
    She rips us off by baiting us
       She the deserving poor
       We the undeserving rich
          (Who daily lose our token women)
    She rips us off by cheating us
       Not so much of money
          (though that too)
    But of the comfort of one warm feminist.

Many women have expressed disappointment and frustration at the
lack of thoughtfulness that pervades many women's groups and that
women seem to accept as a matter of course in feminist relationships
and gatherings.

On the other hand, many women have been socialized to react
almost instinctually to other people's needs, mostly those of men and
children. Women have been drained by a kind of thoughtfulness that is
really lacking in thought to the extent that it is indiscriminately given,
without thinking about the conditions under which it is extended and
the fact that it is left to women in any context to be thoughtful. Here
the thinking is missing from thoughtfulness so that women give and
give, extend themselves constantly, and deal and deal with the needs of
others in what has at times almost amounted to a feminine compulsion. The thoughtfulness that most women are trained to extend in a
hetero-relational context is not born out of Self-directed thinking.
Many women "go into robot" performing "emotional labor" to fulfill
all sorts of others' needs. For women, the cost of this kind of thoughtfulness has been the obliteration of thinking.

A vision of female friendship restores the thinking to thoughtfulness. At the same time, it restores a thoughtfulness to thinking, that is,
a respect and considerateness for another's needs. Only thoughtful-

ness, in its more expanded meaning, can sustain female friendship and give it daily life. A thinking friendship must become a thoughtful friendship in the full sense of the word *thoughtfulness*. Many women may be brilliant thinkers, but that thinking has to be accompanied by a genuine attentiveness and respect for other women if female friendship is to flourish. On the other hand, many women may be caring and considerate of others, but if this thoughtfulness lacks a Self-directed thinking that "prepares us ever anew to meet whatever we must meet in our daily lives,"[31] it reinforces socialized femininity rather than female friendship. The word *thoughtfulness* conveys the meaning of a thinking considerateness and a considerate thinking. It is not accidental that it has such a dual meaning. A woman who truly thinks is, more expansively, full of thought in many realms.

What does it mean to think? Philosophers have often identified thinking with intellectual activity. Aristotle traced the capacity for friendship to *man's* intelligence or thinking capacity. Within the classical western tradition of male philosophy about friendship, women were not recognized as capable of friendship because of their supposed diminished capacity for thinking. It was this emphasis on man's faculty of thought that also led Aristotle to proclaim that friendship could flourish only between persons who are equal in intelligence. Where such an equality exists, he said, minds grow and are always capable of contributing to a common stock of ideas that is necessary for an enriched friendship.

From a different vantage point, Hannah Arendt wrote an entire book, *The Life of the Mind,* in which she talked about a kind of thinking that includes, but that is also distinguished from, intellectual activity. In her framework, thinking and intellect are not concerned with the same things. Thinking is oriented to meaning whereas the intellect searches after truth, a truth that in modern times has been "transformed or, rather, broken down into a string of verities."[32] In other words, the intellect often reduces profound truth to a body of truths or a body of knowledge, while thinking wishes to understand their meaning. The narrow intellectual is concerned with particular facts or truths whereas the thinker searches for the meaning of particular facts or truths. This distinction between knowledge and thinking is particularly significant in the context of vision. A person without vision will place know-how over knowing why. That person may ultimately be satisfied with a knowlege without meaning.

Arendt affirms that thinking is a primary condition of female friendship. Although my use of the word *thoughtfulness* goes beyond

Arendt's discussion of thinking, I agree with many of her basic points about thinking and build on these. With her, I affirm that thinking is not the prerogative of the few professional thinkers. It is

> an ever-present faculty in everybody; by the same token, inability to think is not a failing of the many who lack brain power but an ever-present possibility for everybody—scientists, scholars, and other specialists in mental exercises not excluded. Everybody may come to shun that intercourse with oneself.[33]

"Intercourse with oneself" is crucial to both the idea of thinking and that of friendship, for it is where both come together. Thinking is where I keep myself company, where I find my original friend, if you will. It is the solitude, as opposed to loneliness, where I am alone with, but not lonely in, the companionship of myself. Thinking is where I am at home with myself when, for all sorts of reasons, I withdraw from the world. "The partner who comes to life when you are alert and alone is the only one from whom you can never get away—except by ceasing to think."[34] This is one of the major reasons why women have lost their Selves— because they have stopped thinking. By not thinking, an individual loses her original friendship with her Self. Through thinking, a person discovers that she can be her real Self. In discovering this, she also realizes that the conversation that took place in the duality of thinking activity—that is, the duality of "myself with myself," the "two-in-one," or "the one who asks and the one who answers"—enables conversation with others. When I discover, through thinking, that I can converse with my real Self, I have to realize that such a conversation is possible with others. This is the awakening of female friendship in which the search for others like my Self begins.

As I stated earlier, Aristotle maintained that "the friend is another self." However, until the Self is another friend, it is often difficult for women to have confidence in their power of making and sustaining friends. The conversation of friendship with others can be had only by those who have learned how to think with themselves, to keep themselves company. Conversely, Arendt places the emphasis in the opposite direction. "I first talk with others before I talk with myself, examining whatever the joint talk may have been about, and then discover that I can conduct a dialogue not only with others but with myself as well."[35] The movement, I believe, is dialectical. A woman must be at the same time a friend to her original Self and to others. Which comes first is hard to determine. What is clear is that thinking and friendship go hand in hand.

The classical tradition of friendship was closely connected with thinking. Adolf Harnack pointed out that the "history of the Greek schools of philosophy is at the same time the history of friendship."[36] It was the philosophers of ancient Greece who gave an intellectual development to the idea of friendship. With Socrates, for example, friendship became both the condition and content of an education and educated thought. In other words, the relation between student and teacher was a bond of friendship while, at the same time, friendship was the object of education. That is, it was subjected to philosophical analysis, and its origin, nature, and means of development were investigated.

Arendt follows this tradition in associating friendship with thinking. In the way she has connected the two, she has made a profound and original contribution to the history of thinking, especially in clarifying its quest for meaning and in viewing thinking as the conversation that takes place between "myself and myself." For a specific analysis of female friendship, however, I believe it is necessary to expand Arendt's notion of thinking to thoughtfulness in the way I have already defined. Thinking is made flesh in the lives of women who think, that is, who seek meaning in their lives, but who also know that meaning is material. Thinking, to my way of thinking, is materialized in the thoughtfulness of female friendship. Thoughtfulness is not divorced from thinking but gives flesh to it. The precarious balance between the world of thinking and the world of acting is stabilized by the thoughtfulness of female friendship.

Passion

As female friendship is characterized by thoughtfulness, it is also marked by passion. Friendship is a passion but, in my vision, it is a thoughtful passion. It manifests a thinking heart.

The tension between thinking and feeling, as signified in the phrase "thoughtful passion," is evident in the etymology of the word *passion*. *Passion* derives from Old French and Latin roots meaning "suffering, pain or some disorder of body or spirit." It also means being "affected by external agency." However, etymologies are often multidimensional, and so we find another meaning of *passion* defined as "any kind of feeling by which the mind is powerfully affected or moved . . . an eager outreaching of the mind toward something" (*Oxford English Dictionary*).

A passionate friendship upholds the integrity between thought and passion. In passionate friendship, there is no separation between the two. It is not so much that they merge, but that they have not been fractured to begin with. Emily Dickinson expressed the integrity between thought and passion with her usual eloquent succinctness:

> The Heart is the Capital of the Mind—
> The Mind is a single State—
> The Heart and the Mind together make
> A single Continent—[37]

We have become so accustomed to the dualisms of thought and passion that the idea of a thoughtful passion in which thinking does not rule, but rather suffuses passion (in this case, the passion of friendship), is a strange notion.

This was not always the case. The importance of friendship as a primary passion and its alliance with thinking were part of the Greek tradition of friendship. In pre-Christian times, the tie of friendship was considered the highest form of communion between two persons—always two men—superseding that of marriage. As we have seen, friendship was a homo-relational affair.[38]

Within the tradition of classical friendship, women were judged to be without the passion, sense of individuality, and presence of a common world and worldliness that make friendship possible. Greater than these faults, however, was woman's supposed incapacity for thought—thought being indispensable to the Greek vision of a good friendship. Montaigne is a more modern representative of the Greek philosophical perspective that female friendships are shallow because women do not "appear to be endued [endowed] with firmness of mind to endure the constraint of so hard and durable a knot."[39]

So impressed were the Greeks with the manliness of the passion of friendship, with its power to prompt men to high thought and heroic action, that the love of friendship was set above the love of man for woman. As Aristotle phrased it, the male friend was "another self."[40]

Whereas the man who forms a deep relationship with another man is regarded as "another self," the woman who forms a deep and passionate friendship with another woman is labeled "narcissistic."* Freudian psychology, in particular, has taught that female intimacy is trifling and sentimental, a prelude only to the adult and mature stage of hetero-relational development. Close friendships between women are childish crushes, relics of a bygone time of immaturity, where women have not yet been weaned from the world of women. The world of men is the world of thought and action. The world of women

---

*Always overlooked is the mythological fact that Narcissus was male!

lacks thought and real passion. De Beauvoir, the philosopher, mimics psychological cant in *The Second Sex* by saying that close female friendships smack of the "insipid purity" of girlhood and are narcissistic.[41] Unfortunately, many women still believe this.

I emphasize the Greek tradition of friendship here because it posed an alternative to marriage by affirming friendship as a superior bond, as well as associating it with thinking. It also sanctioned the expression of passion between two friends, even to the point of sexual expression. This is not to say that such passion serves as a model for female friendship, but that there has been a historical recognition of the friendship union as a primary passion associated with thinking.

The reality of friendship as a primary passion and its alliance with thinking in the Greek tradition are important to a vision of female friendship as a thoughtful passion. Not that the Greeks arrived at a unified notion or reality of friendship as a thoughtful passion, but the significance of friendship as a passion and its impact on thinking and the development of philosophy, as well as on all institutions of Greek society, can be considered, expanded, and lived out by female friends in quite different ways.

A thoughtfully passionate friendship is passion at its most active. It keeps passion active and does not allow it to degenerate into its more passive modes. More concretely, it helps two women to become their own person. There is a dynamic integrity of existence in a thoughtful passion that is missing in a more sentimental friendship. Friendship that is characterized by thoughtful passion ensures that a friend does not lose her Self in the heightened awareness of and attachment to another woman.

The loss of Self has happened most frequently in lover relationships. And, in fact, passion is generally associated with lovers, not with friends, or not with friends who aren't lovers. There has been much discussion of passion within the lover relationship, but not much talk of friendship within love. It is my opinion that when a lover finds that she is losing her Self in the heightened awareness of and attachment to another woman in a sexually passionate relationship, the friendship is problematic. Either the friendship wasn't strong initially or it got swallowed up in the sexual passion of the lover relationship. Thus passion deteriorates into its more passive mode, engulfing a necessary friendship and eclipsing its ability to generate a needed thoughtfulness about the friendship that is required for passion to survive and thrive.

In any kind of lover relationship that is committed, one's lover should be one's best friend. And if one's best friend is one's lover, she should also be the primary passion of her lover's life. A truly passionate love life, above all, must be pervaded by a thoughtful passion. The wings of eros are very quickly clipped, especially when eros amounts to desire. The wings of eros become the wings of mere pleasure, short-lived sensual delight, or superficial sentiment when they are divorced from the ground of thoughtfulness. A love relationship which is also a passionate friendship must be a lucid affection.

Passion is not usually associated with friendship. Since the expression of passion has been largely confined to lovers in modern times, one might ask whether my notion of passionate friendship is restricted to lovers. The answer is no. Passion, in this work, is not restricted to lovers, but it is most fully manifested where lovers are friends and, conversely, where friends are lovers.

Of course, any deep friendship is pervaded by powerful feelings—by passion. The distinction that I make between passion and sentiment I would also apply to a passionate friendship in which the friends are not lovers. One must also distinguish between passionate and sentimental friendships. With the latter, such feeling—such passive passion, if you will—contributes to an absence of both intensity of emotion and deep thought. It is a kind of emotion that depends on the feeling of itself feeling. A sentimental or romantic friendship is an example of what I have called the *banality of passion.*

As with lover/friendships, nonlover friendships must also be suffused by thought so that the passion can run deep and not roll off the surface of sentimentality or passive romanticism. Friendship, as a thoughtful passion, creates movement that does not abort passion but brings it to greater heights and depths. The ability of thought to order reality marks the difference between a passionate and a sentimental friendship. A sentimental friendship is based on an intensely romantic yet shallow attachment. It eventually runs its course in the uncentered and disordered diffusion of its feeling. It thrashes its feeling away in a burst. It is passion at its most passive, often camouflaged by activity lacking in forward movement. Finally a sentimental friendship is governed by strong feeling that is separated from thought. It is therefore a thoughtless feeling.

As my use of the term Gyn/affection is meant to expand the political dimensions of affection, so too is it intended to expand the passionate dimensions of affection. In other words, my vision of female friendship does not restrict the expression of passion to a lover relationship where passion is expressed in a sexual/genital way.

Some may question the possibility of a passionate friendship that does not result in the friends becoming lovers. Some women have equated passionate feelings for a woman with a "need" to express such feelings in a sexual/genital way. It is as if passion is experienced as deterministic, and thought is seen as overwhelmed by or submerged in the force of passion. Thus passion has often been used as an excuse not to make choices. Or, more accurately, some women do not call upon their capacity to think through involvement in a passionate friendship so that they can make discerning judgments about what form the friendship will take, given the total circumstances of their lives—for example, commitments to others or the match or mismatch of personalities and purposes that may exist between two women.

Passion is not deterministic, unless one holds a very passive view of passion. One can choose to be passionate friends instead of exercising passion in a sexual/genital way. This is not to say that two women who are passionate friends won't experience certain tensions that pull them, perhaps, in the direction of being lovers.

Like the tension within vision itself, the tension of a passionate friendship may not be easy. However, where thoughtful passion prevails, where thought attends passion like one friend to another and lends it a certain purpose, the possibilities of Gyn/affection are both expanded and deepened.

This is not a "watered-down" version of love. Because passion may not be expressed in a sexual/genital way does not make it immaterial or insignificant. Passionate friendship has its own depth and intensity and is characterized by strong feeling and, often, physical affection. It is also characterized by proper *timing* and *temperature*. When a friend is not a lover, and where intense passion is present, the temperature may initially be difficult to gauge. Sometimes we set the temperature too high when the total climate of the friendship is unsuitable for such a setting—or too low, when we do not invest an intensity and depth that we know the friendship deserves. We hope that we learn by our mistakes.

Women within the parameters of hetero-relations have registered too low a temperature for women. Gyn/affection has not been allowed to expand in either its political or passionate senses. Women's ability to move, stir, arouse, influence other women has been severely diminished. Within other circles of women, the temperature has been set too high. It has been an ethic in some lesbian groups that any intense passion for another woman should always be manifested in a sexual/genital relationship—that passion has an almost innate compulsion to become sexual. And if it isn't sexualized, passion is being falsely repressed—by patriarchal ideals and norms of monogamy, by uptightness, and/or by the making of unnecessary distinctions between friends and lovers. These arguments ignore that passion is not a feeling that can be isolated from other circumstances in a woman's life. A woman must take time to examine her whole life context before exercising passion in certain ways. Passion occurs within the total environment of a woman's life. While it has an ecosystem of its own, it cannot survive outside a larger environment that comprehends connections.

This can take time and timing—an accurate assessment of the weather of the friendship over days, months, and even years. Time is necessary for an acquired wisdom about how to proceed in a passionate friendship. Time becomes a crucial factor in friendship because it conveys a practical wisdom, a prudence, if you will, about what form the friendship should take. It enables a certain thoughtfulness about the friendship, a circumspection that is careful to consider the circumstances and possible consequences of passion. It is an active and creative circumspection, however, that is not wasted in the traditional feminine ways of waiting. Rather, it engages in an arousal of friendship that is both sustaining and sustained by a thoughtful passion. It ultimately reveals how deep the passion runs.

Time provides the context for internal judgment to operate so that discernment in the midst of passion leads to meaningful choices in the friendship and not spent emotion. Where passion may leap to instantaneous union, the time that thought provides reminds us that we don't acquire friendship all at once. It is an ongoing process. Friendship needs to be sustained in and by time.

Friendship also requires the proper timing. Certain circumstances in a woman's life may militate against the forming of a passionate friendship. Friendship has its season. For one party in the friendship, the timing may be right; for another, it may be awry.

Passion is not a "static, inexplicable blob of feeling." It is a "movement rooted in knowledge."[42] At the root of passion is the knowledge and revelation of truth, the truth of one's real Self. In a hetero-relational context, women have lied about passion—with their bodies and their minds, in the first instance often feigning orgasm and in the latter often feigning stupidity. A promiscuity of passion is not the antidote to the lives of repressed passion that women have lived within the confines of hetero-relations. Passion must have truthful consequences. It cannot, as the definition of promiscuity states, be "undiscriminating," "without distinction or order," "done or applied without respect for kind, order, or number." Passion must not be casual or undiscerning. Women must not once again lie with our bodies or our minds, this time to women.

A passionate friendship calls for active, daring, and rigorous discernment. A thoughtful passion entails what Mary Daly has called "creative circumspection." Although she did not use the following words to describe a passionate friendship, they do indeed apply.

> The process is one of creative circumspection, and it becomes possible when a woman has chosen to know E-motionally, that is, to think and live in Fire. It becomes possible when, from this Pyrosophical vantage point, she strives to know outermost circumferences, the cosmic context of circumstances.[43]

Not every friendship, of course, will have the intense feeling of passion that I have described in this section. However, any kind of affection between women must be based on a more ecumenical feminist passion—the passion to move, stir, influence, and affect other women. To repeat, the essential meaning of Gyn/affection is that women affect, move, stir, and arouse each other to full power.

With some women, friendship will be accompanied by deep and thoughtful feeling. Women must then discern where that feeling will be directed. With other women, friendship will take the form of passionately working for women and of actualizing feminist vision.

The philosophers, beginning with Aristotle, maintained that friendship was possible only between equals. Equality is a problematic term, however, because it has such quantitative connotations. Its primary meaning is "measure, quantity, amount." To my way of thinking, it makes more sense to assess the possibilities of female friendship on the basis of another meaning of equality—"capable of meeting the requirements of a situation or task." In other words, are female friends "equal to the task"? What task? The task of building a creative and responsible friendship; the task of two sights-seeing; the task of building a woman-centered existence.

There are different ways of being "equal to the task," different modes in which passion can be manifested, and different kinds of friendship. Like female friendship itself, passion is on a continuum. A passion for women is exercised in multiple ways but is always "something in which a fundamental common character is discernible amid a series of insensible or indefinite variations."[44] Women who may not necessarily experience intense feeling for each other may share passionate commitments to women. Gyn/affection cannot flourish or be sustained without a passion for women which stirs the imagination, memory, thought, and/or feeling in some way. The passion of friendship runs deepest where the personal and political dimensions of affection are brought together and inhabit the same sphere. However, the passion of female friendship is essentially being "equal to the task" of a shared passion for women.

A shared passion for women enables women to live in the world as men have fabricated it while creating the world as women imagine it could be. Unless a woman has some love of the world, why should she seek to change it? The passion of female friendship fuels women's worldliness.

Worldliness

We come back to the question What is the world? What is the world about which women must be both realistic and far-seeing?

As I defined it in the preceding chapter, the world is the "sphere of public activity," where thought becomes concretized and action meaningful. It is "the affairs and conditions of life" or the "state of human affairs." Obviously, men have reserved this world for themselves. Even the word *world* is derived from *vir,* meaning man—thus the world has been defined literally as the "sphere of man." My claim in this chapter is that the sphere of public activity must be reclaimed and re-possessed by women.

A body of feminist literature talks about the world as the larger cosmos, "the system of created things," or as the universe—"the earth and all created things upon it." While I think it is extremely important to hold this worldview—patriarchy having fragmented the world into parts, emphasizing only that which man creates and sustains, a severed anthropocentric perspective—I think it is equally necessary for women not to abscind ourselves from the world of public affairs. I find a disturbing trend in feminist writing that is world-weary or even world-despising. That is, it views the "state of human affairs" and the "public sphere" as corrupt and irretrievably patriarchal. The result has often been to emphasize women's affinity only with the world of Nature. Of course, women must not lose sight of our connections with the world of Nature, or the cosmos, as patriarchy has. Much of my own work has been devoted to this imperative—what one might call an "eco-feminist" perspective. However, this emphasis should not be at the expense of avoiding the world of human affairs or of romanticizing the world of Nature, pitting the latter against the former or characterizing the world of public institutions and human artifacts as inherently patriarchal.

An excellent example of a woman whose love of the world was of both the world of Nature and the "sphere of human affairs" was Rachel Carson. Her writings come from her remarkable love of Nature while at the same time they emerge from a profound knowledge of the world of human affairs.

> Carson used science, out of love for Nature, as a means of protest and reform. She wrote science with a conscience. Breathing passion and poetry into her work, she "broke the dullness barrier of science writing." For both love of Nature and love of the world, she appealed to the world on behalf of Nature and ultimately on behalf of the world — a world that needs the sense of beauty, wonder, awe, and mystery, which Nature arouses. She was, finally, an enormously realistic woman about the power of industry and its lobbies in government.[45]

Carson's most famous work, *Silent Spring,* combines her dual love and knowledge of the world of human affairs and the world of Nature. In it she evokes the sense of Nature being utterly destroyed by the rapaciousness of man's use of pesticides, especially DDT. However, she documents extensively the scientific effects of pesticides while also displaying an immense knowledge of the ways in which the chemical companies collude with government to make their will prevail. She was the first to propose specific concrete measures about how these pesticides could be regulated, and it was because of her work, as Pat Hynes has documented, that the federal Environmental Protection Agency came into being.[46] All through *Silent Spring,* however, and in her books about the sea (*The Sea Around Us* and *The Edge of the Sea*) as well as in her work *The Sense of Wonder,* there is an "elemental" sense of the wonders of Nature. But because Carson writes out of a love of the world both as "the cosmos" and as "the sphere of human affairs," her work can best be described as conveying what Ynestra King has called a "rational reenchantment" with the world.[47] Carson did not retreat from scientific rationalism, but she invested it with its lost, erased, and philosophical depth. As Henry Beston said of her work, she blended "scientific knowledge with the spirit of poetic awareness."[48] The split between the world of Nature and the world of human activity is absent in her work.

The world is what women make of it. This point is crucial — we must make something of it. This presupposes some kind of location in the ordinary world of human affairs, much of which is male-created. Friendship provides a point of crystallization for living in the ordinary world, not the pretense for exiting from it. Friendship does not automatically convey the means of living in the world or of making women into world-builders, but it does provide a location in that world.

In addition to being a personal space, Gyn/affection is a political space, a female enclave created by conscious female effort in the world that men have fabricated. Precisely because friendship can be built where women appear to our Selves and each other, where there is finally an audience for female creation, and where Gyn/affection no longer needs to hide itself or be labeled abnormal, it is a profoundly political act. For it means not only the creation of a world within which a truly feminist life can be lived on the boundary of a man-made world but the construction of the world as women imagine it can be. Gyn/affection is the expanse where a woman can live *as a woman, among women, among men.*

This phrase may strike some as odd. However, it is meant to convey just what it says. When a woman lives as a woman, among women, among men, she at the same time questions the man-made world but does not dissociate from it, assimilate to it, or allow it to define her as a victim in it. She demands her place in it as a woman whose affinities are with women. She takes on the existence of what Mary Daly might refer to as "defiant deviant." Hannah Arendt might have named her a "conscious pariah," and Virginia Woolf would have probably welcomed her into the "Society of Outsiders." I prefer the term *inside outsider* because it helps to make clear the dual tension of women who see the man-made world for what it is and exist in it with worldly integrity, while at the same time seeing beyond it to something different. The term also highlights the reality of women who know that they can never really be insiders yet who recognize the liabilities of the dissociated outsider.

The inside outsider lives in the world with worldly integrity, weaving the strands of feminist wisdom into the texture of the world and paving the way for the entrance of women as women, that is, women on our own terms, into the world. As an inside outsider, a woman's work is characterized by the dual tension between her feminism and her worldliness. Her worldliness is dependent on her feminist vision, yet her feminist vision is actualized in her worldly location. Zora Neale Hurston's words eloquently characterize this tension.

> Ships at a distance have every man's wish on board. For some they come in with the tide. For others they sail forever on the horizon, never out of sight, never landing until the Watcher turns his eyes away in resignation, his dreams mocked to death by Time. That is the life of men.
> Now, women forget all those things they don't want to remember, and remember everything they don't want to forget. *The dream is the truth. Then they act* and do things accordingly. [Italics mine][49]

Female friendship grounds the inside outsider. Because of it, she can lead an existence that is not overwhelmed by the tension of living in the world as men have fabricated it, while working for a world that women imagine. Gyn/affection provides a context of rootedness from which she can orient herself to the world and beyond it, grasp reality and change it, experience history and make it. Worldlessness can be one effect of friendlessness. Deprived of the latter, women have no location among our Selves and thus no location in the world because we more readily lose confidence that we can create some meaning in this world when there is no one to confirm that meaning.

The condition of women who are forced to be for men is that they forget each other, and forget too quickly. Hetero-relations deprive women of a certain type of language characterized by an integrity of reactions, a simplicity of gestures, and an unaffected expression of feeling for each other. Women lose their original Selves and an original world of others like their Selves. This means the rupture of both a private and a public life. Women vanish from each other's sight and vanish from the world as women. Consequently, women's appearance in the world is staged only on men's terms. Sometimes this appearance is taken over completely by men, as when women's genius is absorbed by male creations. The credit due great women writers, philosophers, artists, musicians, scientists has often been usurped by their "bright" brothers, fathers, husbands, or professional collaborators. The case of Rosalind Franklin, whose DNA work was "absorbed" by James Watson and Maurice Wilkins, is but one example.[50] Instead, women are often given "credit" when their "bright boys" turn bad. How many mothers, for example, have been blamed for the perverts, rapists, and murderers of this world or, worse, blame themselves.

The practical question, however, is How and where do women participate in the world? The worldliness I am advocating is not necessarily that of joining the antinuclear movement, the state legislature, or any other such worldly activities on their own terms. The terms of such endeavors are rarely woman-defined or woman-oriented. If participation in such worldly activities, or in others, is to be engaged in with worldly integrity, this participation must be on our terms, not in an absolute sense but in a way that enables woman-identified women to work within these worlds with integrity and with the ability to effect change — in other words, to work as inside outsiders.

If integrity means "that from which nothing can be taken,"[51] women must learn a few lessons from the feminist political past. Historically, women have been the mainstays of the abolitionist movements, peace movements, and other movements for human rights and social justice worldwide. In all of these movements, the feminist question was rarely highlighted. As a result, women did not participate in such movements on our own terms, and a worldly integrity was lacking. There are, of course, exceptions to this, but I am speaking in general.

On a more particular level, it might be helpful to give some concrete examples of how a woman functions as an inside outsider. Or, in other words, how does a woman live and act with worldly integrity? There are individual women and women's groups explicitly dedicated to women's causes. They may work in organizations specifically devoted to battered women, to the feminist campaign against pornography, or in various service organizations that meet women's needs. Or, as individuals, they may defend women in court, institute legislation against rape or for equal pay, or dismantle discriminatory and oppressive structures in which many women live their domestic and work lives. They may edit feminist journals, provide woman-centered health care, and/or teach Women's Studies. All these types of feminist work have made a profound impact on the man-made world, changing, for example, the face of patriarchal legislation, health care, and learning, as well as creating more woman-centered and institutional structures.

As another example of women acting as inside outsiders, let us consider the antinuclear movement. Women have been prominent in the antinuclear movement for years. Helen Caldicott is probably the best-known woman in the U.S. movement, and she has spoken about women's place in the movement. Many of her statements, however, are directed to what she seems to perceive as woman's "natural" role as peacekeeper. All sorts of women's affinity groups have participated in antinuclear demonstrations. These groups, such as lesbian affinity groups, have formed separate enclaves within the wider coalition of groups against nuclearism. These affinity groups have been attempts to move within the larger movement on women's own terms. As such, they have enabled many women who are feminist and who are deeply concerned about the horrendous destructive potency of nuclear weapons and power to participate in such a movement.

What is often missing from women's participation in such movements is the articulation of connections, in the antinuclear case between militarism, nuclearism, and male bonding. The full threat of the militaristic nuclear mentality is the male bonding on which it is based and the fact that all sorts of death have not only been fabricated by men but depend on men's relationships with men — for example, the ways in which, within the system of homo-relations, men must prove their masculinity to other men.

Marxists have not been at all hesitant about demonstrating the role of capitalism in creating and upholding militarism and nuclear weapons. They have made this connection outside of specifically defined Marxist groups, working within the larger context of the antinuclear movement. Feminists must go further and show how, as Joan Sully has phrased it,

> male bonding is a fundamental source of militarism. Militarism also legitimates, protects, backs up, and enhances male bonding. They form a self-feeding cycle from male bonding to militarism and back again . . . To expect to have genuine disarmament while retaining male gender class rule is naive and absurd.[52]

As John Stoltenberg has pointed out, even when militarism is not being actualized in the "hot" or cold wars of the world, nuclear deterrence strategy is itself another form of male bonding.

> Nuclear armament is an extension of men's potency for sadism. Nuclear armament is the capability for the ultimate, masculinity-confirming fuck. It fills the imagination of those who have it and those who don't. And now the fact that more and more nations are obtaining that capability destabilizes homoerotic truces between nations.[53]

When women make explicit the connections between male bonding and militarism, between male bonding and disarmament strategies, women can enter in one important way the world of antinuclearism with worldly integrity and affect the reality that underlies the nuclear mentality and that sustains militarism. Th antinuclear movement claims to be a radical social and political movement. Feminists must test this by articulating the connections between male bonding and nuclearism where there is a claimed social context for doing so. I am not saying that radical movements are paragons of feminist consciousness or even that they are amenable to feminist direction. However, since such movements claim to be "different," women should test that proclaimed difference to see what feminist reality it will accommodate.

The world of men must be shown for what it is, that is, based and sustained in homo-relations. Homo-relations are such a pervasive part of the world as men have made it that only a female friendship that is political and actualized with worldly integrity in the world itself can call forth any genuine nonaggression pacts that do not subsume continued aggression against all women.

Many women would not choose the worldly activity of the antinuclear movement, nor would they choose to work in women's goups or on specifically defined feminist issues as a full-time job. However, day by day, they move in the job or professional world with a worldly integrity that is consistently woman-identified. Although not making explicit feminist statements or articulating feminist politics, such women help to dismantle the artifacts of the man-made world if they have a woman-centered consciousness about what they are doing. If they are college professors, for example, they are aware that they are not the usual instruments of humanist knowledge in a university structure where humanism has consistently meant male-centered thought. If they are scientists, they do not fabricate a destructive science and technology, nor do they promote research in which women bear the burden of its "side effects." Their work may not be accompanied by the articulation of how their work is connected to women or to feminism. However, they manifest their women-centeredness by the very kind of work they do and the consciousness of why they do it.

Of course, there are many women and some men who may also do humane and sensitive work in the world, yet they may not know why they do it beyond the vague feeling that it is the "right" thing to do. The kind of women I have described in the last three examples work in the world because they believe their work breaks the patterns of male bonding and establishes the power of women in a world that men have made and because they ultimately believe that the work they do needs to be done by and for women. As such, they are exemplars of one kind of feminist worldly integrity. As "exemplars" these women show other women that women's work can have consequences, that women can be active in the world, can make decisions that affect the course of the world, and are a force and power with which to be reckoned.

Andrea Dworkin has written, "Creative intelligence . . . demands its right to consequence . . . always it wants recognition, influence, or power; it is an accomplishing intelligence."[54] Women who work day by day in the world with worldly integrity are the living proof that feminist thought, feminist intelligence, has "consequences." Their work may not be the kind that is explicitly devoted to the teaching of Women's Studies, to the campaigns against rape or pornography, or to the writing of women's literature. However, it is work that clearly shows that women can master physical tasks, ideas, culture, and the wider world. It is an accomplishing work that has its creative roots in the world as women imagine it could be because it breaks women out of the world in which men have constricted women's power and work. It is work that is involved in the complexity of the world through direct experience of it. Worldly integrity meets the world on its own *turf*, but not on its own *terms*.

The dissociation, assimilation, and victimism that I spoke about in Chapter IV are false modes of being-in-the-world. All three encourage a worldlessness for women. A genuine worldliness, informed by worldly integrity, works creatively for women on some level.

In the final analysis, worldliness is a materializing of dual vision, of two sights-seeing. Liberation, if it requires "seeing with more than ordinary sight," also requires "seeing with ordinary sight." As vision radically upheaves the existent man-made world, it must at some point give rise to coherent groups, lasting structures, and patterns of worldly activity. As vision disturbs, it must also stabilize. The structures of women living in the world must also be built.

> It is a fact of social/political movements that radicalism does not sustain a movement. For a movement to endure, its broad base and widespread influence must be assured. But radicalism is *essential* for the life of a movement, as it will bring to it the most uncompromising critique of the abusive, exploitative power that the movement seeks to undermine and overcome. It is the presence of radical critique which assures us that the movement will not devolve to simple reform—that is, patchwork on an exploitative, corrupt, and ruthless power structure.[55]

Women must use this radicalism to re-fashion women's existence in the real world. However, without structure and stability, radicalism will be frantic, bursting with energy, but short-lived. In this process, we must keep the tension between movement and stasis. Feminist far-sighted vision is meaningless unless it is accompanied by near-sighted realism which gives it shape and staying power. It is also meaningless unless such dual vision can translate into happiness—a happiness in this world.

Happiness

There has not been much talk or writing about happiness in the women's movement. It is almost as if feminists expected that happiness could come about only in some future life, after the struggle is won and the revolution over. Malraux once noted that in the twentieth century, the so-called intellectuals found in revolution what many others formerly sought in eternal life; that is, the revolution "saves those that make it."

Many women have defined feminism only in political terms, accentuating struggle against male tyranny. They have failed to see that just as feminism is a politics of risk and resistance, it must hold out to women some promise of happiness now. Organized sisterhood against the conditions of female oppression and the feminist fight against all states of atrocities against women serve as a powerful bulwark against the forces and structures of patriarchy. However, a purely political feminism, emphasizing only conflict and resistance, bears too strong a resemblance to religious eschatologies (theologies of the future) that would have women believe that the true happiness is achievable only in some life to come.

What is happiness? We use the term today more in a psychological sense, that is, as a disposition, feeling, or state of being that a person experiences. Originally, however, the term had an ethical meaning. In its earliest philosophical usage, happiness was connected with moral purpose, with teleology. Happiness was found in the fulfillment of some activity, end, or goal of life. Aristotle reminds us that happiness is an activity of the mind, of contemplation. Combining these meanings, happiness has also been defined as the feeling that accompanies the activity of the whole self, or the feeling of self-realization. Along with this, happiness means the harmonious life itself.

My own definition of happiness is an amalgam and rephrasing of these meanings. On the one hand happiness, as I am describing it, is striving for the full use of one's powers. It is attained in fulfilling certain ends or purposes. On the other hand, one must experience happiness. Therefore, it is a state of existence which I think can best be summarized in Nadezhda Mandelstam's translation of the Russian word *zhiznera-dostny* as "life-glad." Literally, she means to be glad in/about/with life. To be "life-glad" adds a certain depth and substance to the word *happiness*. In short, then, happiness is striving for the full use of one's powers that make one "life-glad."

I do not mean to speak about happiness as if it is an all-or-nothing existence. For example, a woman can be happy in her work but unhappy at home. Happiness implies, however, that one is constantly seeking for the integrity of the Self and that it is a process. It is, as I said, a striving. But the more that endeavor is transformed into existence, the more one is "life-glad." It should not be, as Charlotte Brontë noted, a task. "No mockery in this world ever sounds to me so hollow as that of being told to cultivate happiness. What does such advice mean? Happiness is not a potato, to be planted in mould, and tilled with manure."[56]

Female friendship gives women the context in which to be "life-glad." It creates a private and public sphere where happiness can become a reality. It provides encouragement and environment for the full use of one's powers. And since the profession of friendship means that the one who befriends has a greater interest in her friend's happiness than in that of others in general, female friendship strives for the full use of the friend's powers.

Striving for the full use of one's powers means living life with a purposeful energy. There is a quest to experience life to its fullest. Women's powers have been severely diminished within the confines of hetero-relations. The means to the full use of one's powers have been conferred on men. Women have been prohibited from experiencing the intensity of a Self-directed life, so important to happiness. Woman's happiness has been viewed in relation to man's. It has been her job to make him and her children happy. The existence of women "alone," those who remain unattached to men, has been recognized only insofar as they have been judged *not happy* in this state. The very terms "old maid" and "spinster" connote unhappy, unfulfilled women. Within a hetero-relational worldview, a "lesbian" lives her life at "the well of loneliness" or, worse, at the edges of depravity and despair. Nuns have traditionally been portrayed as entering convents because they have been deprived of the "happy" company and care of men. A woman without a man, or without a hetero-relational context, is portrayed as unhappy—to which the happy feminist adage responds: "A woman without a man is like a fish without a bicycle." Loose women are "happily unmarried."

Female friendship is the "life-glad" testament that refutes the still prevalent hetero-relational lie that "loose women" are unhappy. It fosters the full use of a woman's powers. It makes women "life-glad" rather than life-sad. No "half-lives" here.

If we return to one of the earlier definitions of happiness as contemplation, then female friendship is, in a special sense, the activity of contemplating the female Self and others like her Self. This means taking sight seriously and returns us full circle to vision.

Taking Sight Seriously

The necessity for vision is the necessity for women to really see each other. The state of female atrocity presents one view of women—the specter of women who have been molded according to man's image of them. The state of female friendship presents another view of women—the vision of women who have seen their Selves, helped to create other women in their own Self-directed image, and have "seen that it was good." The centrality of sight here is no mere metaphor.

Women's gaze has historically been trained on men. Simone de Beauvoir writes how women's gaze has formed men. "It is especially when he is fixed by the gaze of other persons that he appears to himself as being one."[57] The importance of women's gaze in shaping the male ego has also been noted by Virginia Woolf in her famous words "Women have served all these centuries as looking-glasses possessing the magic and delicious power of reflecting the figure of man at twice its natural size."[58] Woolf goes further and associates the construction of various genres of male reality with the fixing of the female gaze on men.

> . . . mirrors are essential to all violent and heroic action. That is why Napoleon and Mussolini both insist so emphatically upon the inferiority of women, for if they were not inferior, they would cease to enlarge. That serves to explain in part the necessity that women so often are to men. And it serves to explain how restless they are under her criticism . . . For if she begins to tell the truth, the figure in the looking-glass shrinks; his fitness for life is diminished . . . *The looking-glass vision is of supreme importance because it charges the vitality; it stimulates the nervous system.* [Italics mine][59]

For men, then, it has been women's gaze that has endowed them with subjectivity. Of course men gaze at women or, to phrase it more accurately, stare or often leer at women. It is this stare that forms the man-made woman. Men's stare, however, objectifies women. It makes of her an object, not a subject.

The focused eye of the female beholder confers on men a sense of acting in and on the world. Women are taught to fixate on men. The eyes of women mold men because men have assured themselves of women's continued gaze.

Furthermore, in a world where women are primed to look at and to men, it is women's gaze that also fixes male bonding. Women have been cast in the role of eternal onlookers at the rituals of homo-relations. Homo-relations can remain strong only in a world where women are forced into the role of passive spectators of the things that men do with other men—the man-to-man stunts, feats, or other boy wonders whose potency is derived from the watchfulness of women. The spectacle of male bonding can be displayed only in the real or fantasized presence of women. The real bodies of women are raped, often in a "gang bang" context. Susan Brownmiller writes how "men in war tend to rape in groups in which they are anonymous and secure, and against the backdrop of an all-male army to which they have a strong male allegiance. In domestic group rape, male bonding is similarly operative."[60] Through interview data, Brownmiller documents how men arrested for group rape spoke of it as though "the sexual feeling in the . . . rape experience was largely a relationship between the boys rather than between any of the boys and the girl involved."[61] In addition, the real bodies of women in pornography, in their male fantasized positions, solidify male bonding in automobile garages, men's clubs, and among young boys who learn their sexuality not only through reading such porn but in concert with each other as they leer.

Women watching solidifies men acting. Men prove they are agents in this world only in contrast to the passivity of those who watch and are thus acted upon. Yet women who watch are never really passive. They are active in consolidating the spectacle of male bonding. Without women watching, male activity of any sort would be recognized for what it often is — passivity.

When women avert their eyes from men, men will have to see each other for what they really are. This may be the beginning of men's salvation or final self-destruction. More important, when women turn their eyes toward their Selves and other women, they put the world in perspective. The invisibility of women to each other has been the condition of women in a hetero-relational society and affects women's total loss of sensation for their Selves and other women. Women can choose their line of vision. Women can choose to see each other.

Female friendship takes our original sight of our Selves and each other seriously. It is always a dual vision that is exercised with tension, but also with thoughtfulness and passion. It gives women a world in which we can be truly happy. Anna-Natalia Malachowskaja, a Russian feminist now living in Austria, writes profoundly of what happens when women's gaze is directed toward their Selves and other women.

No, love is not blind, as they say: . . . The loving gaze does not idealize, on the contrary, it tears the covering of pseudo-reality . . . the loving gaze does not only see, it also creates, projects into daily life what it sees in moments of illumination . . . You form me through your gaze, under its rays *I can no longer remain as I was* . . . you have led me to the sunny side, where *growth is a matter of course.*[62]

Notes

Introduction

1. The phrase is Kate Clinton's. Her first album, entitled *Making Light,* can be obtained from Making Light Productions, P.O. Box 93, Cazenovia, NY 13035. Clinton defies the boundaries of hetero-relational humor and reclaims a true women's wit. She is not only a practitioner of humor but a theorist as well. See Kate Clinton, "Making Light: Another Dimension, Some Notes on Feminist Humor," *Trivia: A Journal of Ideas* 1 (Fall 1982): 37–42.

2. Lily Tomlin, *On Stage,* Arista Records (1977).

3. Olga Carlisle, "In Praise of Old Nantucket," *New York Times Magazine,* 8 August 1982, p. 28.

4. Douglas Johnson, "Managing the Great Man's Memory," review of *Adieux: A Farewell to Sartre,* by Simone de Beauvoir, in *New York Times Book Review,* 6 May 1984, p. 11.

5. Virginia Woolf, *A Room of One's Own* (New York: Harcourt, 1929), p. 88.

6. Daly uses this term in *Gyn/Ecology: The Metaethics of Radical Feminism* (Boston: Beacon, 1978) to indicate the way in which women have been deprived of our history and traditions and encouraged to forget by "patriarchal erasure of our tradition." As the female body has been dismembered, so too has women's memory of our heritage.

7. Again I use Mary Daly's device of capitalizing *Self* to distinguish between the man-made feminine self—"the imposed/internalized false 'self'" of women—and the authentic Self which women are re-creating.

8. Doris Faber, *The Life of Lorena Hickok, E.R.'s Friend* (New York: Morrow, 1980), esp. pp. 330–32.

9. Simone de Beauvoir, *The Second Sex,* trans. and ed. H. M. Parshley (New York: Bantam, 1952), p. 174.

10. Toni Morrison, "What the Black Woman Thinks About Women's Lib," *New York Times Magazine,* 22 August 1971, p. 63.

11. Alix Dobkin with Kay Gardner, "The Woman in Your Life Is You," recorded on *Lavender Jane Loves Women* (1975), Ladyslipper Music, Box 3124, Durham, NC 27705. Dobkin, one of the first feminist and lesbian singers to write and perform women's music, is one of the remnant of feminist musicians who still creates strong Gyn/affective lyrics with both a personal and political message.

12. Michael Walzer, *Radical Principles* (New York: Basic, 1980), p. 13.

13. Nancy Arnold, "Toward a Personal Feminist Theory" (paper in feminist theory, University of Massachusetts, 1983), p. 3.

14. Andrea Dworkin, *Pornography: Men Possessing Women* (New York: Perigee, 1981), p. 61.

15. Daly, *Gyn/Ecology,* p. 63.

16. Mary Catherine Bateson, *With a Daughter's Eye: A Memoir of Margaret Mead and Gregory Bateson* (New York: Morrow, 1984), p. 34.

17. I have often asked students in my Women and Health Issues courses how many of them would want their mothers present if they chose to give birth. Very few students answer in the affirmative.

18. De Beauvoir, *Second Sex,* p. 65.

19. De Beauvoir, *Second Sex,* p. xvi, quoting Benda, *Rapport d'Uriel.*

20. Alice Walker uses this word in a variety of ways. In its primary meaning, she applies it to black women, "usually referring to outrageous, audacious, courageous or *willful* behavior . . . In charge. *Serious.*" In its secondary sense, Walker defines "womanist" as "a woman who loves other women, sexually and/or nonsexually. Appreciates and prefers women's culture, women's emotional flexibility . . . and women's strength." *In Search of Our Mothers' Gardens: Womanist Prose* (New York: Harcourt, 1983), pp. xi–xii.

21. I use the capital letter *L* to indicate, as Mary Daly has pointed out, the difference between woman-identified Lesbians and those lesbians (indicated by a small *l*) who, although they relate genitally to women, are governed by what I call hetero-relational standards.

22. Barbara Smith, "Toward a Black Feminist Criticism," *Conditions* 2 (1977): 33.

23. Adrienne Rich, "Compulsory Heterosexuality and Lesbian Existence," *Signs: Journal of Women in Culture and Society* 5 (1980): 648.

24. Rich, "Compulsory Heterosexuality," p. 648.

25. Blanche Wiesen Cook, "Female Support Networks and Political Activism: Lillian Wald, Crystal Eastman, Emma Goldman," *Chrysalis* 3 (Spring 1978): 48.

26. Several years ago, I devised the phrase *Lesbian continuum* to illustrate the woman-identified relationships that Rich, Smith and Cook describe. In my view at that time, friendship that was on a Lesbian continuum was imbued with Lesbian meaning, as characterized by the above writers. Now, however, I would prefer to use *Gyn/affection* and think that it more adequately describes all of the complexities involved.

27. Conversation, June 1981.

28. Conversation with Pat Hynes, Gloucester, Mass., March 1981.

29. The work of Michel Foucault has been helpful in elucidating just what genealogy is and does. However, much of Foucault's philosophy of history is rooted in a "philosophized" pornographic world view. I discuss at length in Chapter I Foucault's disdain for women that is present, *sub rosa,* in his theories of language and history and not so hidden in his adulation of Sade and Bataille.

30. Dale Spender, *Women of Ideas and What Men Have Done to Them* (London: Routledge, 1982), p. 14.

31. The word is used in Michel Foucault, *Language, Counter-Memory, Practice: Selected Essays and Interviews,* ed. Donald F. Bouchard and Sherry Simon, trans. Donald F. Bouchard (Ithaca, N.Y.: Cornell University Press, 1977).

32. Foucault, *Language,* p. 139.

33. Vera Brittain, *Testament of Friendship: The Story of Winifred Holtby* (London: Macmillan, 1947), p. 2.

34. Elizabeth Gould Davis, *The First Sex* (Baltimore: Penguin, 1971), p. 240.

35. See Robin Morgan, ed., *Sisterhood Is Global* (New York: Anchor, 1984).

I. The Origins of Female Friendship: In The Beginning Was Woman

1. Emile Durkheim, *The Division of Labor in Society,* trans. George Simpson (New York: Free Press, 1933), p. 61.

2. Otto Weininger, *Sex and Character* (New York: Putnam, 1975), p. 299.

3. Paula Giddings, *When and Where I Enter: The Impact of Black Women on Race and Sex in America* (New York: Morrow, 1984), p. 108.

4. Giddings, *When and Where,* p. 109.

5. Giddings, *When and Where,* p. 111.

6. With thanks to Pat Hynes, who first drew my attention to this female pattern of "professional lineage."

7. See Margaret Rossiter, *Women Scientists in America: Struggles and Strategies to 1940* (Baltimore: Johns Hopkins University Press, 1984), pp. 18–22. Rossiter gives excessive visibility and significance to married women scientists despite the fact that her statistics show that a small fraction of women scientists were married in the period of her investigation. One would have expected her to focus on the majority—for once single women. Important questions to be asked might have been What were the strategies such women used to survive and succeed professionally? With whom did they collaborate? With whom did they retire? Did they have female colleagues, friends, and/or lovers who affected their professional lives? Instead, Rossiter devotes pages and statistical tables to documenting who married whom of the small percent that were married and what sciences had what percent of the female faculty who were married. In a table entitled "Notable Couples in Science before 1940," Rossiter lists the married couples by the wife's field of science. It is ironic to see Ruth Benedict and Margaret Mead listed with their respective husband scientists, *but not with each other,* a relationship that certainly lasted longer than Benedict's marriage to Stanley Benedict and even outlasted the total years of Mead's three marriages. Rossiter's book does predate the 1984 biographies of Mead written by Mary Catherine Bateson and Jane Howard, but certainly this information was known by many before the actual publication of these two works and could have been

investigated with the careful and considered attention that Rossiter gives to the married scientists' relationships. See esp. pp. 141–43.

8. See Edward Hyams, *Soil and Civilization* (New York: Harper Colophon, 1976), esp. pp. 210–12.

9. See, for example, Robert Briffault, *The Mothers: A Study of the Origins of Sentiments and Institutions*, 3 vols. (New York: Macmillan, 1927); and Lewis Henry Morgan, *Ancient Society* (New York: World, 1963).

10. See H. J. Mozans, *Woman in Science* (Cambridge: MIT Press, 1974), esp. chaps. 1–9.

11. Mozans, *Woman in Science*, chap. 10.

12. Raymond Williams, "Culture and Civilization," *The Encyclopedia of Philosophy* (reprint, New York: Macmillan—The Free Press, 1972) 2: 273.

13. Women's culture has not been valued or extolled as have many ethnic and racial cultural traditions. Recent feminist attempts to do so have often met with the demeaning of what has come to be called "cultural feminism."

14. Debra Seidman, "The Voices of Women Surviving: The Holocaust, Women and Resistance" (Division III thesis, Hampshire College, 1982), p. 87.

15. Seidman, "Voices," p. 96.

16. Seidman, "Voices," p. 89.

17. Seidman, "Voices," p. 86.

18. Seidman, "Voices," pp. 71–72.

19. Seidman, "Voices," pp. 102–3.

20. Seidman, "Voices," pp. 103–4.

21. Alice Walker, *The Color Purple* (New York: Harcourt, 1982), p. 5.

22. Walker, *The Color Purple*, p. 9.

23. Walker, *The Color Purple*, p. 108.

24. Conversation with Anne Dellenbaugh, Gloucester, Mass., October 1980.

25. See Carroll Smith-Rosenberg, "The Female World of Love and Ritual: Relations Between Women in Nineteenth Century America," *Signs: Journal of Women in Culture and Society* 1 (Autumn 1975): 1–29.

26. Toni Morrison, *Sula* (New York: Knopf, 1974), p. 195.

27. Morrison, *Sula*, p. 174.

28. See Nina Auerbach, *Communities of Women: An Idea in Fiction* (Cambridge: Harvard University Press, 1978), p. 63.

29. See Michel Foucault, *The Archaeology of Knowledge*, trans. A. M. Sheridan Smith (New York: Harper, 1972); and *Language*.

30. Dale Spender, *Women of Ideas and What Men Have Done to Them* (London: Routledge, 1982), p. 12.

31. Conversation with Pat Hynes, Gloucester, Mass., November 1980.

32. Foucault, *Language*, p. 171.

33. Foucault, *Language*, pp. 60–61.

34. Foucault, *Language*, p. 33.

35. Andrea Dworkin, *Pornography: Men Possessing Women* (New York: Perigee, 1981), p. 70.

36. Foucault, *Language*, p. 45.

37. Foucault, *Language,* p. 45.
38. Sigmund Freud, "Some Psychological Consequences of the Anatomical Distinctions Between the Sexes," *Collected Papers* 5:190.
39. Freud, "Some Psychological Consequences," p. 193.
40. Freud, "On the Sexual Theories of Children," *Collected Papers* 2:67.
41. Freud, "The Transformations of Puberty," *Collected Papers,* 613.
42. Dorothy Dinnerstein, *The Mermaid and the Minotaur* (New York: Harper, 1976), p. 44.
43. Dinnerstein, *Mermaid,* p. 46.
44. Dinnerstein, *Mermaid,* p. 65.
45. Dinnerstein, *Mermaid,* p. 225.
46. Helene Deutsch, *The Psychology of Women,* quoted in Nancy Chodorow, *The Reproduction of Mothering* (Berkeley: University of California Press, 1978), p. 191.
47. Chodorow, *Reproduction,* p. 193.
48. Chodorow, *Reproduction,* p. 140.
49. Chodorow, *Reproduction,* p. 140.
50. Chodorow interprets Freud on this subject. Citing his essay "Female Sexuality" (1931), she says: "Freud speaks to the way women seek to recapture their relationship with their mother in heterosexual relationships. He suggests that as women 'change object' from mother to father, the mother remains their primary internal object, so that they often impose on their relation to their father, and later to men, the issues which preoccupy them in their internal relation to their mother. They look in relations to men for gratifications that they want from a woman." *Reproduction,* pp. 194–95.
51. Chodorow, *Reproduction,* p. 195.
52. Chodorow, *Reproduction,* p. 195. Carrying this point further, one might ask how many women do really know the men they supposedly love. This lack of real knowledge is thrown into bolder relief by de Beauvoir's remarks about the insincerity of what I call hetero-relations: "Man and woman—even husband and wife—are in some degree playing a part before one another, and in particular woman, upon whom the male always imposes some requirement; virtue beyond suspicion, charm, coquettishness, childishness, or austerity. Never in the presence of husband or lover can she feel wholly herself." Simone de Beauvoir, *The Second Sex,* trans. and ed. H. M. Parshley (New York: Bantam, 1952), p. 394.
53. Chodorow, *Reproduction,* p. 198.
54. Chodorow, *Reproduction,* p. 197.
55. Dworkin, *Pornography,* p. 151.
56. Chodorow, *Reproduction,* p. 200.
57. Chodorow, *Reproduction,* p. 200.
58. Adrienne Rich, "Compulsory Heterosexuality and Lesbian Existence," *Signs: Journal of Women in Culture and Society* 5 (1980): 648.
59. Chodorow, *Reproduction,* pp. 203–4.
60. Chodorow, *Reproduction,* p. 208.

61. Chodorow, *Reproduction,* p. 218.

62. Dinnerstein, *Mermaid,* pp. 148–49.

63. Given the fact that many men have no idea of or training for consistent and responsible parenting, women, having been enjoined to relinquish the primary mothering of children, may now find that they will have to "mother" men into male mothering.

64. I use the words *visible* and *immediate* purposefully. Mothers, while being the visible and immediate conduits of hetero-relations, are not the primary conduits. Chodorow notes: ".... from both psychoanalytic clinical reports and from social psychological research,... fathers generally sex-type their children more consciously than mothers along traditional gender-role lines and... they encourage feminine heterosexual behavior in young daughters." *Reproduction,* p. 118. However, fathers' encouragement of hetero-relations is frequently less visible than mothers' because the former are most often the distant and invisible parent.

65. De Beauvoir, *Second Sex,* p. 360.

66. Duncan as quoted in de Beauvoir, *Second Sex,* p. 360.

67. De Beauvoir, *Second Sex,* p. 360.

68. Bruno Bettelheim, *The Uses of Enchantment* (New York: Knopf, 1976), p. 219.

69. Phyllis Chesler, *Women and Madness* (New York: Doubleday, 1972), pp. 46–47.

70. Shere Hite, *The Hite Report: A Nationwide Study of Female Sexuality* (New York: Dell, 1981).

71. "60,000 Women Tell Ann Landers Sex Is Not Fulfilling," *Greenfield Recorder,* 15 January 1985, p. 1.

72. "60,000 Women," p. 12. Of course, the "experts" responded by saying that the Landers poll was "dangerous," "misleading," and "threatened to take us back to the Victorian age." See "Sex Experts: Landers Reader Poll Dangerous," *Greenfield Recorder,* 16 January 1985, p. 8.

73. I am not advocating the development or use of these technologies. Indeed, elsewhere in my published and activist work, I have opposed their use and development. Rather, I am challenging the "naturalness" or biologism of the so-called natural reproductive argument which, I contend, is refuted by the existence of the technologies.

74. Dworkin, *Pornography,* p. 187.

75. Barbara Deming, *We Cannot Live Without Our Lives* (New York: Grossman, 1974), p. 55.

76. Deming, *We Cannot Live,* p. 57.

77. Charlotte Brontë, Introduction, *The Poems of Emily Jane Brontë and Anne Brontë,* ed. Thomas J. Wise and J. Alex Symington (Oxford: Shakespeare Head, 1934), p. xxii.

78. Charlotte Brontë, "Biographical Notice of Ellis and Acton Bell," Emily Brontë, *Wuthering Heights: An Authoritative Text with Essays in Criticism,* ed. William M. Sale, Jr. (New York: Norton, 1963), p. 7.

79. De Beauvoir, *Second Sex,* p. 144.

80. Mary Catherine Bateson, *With a Daughter's Eye: A Memoir of Margaret Mead and Gregory Bateson* (New York: Morrow, 1984), p. 102.

81. Barbara Macdonald with Cynthia Rich, *Look Me in the Eye: Old Women, Aging and Ageism* (San Francisco: Spinsters Ink, 1984), p. 19.

82. Lillian Faderman, *Surpassing the Love of Men: Romantic Friendship and Love Between Women from the Renaissance to the Present* (New York: Morrow, 1981), p. 351.

83. Cited in Kathleen Barry, "The Network Defines Its Issues: Theory, Evidence and Analysis of Female Sexual Slavery," in *International Feminism: Networking Against Female Sexual Slavery,* ed. Kathleen Barry, Charlotte Bunch, and Shirley Castley (New York: International Women's Tribune Centre, 1984), p. 48.

84. K. J. Dover, *Greek Homosexuality,* (New York: Vintage, 1978), p. 20, n. 2.

85. Dover, *Greek Homosexuality,* p. 172.

86. Dover, *Greek Homosexuality,* p. 172.

87. Dover, *Greek Homosexuality,* p. 172.

88. Demosthenes, as quoted in Dolores Klaich, *Woman + Woman: Attitudes Toward Lesbianism* (New York: Morrow, 1979), pp. 130–31.

89. Klaich, *Woman + Woman,* p. 133.

90. Klaich, *Woman + Woman,* p. 133.

91. Dover, *Greek Homosexuality,* pp. 183–84.

92. Quoted in Klaich, *Woman + Woman,* p. 134.

93. Klaich, *Woman + Woman,* p. 134.

94. De Beauvoir, p. 178.

95. Havelock Ellis and John Addington Symonds, *Sexual Inversion* (1897; reprint, New York: Arno, 1975), p. 101.

96. The motives for such studies by men are apparent in Frank Caprio's work *Female Homosexuality: A Psychological Study of Lesbianism* (New York: Citadel, 1954). "We need less moral condemnation and greater scientific understanding of human frailties . . . We need to become sexwise. Knowledge is power. *We develop greater power only by attempting to understand that which needs to be controlled."* [Italics mine], p. 93.

97. Harold Greenwald, *The Call Girl: A Social and Psychoanalytic Study* (New York: Ballantine, 1958), p. 134.

98. Greenwald, *Call Girl,* p. 134.

99. Caprio, *Female Homosexuality,* Introduction.

100. Socrates, as quoted in Fernando Henriques, *Prostitution and Society* (New York: Citadel, 1962), p. 23.

101. Sozomen, as quoted in Henriques, *Prostitution,* p. 23.

102. Mary Daly, in *Gyn/Ecology: The Metaethics of Radical Feminism,* used the term "loose women" in defining *Gyn/Ecology* as "the process of know-ing, of 'loose' women who choose to be subjects and not mere objects of enquiry . . . That is, it is about dis-covering, de-veloping the complex web of living/loving relationships *of our own kind"* (pp. 10–11).

II. *Varieties of Female Friendship: The Nun as Loose Woman*

1. Letter of Martin Luther, 6 August 1524, quoted in Julia O'Faolain and Laura Martines, eds., *Not in God's Image: Women in History from the Greeks to the Victorians* (New York: Harper, 1973), p. 196.

2. Lina Eckenstein, *Women Under Monasticism* (1896; reprint, New York: Russell & Russell, 1963), p. 3. This has been an invaluable source. It is an extensive history of nuns and convents from A.D. 500 to 1500, and much of it is quite originally written.

3. Eileen Power, "The Position of Women," in *Women: From the Greeks to the French Revolution,* ed. Susan Groag Bell (Stanford: Stanford University Press, 1973), p. 168.

4. Eckenstein, *Women Under Monasticism,* p. 4.

5. Marcia Guttentag and Paul F. Secord, *Too Many Women? The Sex Ratio Question* (Beverly Hills, Calif.: Sage, 1983), p. 65.

6. Guttentag and Secord, *Too Many Women?,* p. 66.

7. I visited the Beguinages of Bruges in April 1984. These dwellings are elegant in their simple construction and obviously built with the right mixture of privacy and community in mind. They form a distinct section of the town of Bruges.

8. Dayton Phillips, *Beguines in Medieval Strasbourg: A Study of the Social Aspect of Beguine Life* (Stanford: Stanford University Press, 1941), p. 227.

9. Quoted in Rufus M. Jones, *Studies in Mystical Religion* (London: Macmillan, 1909), p. 197.

10. R. W. Southern, *Western Society and the Church in the Middle Ages* (Baltimore: Penguin, 1970), p. 321.

11. Southern, *Western Society,* pp. 328–29.

12. Southern, *Western Society,* p. 329.

13. Jones, *Studies in Mystical Religion,* p. 207.

14. Eckenstein, *Women Under Monasticism,* p. 5.

15. Cited in Eckenstein, *Women Under Monasticism,* pp. 32–33.

16. Eckenstein, *Women Under Monasticism,* p. 32.

17. Kenneth Scott Latourette, *The Thousand Years of Uncertainty,* vol. 2 in *A History of Christianity* (New York: Harper, 1938), p. 397.

18. Latourette, *Thousand Years,* p. 365.

19. Guttentag and Secord, *Too Many Women?,* p. 70.

20. Sara Maitland, *A Map of the New Country: Women and Christianity* (London: Routledge, 1983), p. 49.

21. Havelock Ellis and John Addington Symonds, *Sexual Inversion* (1897; reprint, New York: Arno, 1975), p. 101.

22. Edmond and Jules de Goncourt, *The Woman of the Eighteenth Century,* trans. Jacques Le Clercq and Ralph Roeder (New York: Minton, Balch, 1927), pp. 10–11.

23. Guttentag and Secord, *Too Many Women?,* p. 58.

24. John McNeill, *Makers of Christianity* (New York: Holt, 1935), p. 72.

25. Guttentag and Secord, *Too Many Women?*, p. 63.

26. Guttentag and Secord, *Too Many Women?*, p. 64.

27. Eckenstein, *Women Under Monasticism*, p. 478.

28. Guttentag and Secord, *Too Many Women?*, p. 61.

29. Guttentag and Secord, *Too Many Women?*, p. 63.

30. Eckenstein, *Women Under Monasticism*, p. 165.

31. Eckenstein, *Women Under Monasticism*, p. 161.

32. Quoted in Eckenstein, *Women Under Monasticism*, p. 224.

33. Mary Daly, *Gyn/Ecology: The Metaethics of Radical Feminism* (Boston: Beacon, 1978), pp. 3–4.

34. Louise Seymour Houghton, "Women's Work in the Church," in *The New Schaff-Herzog Encyclopedia of Religious Knowledge* (1912) 12:415.

35. Eleanor Commo McLaughlin, "Equality of Souls, Inequality of Sexes: Woman in Medieval Theology," in *Religion and Sexism: Images of Woman in the Jewish and Christian Traditions,* ed. Rosemary Radford Ruether (New York: Simon and Schuster, 1974), p. 237.

36. McLaughlin, "Equality of Souls," p. 237.

37. Houghton, "Women's Work," pp. 416.

38. Pie de Langogne, "Abbesses," in *Dictionnaire de Théologie Catholique* (1909), Tome Premier 21, originally translated by Janice G. Raymond for "The Effects of Patriarchy upon Roman Catholic Religious Communities of Women: An Alternative" (M.A. thesis, Andover Newton Theological School, Newton, Mass., 1971), p. 55.

39. De Langogne, "Abbesses," p. 55.

40. Houghton, "Women's Work," p. 416.

41. Elsie Thomas Culver, *Women in the World of Religion* (New York: Doubleday, 1967), p. 87.

42. Douglass Roby, Introduction in Aelred of Rievaulx, *Spiritual Friendship,* trans. Mary Eugenia Laker, S.S.N.D. (Kalamazoo, Mich.: Cistercian Publications, 1977), p. 37.

43. Roby, Introduction, p. 38.

44. Jean Leclercq, *The Love of Learning and the Desire for God: A Study of Monastic Culture,* trans. Catharine Misrahi (New York: Fordham University Press, 1961), p. 106.

45. Aelred, *Spiritual Friendship,* p. 72.

46. Aelred, *Spiritual Friendship,* p. 93.

47. Aelred, *Spiritual Friendship,* p. 95.

48. Aelred, *Spiritual Frienship,* p. 92.

49. Aelred, *Spiritual Friendship,* p. 84.

50. R. W. Southern, *Saint Anselm and His Biographer: A Study of Monastic Life and Thought 1059–c. 1130* (Cambridge: Cambridge University Press, 1963), p. 69.

51. Anselm, quoted in Southern, *Saint Anselm,* p. 72.

52. Southern, *Saint Anselm,* p. 70.

53. Lillian Faderman, *Surpassing the Love of Men: Romantic Friendship and Love Between Women from the Renaissance to the Present* (New York: Morrow, 1981), p. 84.

54. Roby, Introduction, pp. 21–22.

55. Sisters of Mercy, *Constitutions of the Institute of the Religious Sisters of Mercy of the Union in the United States of America* (Bethesda: General Motherhouse, 1955), p. 64.

56. Teresa of Avila, *Way of Perfection*, vol. 2 in *The Complete Works of Saint Teresa of Jesus,* ed. E. Allison Peers (New York: Sheed & Ward, 1946), p. 18.

57. Teresa of Avila, *Way of Perfection,* pp. 30–31.

58. Sisters of Mercy, *Customs and Guide of the Institute of the Religious Sisters of Mercy of the Union in the United States of America* (Bethesda: General Motherhouse, 1957), p. 226.

59. Teresa of Avila, *Way of Perfection,* p. 17.

60. Sisters of Mercy, *Constitutions,* p. 40, no. 108.

61. Suzanne Campbell-Jones, *In Habit: A Study of Working Nuns* (New York: Pantheon, 1978), p. 86.

62. Derwas J. Chitty, *The Desert a City: An Introduction to the Study of Egyptian and Palestinian Monasticism Under the Christian Empire* (Oxford: Basil Blackwell, 1966), p. 66.

63. Chitty, *The Desert a City,* p. 66.

64. Roby, Introduction, p. 17.

65. McLaughlin, "Equality of Souls," pp. 252–53.

66. M. Basil Pennington, "Aelred in the Tradition of Monastic Friendship," in Aelred of Rievaulx, *Spiritual Friendship,* trans. Mary Eugenia Laker, S.S.N.D. (Kalamazoo, Mich.: Cistercian Publications, 1977), p. 40.

67. Erasmus, *Colloquies,* trans. Craig R. Thompson (Chicago: The University of Chicago Press, 1965).

68. Vita Sackville-West, *The Eagle and the Dove* (New York: Doubleday, Doran, 1944), p. 19.

69. Teresa of Avila, *Way of Perfection,* p. 31.

70. Jane F. Becker, "Overcoming Problems in Friendship," *Sisters Today* 49 (May 1978): 605.

71. Becker, "Overcoming Problems," p. 603.

72. Becker, "Overcoming Problems," p. 603.

73. Becker, "Overcoming Problems," p. 604.

74. Becker, "Overcoming Problems," p. 604.

75. Becker, "Overcoming Problems," p. 605.

76. John Calvin, *Opera,* 15:92, 125. In this opinion, Calvin joined with his ardent disciple John Knox.

77. See, for example, Southern, *Western Society,* pp. 310–18.

78. Eckenstein, *Women Under Monasticism,* p. 193.

79. Eckenstein, *Women Under Monasticism,* p. 193.

80. Eckenstein, *Women Under Monasticism,* p. 198.

81. Houghton, "Women's Work," p. 416.

82. Conversation with Pat Hynes, Gloucester, Mass., May 1981.

83. Eckenstein, *Women Under Monasticism,* p. 202.

84. Eckenstein, *Women Under Monasticism,* p. 202.

85. Quoted in Fernando Henriques, *Prostitution in Europe and the Americas* (New York: Citadel, 1968), p. 38.

86. Cited in Eckenstein, *Women Under Monasticism,* p. 200.

87. Faderman, *Surpassing the Love of Men,* p. 333.

88. Houghton, "Women's Work," pp. 416-17.

89. John Calvin, *Opera* 28:149. Ser. on Deut. 24:1-4.

90. Houghton, "Women's Work," p. 417.

91. Cited in Henriques, *Prostitution,* p. 38.

92. Quoted in Henriques, *Prostitution,* p. 37.

93. Eckenstein, *Women Under Monasticism,* p. 433.

94. Eckenstein, *Women Under Monasticism,* p. 434.

95. Quoted in Eckenstein, *Women Under Monasticism,* p. 468.

96. Geoffrey Baskerville, *English Monks and the Suppression of the Monasteries* (New Haven: Yale University Press, 1937), p. 217.

97. Eckenstein, *Women Under Monasticism,* p. 452.

98. Quoted in Eckenstein, *Women Under Monasticism,* p. 468.

99. Eckenstein, *Women Under Monasticism,* pp. 473-74.

100. The Protestant Truth Society, "The Ruin of Girls in Convent Schools," inside cover, n. d.

101. Eckenstein, *Women Under Monasticism,* p. 483.

102. Maitland, *Map of the New Country,* p. 56.

103. "Convent Values Transformed into Lesbian Ethics: Conversation with H. Patricia Hynes and Janice Raymond," in *Lesbian Nuns: Breaking Silence,* ed. Rosemary Curb and Nancy Manahan (Tallahassee, Fl.: Naiad, 1985), pp. 351-52.

104. "Convent Values," p. 352.

105. Hester Brown, "Get Thee to the Mother House," *Heresies: A Feminist Publication of Art and Politics* 2 (Spring 1979): 78.

106. Kathleen Barry, *Female Sexual Slavery* (Englewood Cliffs, N.J.: Prentice-Hall, 1979), p. 227.

107. Barry, *Female Sexual Slavery,* p. 227.

108. Audre Lorde, "Uses of the Erotic: The Erotic as Power," in *Sister Outsider* (Trumansburg, N.Y.: Crossing, 1984), p. 54.

109. Ortega y Gasset, quoted in Robert A. Nisbet, *Community and Power* (London: Oxford University Press, 1953), p. 61.

110. Lucinda San Giovanni, *Ex-Nuns: A Study of Emergent Role Passage* (Norwood, N.J.: Ablex, 1978), p. 101.

111. "Convent Values," p. 354.

112. "Convent Values," pp. 354-55.

III. More Loose Women: The Chinese Marriage Resisters

1. Leila Ahmed, "Western Ethnocentrism and Perceptions of the Harem," *Feminist Studies* 8, no. 3 (Fall 1982): 524.
2. Susan Mann, "Suicide and Chastity: Visible Themes in the History of Chinese Women" (Paper presented at the Sixth Berkshire Conference on the History of Women, Smith College, Northampton, Mass., 1984), pp. 4–5, citing the work of Margery Wolf, *Women and the Family in Rural Taiwan* (Stanford: Stanford University Press, 1972).
3. Marjorie Topley, "The Organisation and Social Function of Chinese Women's *Chai T'ang* in Singapore" (Ph.D. diss., University of London, 1958), p. 161. Without Topley's ground-breaking work on marriage resistance, this chapter could not have been written.
4. Francis L. K. Hsu, *Under the Ancestor's Shadow* (New York: Columbia University, 1948), p. 2.
5. E. A. Wrigley, *Population and History* (New York: McGraw-Hill, 1969), p. 90.
6. Maxine Hong Kingston, *The Woman Warrior: Memoirs of a Girlhood Among Ghosts* (New York: Vintage, 1975), pp. 54–55.
7. Hong Kingston, *Woman Warrior*, p. 56.
8. Su Hua Ling Chen, *Ancient Melodies*, with an introduction by Vita Sackville-West (London: Hogarth, 1969), p. 201. Sometime during 1938–39, Su Hua began correspondence with Virginia Woolf. She sought Woolf's advice about writing and also about books to read in English. Woolf sent her many books and wrote her several letters giving writing counsel. In time, Su Hua sent Woolf a manuscript, and Woolf wrote back: "Please go on; write freely; do not mind how directly you translate the Chinese into English. In fact, I would advise you to come as close to the Chinese both in style and in meaning as you can. Give as many natural details of life, of the house, of furniture, as you like. And always do it as you would were you writing for the Chinese" (p. 8). Su Hua arrived in London in 1947, wrote to Vita Sackville-West by chance, not knowing that she and Woolf had been friends, and asked Sackville-West to write the introduction to her book, which the Hogarth Press had agreed to publish. In *Ancient Melodies*, as Vita Sackville-West wrote in her introduction, Su Hua brings "with her the flavour of a forgotten world in which the desire for the good life of peaceable contemplation and exquisite thoughts was axiomatic." *Ancient Melodies* is one of the earliest northwestern records we have of a woman's impressions of her own culture whose publication was made possible by other women.
9. Arthur Smith, *Village Life in China: A Study in Sociology* (New York: Revell, 1899), p. 287.
10. Hong Kingston, *Woman Warrior*, p. 35.
11. Hong Kingston, *Woman Warrior*, p. 23.
12. Hong Kingston, *Woman Warrior*, p. 24.

13. I thank Charlotte Boynton for bringing this popular culture to my attention.

14. Elisabeth Croll, *Feminism and Socialism in China* (London: Routledge, 1978), p. 39.

15. Croll, *Feminism and Socialism*, p. 40

16. Croll, *Feminism and Socialism*, p. 64.

17. Croll, *Feminism and Socialism*, p. 66.

18. Quoted in Croll, *Feminism and Socialism*, pp. 68–69.

19. Croll, *Feminism and Socialism*, p. 69.

20. Ch'iu Chin, "To the Tune 'The River Is Red,'" in *The Orchid Boat: Women Poets of China*, trans. and ed. Kenneth Rexroth and Ling Chung (New York: Seabury, 1972), p. 83. New edition (Newton, N.J.: New Directions Press, 1982).

21. Ch'iu Chin, "Two Poems to the Tune 'Narcissus by the River,'" in *Orchid Boat*, p. 82.

22. Cited in Robert K. Douglas, *Society in China* (London: Innes, 1894), p. 215.

23. Maria H. A. Jaschok, "On the Lives of Women Unwed by Choice in Pre-Communist China: Research in Progress," *Republican China* (Fall 1984): 42–43.

24. Jaschok, "On the Lives of Women," p. 43.

25. Cited in Topley, "Organisation and Social Function," p. 177.

26. Quoted in Marjorie Topley, "Marriage Resistance in Rural Kwangtung," in *Women in Chinese Society*, ed. Margery Wolf and Roxane Witke (Stanford: Stanford University Press, 1975), p. 75.

27. Topley, "Marriage Resistance," p. 75.

28. Benjamin Henry, *Ling-Nam: or, Interior Views of Southern China* (London, 1886), p. 68.

29. Topley, "Organisation and Social Function," p. 179.

30. Susan Mann in "Suicide and Chastity: Visible Themes in the History of Chinese Women" writes that the " 'local gazetteers' (*difang zhi*) . . . are really semi-official histories of counties throughout the Chinese empire . . . gazetteer staff writers presented material on 'local customs,'. . . women appear in chapters entitled 'Exemplary Women,' under two main headings: 'faithful widows' (*jiefu*) and 'chaste maidens' (*zhengnu*)" (p. 6). Evidently, gazetteers included ceremonials of sworn sisters under the heading "chaste maidens."

31. Quoted in Topley, "Marriage Resistance," p. 76.

32. Topley, "Organisation and Social Function," p. 180.

33. Quoted in Topley, "Marriage Resistance," p. 76.

34. Topley, "Marriage Resistance," p. 83.

35. Quoted in Mrs. E. T. Williams, "Some Popular Religious Literature of the Chinese," *Journal of the China Branch of the Royal Asiatic Society* 33 (1900–01): 28–29.

36. Topley, "Organisation and Social Function," p. 169.

37. Smith, *Village Life in China*, pp. 287–88.

38. Topley, "Organisation and Social Function," p. 40.
39. Topley, "Organisation and Social Function," p. 40.
40. Mann, "Suicide and Chastity," p. 11.
41. Douglas, *Society in China,* p. 215.
42. Topley, "Organisation and Social Function," p. 43.
43. Topley, "Organisation and Social Function," p. 39.
44. Lady Hosie (Dorothea Soothill), *The Pool of Ch'ien Lung* (London: Hodder, Stoughton, 1948), p. 157.
45. Hosie, *Pool of Ch'ien Lung,* p. 158.
46. Hosie, *Pool of Ch'ien Lung,* p. 160.
47. Topley, "Organisation and Social Function," pp. 45–46.
48. Topley, "Organisation and Social Function," p. 46.
49. Agnes Smedley, *Portraits of Chinese Women in Revolution,* ed. Jan MacKinnon and Steve MacKinnon (Old Westbury, N.Y.: Feminist Press, 1976), p. 105.
50. Smedley, *Portraits,* p. 107.
51. Smedley, *Portraits,* pp. 107–8.
52. Smedley, *Portraits,* p. 108.
53. Smedley, *Portraits,* p. 107.
54. Topley, "Organisation and Social Function," p. 46.
55. Topley, "Marriage Resistance," p. 76.
56. Quoted in Ch'en Tung-yuan, *Chung-kuo fu-nü sheng-huo shih* (History of Women's Life in China) (Shanghai, 1928), from sec. 11, chap. 8, translated by Charlotte Boynton.
57. Ch'en, *Chung-kuo*
58. Topley, "Marriage Resistance," p. 85.
59. Topley, "Marriage Resistance," p. 85.
60. Jaschok, "On the Lives of Women," p. 43.
61. Topley, "Marriage Resistance," p. 85.
62. Topley, "Organisation and Social Function," p. 52.
63. Topley, "Organisation and Social Function," p. 55.
64. Topley, "Organisation and Social Function," p. 64.
65. Topley, "Marriage Resistance," p. 85.
66. Cited in Topley, "Marriage Resistance," p. 68.
67. Topley, "Organisation and Social Function," p. 183. It should be noted that in Topley's more recent published work "Marriage Resistance in Rural Kwangtung," which summarizes and, presumably, updates her dissertation, Topley presents a more positive political assessment of the resistance movement.
68. Croll, *Feminism and Socialism,* p. 44.
69. Topley, "Marriage Resistance," p. 88.
70. Graham E. Johnson, "Rural Chinese Social Organization, Tradition and Change," *Pacific Affairs* 46 (Winter 1973–74): 557–64. Johnson himself does not attribute these advances in women's status to the legacy left by resistance women. He finds the reasons for these localized advances "com-

plex" and adds that "in order to unravel the complexity, a lengthy period of residence . . . is fundamental" (p. 564).

71. This is an eternal complaint made about loose women. It surfaces in many disparate places. For example, in discussing the principle of equal pay for equal work, Margaret Rossiter in *Women Scientists in America: Struggles and Strategies to 1940* (Baltimore: Johns Hopkins University Press, 1984), p. 198, cites a 1928 study done at the University of Nebraska comparing the spending habits of 29 unmarried faculty women with those of 155 married faculty, most of whom would have been men. The study found that the single women "spent twice as high a percentage of their income (not actual amount) on savings, gifts, churches, charity, recreation, and travel" as did the sample of 155 married faculty. The two female authors of the study concluded that the unattached women faculty spent more money than the married ones on "luxury" items and opined that the enjoyment of such luxuries may be considered "compensations for their lack of family life." Finally, they suggested that equal pay for equal work unjustly favors single women and that salary in academia should be determined by the number of persons dependent on the salary earner.

72. Ahmed, "Western Ethnocentrism," p. 528.

73. Ahmed, "Western Ethnocentrism," p. 529.

74. Ahmed, "Western Ethnocentrism," p. 531.

75. Ahmed, "Western Ethnocentrism," p. 532.

76. Janice G. Raymond, "Women's Studies: A Knowledge of One's Own," *Union Seminary Quarterly Review* 35 (Fall/Winter 1979–1980): 41.

IV. Obstacles to Female Friendship

1. Cited in Joel Block, *Friendship* (New York: Macmillan, 1980), p. 33.

2. I am enormously indebted to Hannah Arendt's typologies of dissociation from and assimilation to the world which she develops in much of her work on the Jews and Judaism. See, for example *The Jew as Pariah,* ed. and intro. Ron H. Feldman (New York: Grove, 1978). I have drawn on many of her ideas in this chapter.

3. Arendt, *Jew as Pariah,* pp. 89–90.

4. Arendt, *Jew as Pariah,* p. 27.

5. Hannah Arendt, "On Humanity in Dark Times," in *Men in Dark Times* (New York: Harcourt, 1968), p. 23.

6. Janice G. Raymond, *The Transsexual Empire* (Boston: Beacon, 1979); see especially chap. 4, "Therapy as a Way of Life."

7. Michel Foucault, *The History of Sexuality* (New York: Pantheon, 1978) 1:59.

8. Foucault, *History of Sexuality,* p. 60.

9. Sara Scott and Tracey Payne, "Underneath We're All Lovable: Therapy and Feminism," *Trouble and Strife* 3 (Summer 1984): 22.

10. Hannah Arendt, *Rahel Varnhagen: The Life of a Jewish Woman* (New York: Harcourt, 1974), p. 16.

11. Interview, *Boston Globe,* 26 August 1984, p. A3.

12. Scott and Payne, "Underneath We're All Lovable," p. 24.

13. Conversation with Pat Hynes, Montague, Mass., July 1984.

14. Mary Daly, *Pure Lust: Elemental Feminist Philosophy* (Boston: Beacon, 1984), pp. 200–201.

15. Daly, *Pure Lust,* p. 204.

16. Virginia Woolf, *A Room of One's Own* (New York: Harcourt, Brace, & World, 1929), p. 35.

17. Robert Jay Lifton, *Thought Reform and the Psychology of Totalism* (New York: Norton, 1961), p. 426.

18. Kathleen Barry, " 'Sadomasochism': The New Backlash to Feminism," *Trivia: A Journal of Ideas* 1 (Fall 1982): 86–87.

19. See Jean Bethke Elshtain, "Feminists Against the Family," *The Nation,* 17 November 1979, p. 497. I cite Elshtain here because it is important to distinguish between well-placed and "displaced" critiques of "the personal is political." In my opinion, Elshtain's is an example of the latter. Her critique can be summed up in her own words:

> Note that the claim is not that the personal and the political are interrelated in important and fascinating ways not yet fully explored and previously hidden to us by patriarchal ideology and practice; nor that the personal and the political may be fruitfully examined as analogous to one another along certain touchstones of power and privilege, but that the personal *is* political. (p. 497)

It is nothing other than bad faith to critique an abbreviated adage for failing to convey the complexities that Elshtain speaks about. Does Elshtain seriously believe that feminists who have used this insight in political theory and organizing are all simpleminded reductionists? Of course, many feminists realize the multidimensionality of "the personal is political." For years, many of us have understood the complexity of "the personal is political." It is because we understand its complexity that we do the particular kind of political analysis that we do.

The statement "the personal is political" can be compared to a metaphor that suggests an analogy but that cannot be reduced to it. It is meant to be taken seriously but not reductionistically. When someone says that she has been "in the dumps" all day, we do not presume that there is a literal reduction in these words. Rather we understand that one situation can be construed in terms of another. I am not saying that "the personal is political" *is* a metaphor. I do maintain that it is *like* a metaphor in that the analogy it presents allows for both similarity and difference and that it is wrong to collapse the two terms in a reductionistic way. As Anne Koedt wrote in her essay "Lesbianism and Feminism" in the classic anthology *Radical Feminism*:

The original genius of the phrase "the personal is political" was that it opened up the area of women's private lives to political analysis. Before that, the isolation of women from each other had been accomplished by labeling a woman's experience "personal." Women had thus been kept from seeing their common oppression by men.

However, opening up women's experience to political analysis has also resulted in a misuse of the phrase. While it is true that there are political implications in everything a woman *qua* woman experiences, it is not therefore true that a woman's life is the political property of the women's movement. Anne Koedt, "Lesbianism and Feminism," in *Radical Feminism* ed. Anne Koedt, Ellen Levine, and Anita Rapone (New York: Quadrangle/New York Times Book Co., 1973, p. 255.)

Koedt wrote these words in 1971, yet Elshtain shows no familiarity with her work. One would think that Elshtain invented the insight that "the personal is political" can be perverted.

20. Thomas J. Cottle, "Our Soul-Baring Orgy Destroys the Private Self," *Psychology Today* (October 1975): 22.
21. Personal correspondence to Janice Raymond, 1978.
22. Quoted in Paula Caplan, *Barriers Between Women* (New York: SP Medical and Scientific Books, 1981), pp. 125–26.
23. Andrea Dworkin, *Right-Wing Women* (New York: Perigee, 1983), p. 227.
24. Judy Foreman, "Men Are Resisting Sweeping Changes," *Boston Globe*, 23 December 1980. "Today's husbands, according to four new advertising studies and some new academic research, are taking over more of the housework than they used to—through still less than half the workload—and they're hating every minute of it.

"When husbands do share the housework burden, it is almost always only when they are married to women who are full-time workers in the paid labor force.

"...It isn't the sheer number of hours spent in housework but the continued inequality of the burden which causes the most stress for working couples, says Wellesley researcher Joseph Pleck.

"...a new Pleck study shows, 'men's time in total work, combining both paid work and family work, (actually) decreases when their wives are employed'" (pp. 19, 21).
25. Shulamith Firestone, *The Dialectic of Sex* (New York: Morrow, 1970), p. 168.
26. Firestone, *Dialectic*, pp. 166–67.
27. John Stoltenberg, "Sadomasochism: Eroticized Violence, Eroticized Powerlessness," in *Against Sadomasochism* ed. Robin Ruth Linden et al. (East Palo Alto, Calif.: Frog in the Well, 1982), p. 125.
28. Stoltenberg, "Sadomasochism," p. 127.
29. Stoltenberg, "Sadomasochism," p. 128.

30. Dworkin, *Right-Wing Women,* p. 52.

31. Dworkin, *Right-Wing Women,* p. 52.

32. Hilde Hein, "Sadomasochism and the Liberal Tradition," in Linden, *Against Sadomasochism,* p. 88.

33. See Raymond, *Transsexual Empire,* esp. pp. 175–77 on " 'Repressive Tolerance' and Sensitivity."

34. Herbert Marcuse, "Repressive Tolerance," in Robert Paul Wolff, Barrington Moore, Jr., and Herbert Marcuse, *A Critique of Pure Tolerance* (Boston: Beacon, 1965), p. 82.

35. Joreen, "The Tyranny of Structurelessness," in Koedt, Levine, and Rapone, *Radical Feminism,* p. 287.

36. Alice Walker, "*One* Child of One's Own," in *In Search of Our Mothers' Gardens: Womanist Prose* (New York: Harcourt, 1983), p. 379.

37. Cicero, *De Amicitia* (On Friendship) 1.85, trans. and intro. Harry G. Edinger (New York: Bobbs-Merrill, 1967), p. 73.

38. Personal correspondence, Julie Melrose to Janice Raymond, 23 May 1984.

39. Joseph P. Lash, *Helen and Teacher: The Story of Helen Keller and Anne Sullivan Macy* (New York: Delacorte, 1980), p. 332.

40. Lash, *Helen and Teacher,* p. 295.

41. Virginia Woolf, *A Room of One's Own* (New York: Harcourt, 1929), p. 86.

42. Freud quoted in Daly, *Pure Lust,* p. 250.

43. Daly, *Pure Lust,* p. 251.

44. Personal correspondence, Julie Melrose to Janice Raymond.

45. Personal correspondence, Denice Yanni to Janice Raymond, April 1984.

46. Dworkin, *Right-Wing Women,* p. 159.

47. Dworkin, *Right-Wing Women,* p. 25.

48. Simone de Beauvoir, *The Second Sex,* trans. and ed. H. M. Parshley (New York: Bantam, 1952), p. 307.

49. Tania Modleski, *Loving with a Vengeance: Mass-Produced Fantasies for Women* (Hamden, Conn.: Archon, 1982), p. 88.

50. Daly, *Pure Lust,* esp. pp. 232–35.

51. Elizabeth Janeway, *The Powers of the Weak* (New York: Knopf, 1980), p. 144.

52. Barry, *Female Sexual Slavery* (Englewood Cliffs, N.J.: Prentice-Hall, 1979), p. 35.

53. Alice Walker, "*To* the Black Scholar," in *In Search of Our Mothers' Gardens,* p. 322.

54. Adrienne Rich, *Of Woman Born* (New York: Norton, 1976), p. 226.

55. Nancy Richard, "Mothers and Daughters" (Advanced Seminar Paper in Women's Studies, University of Massachusetts, Fall 1982), p. 1.

56. Richard, "Mothers and Daughters," p. 1.

57. Hannah Arendt, *The Life of the Mind* (New York: Harcourt, 1978); see especially vol. 1, "Thinking."

58. Louise Bernikow, *Among Women* (New York: Harmony, 1980), p. 66.

59. Colette, *Earthly Paradise,* ed. Robert Phelps (New York: Farrar, 1966), pp. 35–36.

60. Colette, *Break of Day* (London: Secker and Warburg, 1961), p. 6.

61. Richard, "Mothers and Daughters," p. 12.

62. Personal correspondence, Denice Yanni to Janice Raymond.

63. Personal correspondence, Denice Yanni to Janice Raymond.

64. Daly, *Gyn/Ecology: The Metaethics of Radical Feminism* (Boston: Beacon, 1978), p. 9.

65. Barry, " 'Sadomasochism,' " p. 81.

66. Friedrich Nietzsche, *Beyond Good and Evil,* trans. Walter Kaufmann (New York: Vintage, 1966), pt. 4, 1.169.

67. Lifton, *Thought Reform,* p. 427.

68. This is Christine Delphy's phrase. See "The Main Enemy," in *Close to Home: A Materialist Analysis of Women's Oppression,* trans. and ed. Diana Leonard (Amherst: University of Massachusetts Press, 1984), pp. 57–77.

69. Arendt, "On Humanity in Dark Times," pp. 16–17.

70. H. Patricia Hynes, "On 'Racism and Writing,' " *Sinister Wisdom* 15 (Fall 1980): 105.

71. Hynes, "On 'Racism and Writing,' " p. 108.

72. Lucy Dawidowich, *The Holocaust and the Historians* (Cambridge: Harvard University Press, 1981), pp. 13–14.

73. Bonnie Mhine (Feminist Theory class paper, University of Massachusetts, Fall 1983).

74. Walker, "*One* Child of One's Own," in *In Search of Our Mothers' Gardens,* p. 379.

75. Walker, "*One* Child," p. 379.

76. Walker, "*One* Child," pp. 379–80.

77. Andrea Dworkin, *Pornography: Men Possessing Women* (New York: Perigee, 1981), p. 217.

78. Paul Tillich, *Love, Power, and Justice* (London: Oxford University Press, 1954), p. 40.

79. Sherry McCoy and Maureen Hicks, "A Psychological Retrospective on Power in the Contemporary Lesbian-Feminist Community," *Frontiers: A Journal of Women's Studies* 4 (Fall 1976): 68.

80. McCoy and Hicks, "Psychological Retrospective," pp. 66–67.

81. McCoy and Hicks, "Psychological Retrospective," p. 68.

82. McCoy and Hicks, "Psychological Retrospective," p. 68.

83. Daly, *Pure Lust,* p. 112.

84. Dworkin, *Pornography,* p. 67.

85. Renate Duelli Klein, "Rethinking Sisterhood: Unity in Diversity," editorial, *Women's Studies International Forum* 8 (1985): iv.

86. Daly, *Pure Lust,* p. 261.

87. Walker, "The Civil Rights Movement: What Good Was It?" in *In Search of Our Mothers' Gardens,* pp. 125–26.

V. A Vision of Female Friendship: Two Sights-Seeing

1. My use of *vision* goes far beyond its physiological meaning of physical sight. Helen Keller did not have the capacity of physical sight, but she had the dual vision of which I write. Nor am I basing the concept of vision in a white western philosophical tradition of idealism such as Judith Butler accuses Marilyn Frye of doing in her *Conditions* review of Frye's *The Politics of Reality.* I find Butler's review utterly ignorant of the critical idealism contained, for example, in the work of black and white *women,* such as Zora Neale Hurston, Virginia Woolf, and Alice Walker. To imply, as Butler does, that "the metaphor of sight looms large in Frye's theory *because* she believes, like the Anglo-American philosophers who trained her, that perception constitutes reality" is a gross distortion not only of Frye's work but of the work of many women whose dual *vision* enabled them to change the material conditions of their lives. Judith Butler, review of *The Politics of Reality: Essays in Feminist Theory* by Marilyn Frye, in *Conditions* 3 (1984): 167.

2. Keith Melville, *Communes in the Counter Culture: Origins, Theories, Styles of Life* (New York: Morrow, 1972), p. 30.

3. Lester Thurow, quoted in *Second Century Radcliffe News* (April 1982).

4. Dianne Dumanoski, "The New Poor: Women, Children," *Boston Sunday Globe,* 14 December 1980, pp. 18–19.

5. United Nations, "Review and Evaluation of Progress Made and Obstacles Encountered at the National Level in Attaining the Objectives of the World Plan of Action," item 8a of the Provisional Agenda 80-14909, World Conference of the United Nations Decade for Women: Equality, Development, and Peace, Copenhagen, Denmark, 1980.

6. United States Department of Commerce, Table 12, Comparison of Median Earnings of Year Round Full Time Workers by Sex, 1955–1978, in *Money Income of Families and Persons in the U.S., Current Population Reports, 1957–1977; Money Income and Poverty Status of Families and Persons in the U.S.;* 1980 census.

7. United Nations, "Program of Action for the 2nd Half of the U.N. Decade for Women: Equality, Development, and Peace," item 9 of the Provisional Agenda 80-12383, World Conference of the United Nations Decade for Women: Equality, Development, and Peace, Copenhagen, Denmark, 1980.

8. United States Department of Justice, *F.B.I. Uniform Crime Reports: Crime in the United States,* 1980.

9. D. Moore, *Battered Women* (Beverly Hills, Calif.: Sage, 1979).

10. Conversation with Pat Hynes, Gloucester, Mass., 1981.

11. Virginia Woolf, review of *La Femme Anglaise au XIXième Siècle et son Evolution d'après le Roman Anglais Contemporain,* by Léonie Villard, in *The Times Literary Supplement,* 18 March 1920, reprinted in *Virginia Woolf: Women and Writing,* ed. Michele Barrett (New York: Harcourt, 1979), p. 67.

12. Karl Jaspers, *Philosophy* (Chicago: University of Chicago Press, 1970), 1:246.

13. I do not wish to enter into a discussion about the intricacies of philosophical theories of idealism. I am using the term "critical idealism" to mean that ideas or rational knowledge alone do not give one access to the world. On the other hand, my use of the term "critical materialism" signals that sense experience and material existence do not give one access either since, as Kant held, in the absence of interpretation, sense experience and matter are "unreal."

14. Ernst Bloch, "Incipit Vita Nova," in *Man on His Own: Essays in Philosophy of Religion,* trans. E. B. Ashton (New York: Herder and Herder, 1970), p. 90.

15. Max Horkheimer, Foreword in Martin Jay, *The Dialectical Imagination: A History of the Frankfurt School and the Institute of Social Research 1923–1930* (Boston: Little, Brown, 1973), p. xiv.

16. The phrase is Ernst Bloch's. See Ernst Bloch, "Man as Possibility," in *The Future of Hope,* ed. Walter H. Capps (Philadelphia: Fortress), p. 64.

17. Michael Novak, *Ascent of the Mountain, Flight of the Dove* (New York: Harper, 1971), p. 5.

18. Daly, *Gyn/Ecology: The Metaethics of Radical Feminism* (Boston: Beacon, 1978), p. 1.

19. Mary Catherine Bateson uses these words to describe how her mother, Margaret Mead, explained the difference between religious believers and those who do not believe. The words are appropriate in this context also Mary Catherine Bateson, *With a Daughter's Eye: A Memoir of Margaret Mead and Gregory Bateson* (New York: Morrow, 1984), p. 87.

20. Alice Walker, "From an Interview," in *In Search of Our Mothers' Gardens: Womanist Prose* (New York: Harcourt, 1983), pp. 251–52.

21. Hannah Arendt, "Tradition and the Modern Age," in *Between Past and Future: Eight Exercises in Political Thought* (New York: Penguin, 1961), p. 25.

22. This is one of the major themes running throughout Hannah Arendt, *The Life of the Mind* (New York: Harcourt, 1978).

23. Arendt, *Life of the Mind,* p. 6.

24. Andrea Dworkin, *Right-Wing Women* (New York: Perigee, 1983), pp. 50–51.

25. Dale Spender, *Women of Ideas and What Men Have Done to Them* (London: Routledge, 1982), p. 18.

26. Mary Daly, *Pure Lust: Elemental Feminist Philosophy* (Boston: Beacon, 1984), p. 321.

27. Spender, *Women of Ideas,* p. 18.

28. The famous phrase of Abbie Hoffman.

29. Robert Jay Lifton, *Thought Reform and the Psychology of Totalism* (New York: Norton, 1961), p. 429.

30. Nadezha Mandelstam, *Hope Abandoned,* trans. Max Hayward (New York: Atheneum, 1974), p. 74.

31. Arendt, quoted in Elisabeth Young-Bruehl, *For Love of the World* (New Haven: Yale University Press, 1982), p. 452.

32. Arendt, *Life of the Mind,* p. 55.

33. Arendt, *Life of the Mind,* p. 191.

34. Arendt, *Life of the Mind,* p. 188.

35. Arendt, *Life of the Mind,* p. 189.

36. Adolf Harnack, quoted in W. M. Rankin, "Friendship," *Encyclopaedia of Religion and Ethics,* ed. James Hastings, 4:132.

37. Emily Dickinson, *The Complete Poems of Emily Dickinson,* ed. Thomas Johnson (Boston: Little, Brown, 1960), c. 1876, p. 585.

38. Christianity endowed marriage with the esteem that the Greeks had given to friendship between men. It asserted that, in doing this, it placed a higher value on women and married life. This claim was true only within a very limited and limiting sphere for women. Neither classical friendship nor Christian marriage sanctified friendship, or love relationships, between two women.

39. Michel de Montaigne, "On Friendship," in *Works of Michel de Montaigne* trans. W. Hazlitt, ed. O. W. Wright, 1:269.

40. Aristotle, *Nicomachean Ethics* 9, 4:1.31.

41. Simone de Beauvoir, *The Second Sex,* trans. and ed. H. M. Parshley (New York: Bantam, 1952), see chap. 15, "The Lesbian."

42. Daly, *Pure Lust,* p. 198.

43. Daly, *Pure Lust,* p. 272.

44. See the definition of *continuum* in Webster's *New Collegiate Dictionary,* 9th ed. (1983).

45. H. Patricia Hynes, "Ellen Swallow, Lois Gibbs, and Rachel Carson: Catalysts of the American Environmental Movement," *Women's Studies International Forum* 8, no. 4 (1985): 56.

46. Hynes, "Ellen Swallow," pp. 57–58. "Thanks to the moral persuasion of *Silent Spring* and Carson's subsequent testimony before Senate subcommittees and Presidential commissions. DDT was banned from use in the United States. The responsibility for regulating the manufacture and use of pesticides passed from the Department of Agriculture to a newly created federal environmental agency, the Environmental Protection Agency (EPA). Major pieces of legislation were passed which gave EPA the power to prohibit or limit the manufacture, processing, distribution, use, and disposal of any chemical substances which present a risk of injury to human health or the environment . . . What is needed, if these statutes are to fulfill their inherent potential, is no less than the same moral clarity and intellectual courage with which Rachel Carson lived."

47. Ynestra King, "Feminism and the Revolt of Nature," *Heresies* 4, issue 13, "Feminism & Ecology" (1981): 14.

48. Henry Beston, quoted in Frank Graham, Jr., *Since Silent Spring* (Boston: Houghton Mifflin, 1970), p. 3.

49. Zora Neale Hurston, *Their Eyes Were Watching God* (Philadelphia: Lippincott, 1937), p. 9.

50. Rosalind Franklin made an initial and major contribution to the discovery of the structure of DNA yet was not part of the group that received the Nobel Prize for this discovery. See Anne Sayre, *Rosalind Franklin and DNA* (New York: Norton, 1975), for the complete account of how Franklin's early discovery was used without her knowledge and appropriated by Watson and Wilkins.

51. See Raymond, *The Transsexual Empire* (Boston: Beacon, 1979), chap. 6, for a fuller definition and description of *integrity.*

52. Joan Sully, "A Heritage of War: Male Bonding and Militarism" (Division III thesis, Hampshire College, Amherst, Mass., 1982), pp. 92–93.

53. John Stoltenberg, *Disarmament and Masculinity* (Palo Alto, Calif.: Frog in the Well, 1978), p. 3.

54. Andrea Dworkin, *Right-Wing Women,* p. 51.

55. Kathleen Barry, " 'Sadomasochism': The New Backlash to Feminism," *Trivia: A Journal of Ideas* 1 (Fall 1982): 78.

56. Charlotte Brontë, *Villette* (New York: Harper Colophon Books, 1972), p. 243.

57. De Beauvoir, *Second Sex,* p. 250.

58. Virginia Woolf, *A Room of One's Own* (New York: Harcourt, 1929), p. 35.

59. Woolf, *Room of One's Own,* p. 36.

60. Susan Brownmiller, *Against Our Will: Men, Women and Rape* (New York: Simon and Schuster, 1975), p. 187.

61. Brownmiller, *Against Our Will,* p. 190.

62. Natalia Malachowskaja, unpublished essay, "Human Hope" (Leningrad, 1980), translated from the German by Lise Weil.

Index